do you know things i don't know?

prose poems + drawings by

ellin randel

Small Batch Books
Amherst, Massachusetts

Printed in the United States of America
on acid-free paper

ILibrary of Congress Control Number 2011937069
ISBN: 978-1-937650-00-1

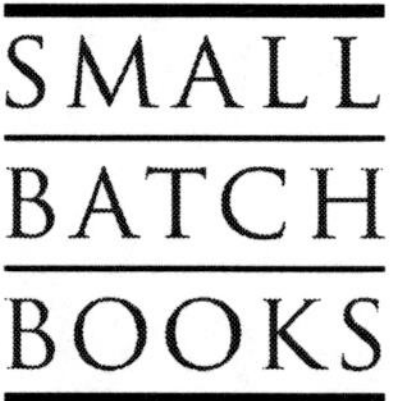

493 South Pleasant Street
Amherst, Massachusetts 01002
413.230.3943
SmallBatchBooks.com

*To my Guru, Swami Muktananda (known to all as Baba),
my children Jonathan and Amy, and my grandchildren
Benjamin, Nikola, Madison, and Julian.*

Contents

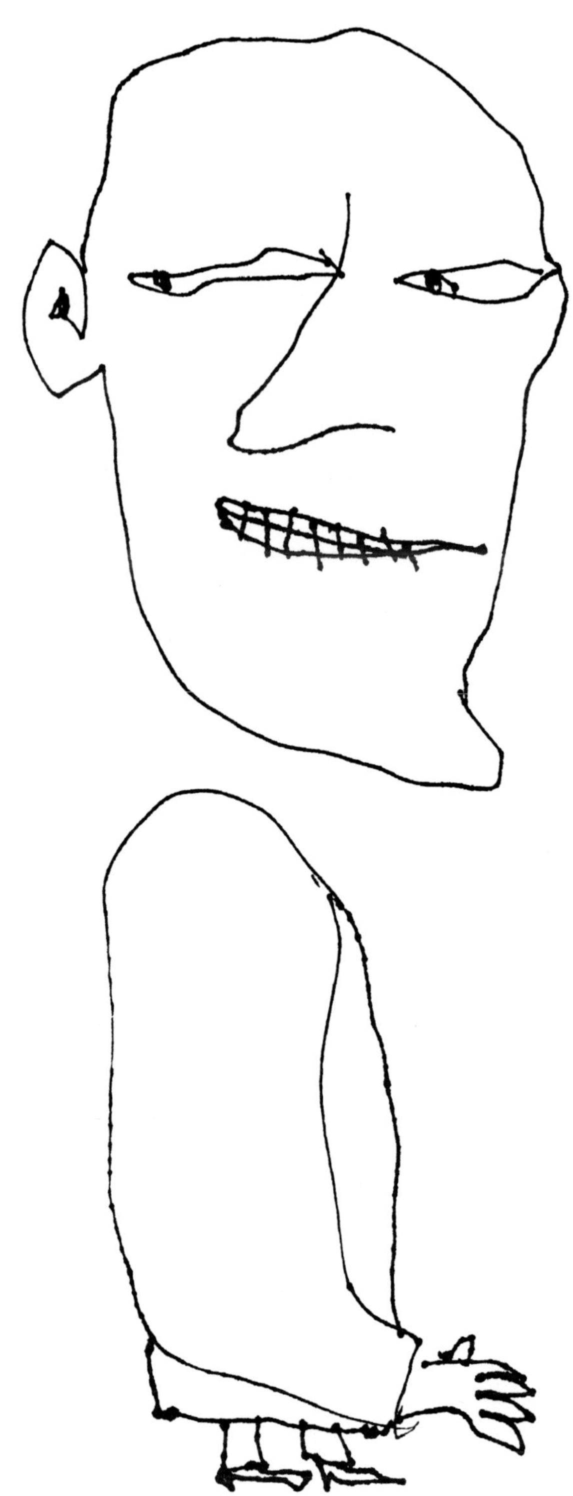

A Note About the Drawings

About 15 years ago I began drawing with my left hand, hoping to go beyond the limits of my dominant right hand. I was instantly plunged into another way of drawing, a way that spoke to me and allowed me to say things I hadn't been able to say before. I continued to draw with both hands, but the left hand became increasingly freer. The drawings in this book are examples of both, but the drawings that are shaky and come from a different and more primitive source are recognizable as left-handed works.

A stroke intervened recently, leaving me with only the use of my left hand. Now that I can only use that side, it seems that my years of efforts were preparation for what was to come.

–Ellin Randel

 there is always a white page waiting for words,
and words waiting for the white page. Words accumulating, crowding, piling up, lining
up, waiting their turn, ready to come out, to issue forth, to spill onto the white page and
make room for others.

Everything becomes a word—every moment that passes, or rather that bumps into us,
becomes a word and goes where the words go, where words wait to come out and line
themselves up on the white page, black on white, row on row, now waiting to be read. And
once they go more words fill the spaces, packed moments packing themselves into packed
spaces, suitcases packed and ready to go, to issue forth and make room for more words.

And once they are out and waiting to be read they line themselves up, page upon
page, piles of pages waiting to be read, sitting there solid as a rock, not going anywhere.
Piles of pages taking up room, taking up rooms, condensed thoughts taking form in
words, every word packed with meaning, the meaning of every moment encountered in
a life, in many lives, in every life. Meaning flows through moments into mind, through
words onto pages in piles, packed in rooms, waiting to be read. My meaning, your mean-
ing, all meanings, do you get my meaning? Meaning and purpose dance round in spirals
spinning off into matter like butter in a churn.

Meaning and matter, purposeful spirals, strings of DNA twirling within us, packed
with words, packed with meaning. Lifetimes of meaning drift through intergalactic inky
space and sift silently into strings of matter, a blueprint for a form, my form, your form.
Who knows how many words are packed inside this form,
and what they mean, and why.

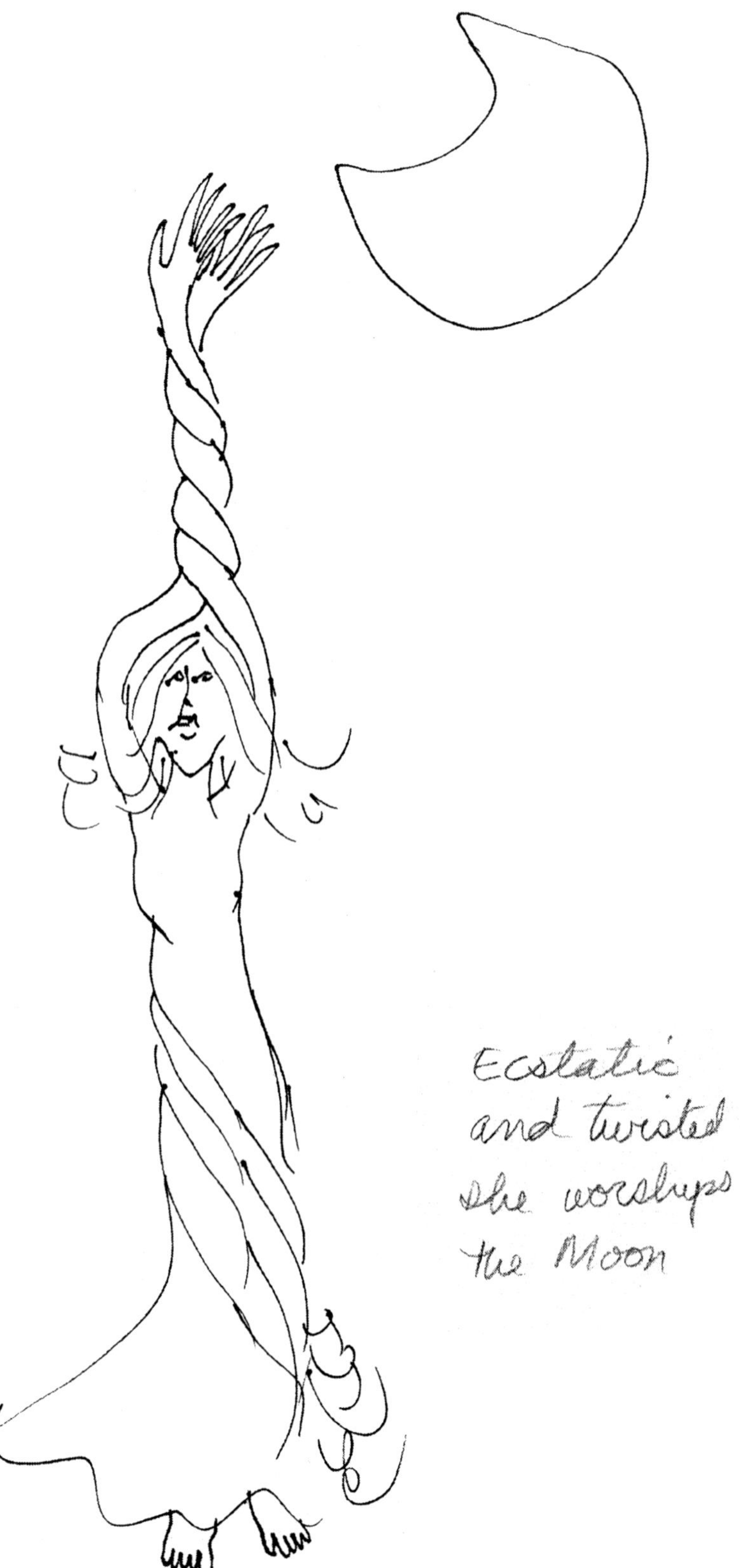

Ecstatic
and twisted
she worships
the Moon

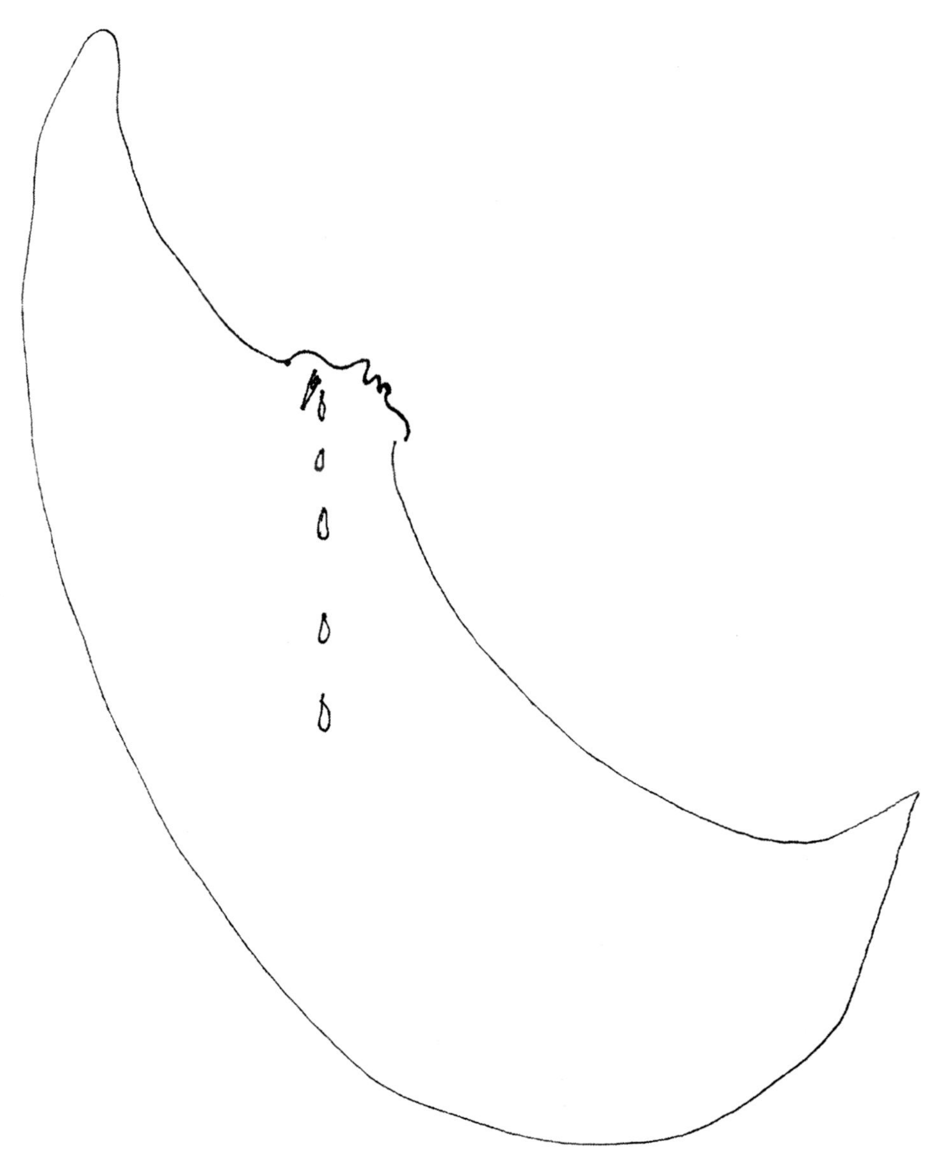

Her tears fell like liquid
crystals in the night

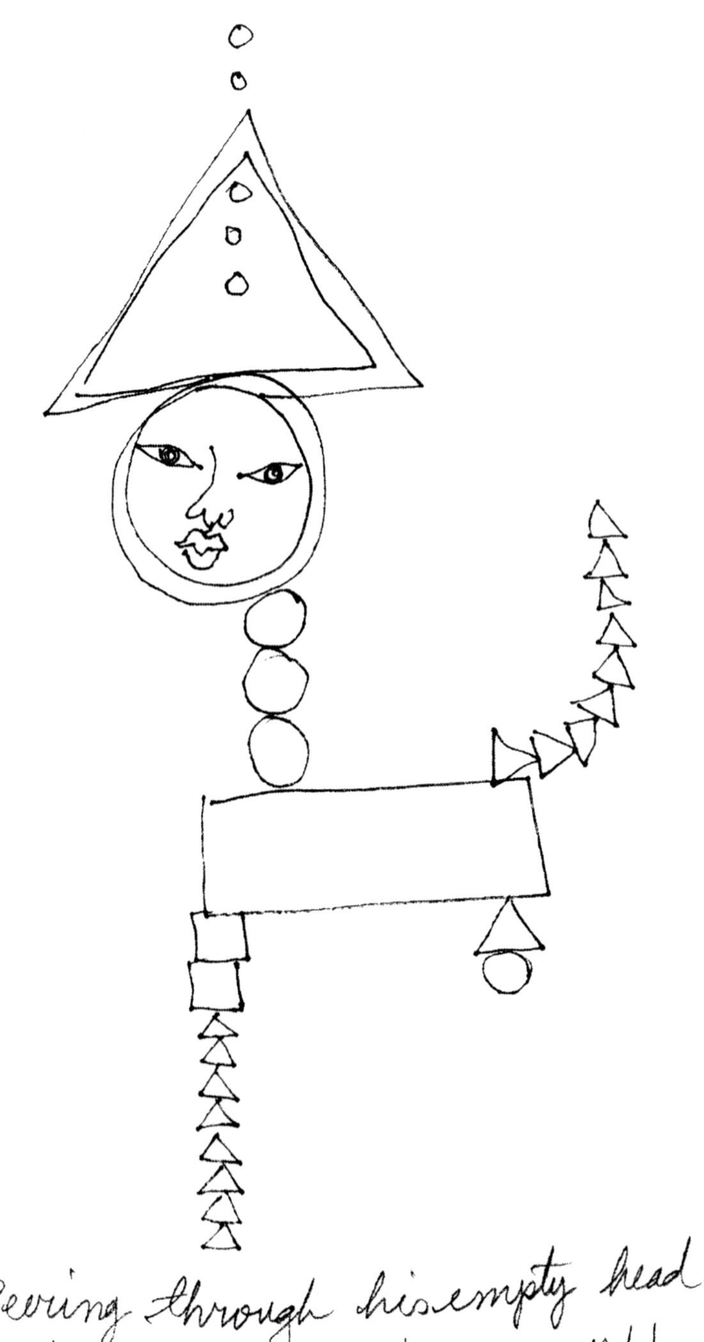

Peering through his empty head is
a face from another world.

I'd like a word with you.

In the beginning was the word. Then two words, then three. Words for things. Then words for doing things. Then words to tell one thing from another the same thing. The pretty one the ugly one the big one the yellow one. Judgments come into it, and preferences. I'd rather have the yellow one. It suits me, don't you think? Somehow I don't see me as blue.

There I am, I'm different from you. The yellows against the blues. Cell division. Word division. Language. The Tower of Babel. We all talk and talk, but we can't understand each other. Not through the words.

Paint a picture with words. Not with colors. A different kind of picture. Words as paint. Once upon a time. Listen my children. In the beginning. Call me Ishmael.

A man walks to a rock. It's rough and gray, taller than he is. He stands before it, looks at it, puts his hands on it. It's cool and hard to the touch. Does he want to move it? It's too big. He climbs up on top of it and looks down. The view is different from here. He looks around—he can see farther.

There is power in this. He has added the stone's power to his own. The stone has become his ally. He wants to take it with him, but it's too big. He sits beside it, absorbing its strength. He gathers leaves from the trees and sets them before the stone in offering. He and the stone are linked now. Part of him stays with the stone. Some of the stone's power goes with him. He walks tall as he leaves. He feels himself increased.

Above the tall trees in the jungle the thunder rumbles. Distant lightning cuts through the shadows from time to time. The leaves rustle as a beginning breeze passes through the trees. The air smells humid, the birds call, their cries sounding hollow under the roof of treetops. A faint scent of fragrant flower is carried on the breeze.

On the soft leafy path a woman puts one brown foot after another. She walks silently, sending her thoughts ahead on the path to feel out what is there. Her ears are alert for sounds beside her or behind her. The moon slips from behind a cloud and lights the path. The woman slips into the leafy shadows and squats silently. Her eyes look straight ahead through half-open lids.

Wherever I look there's a story. They spring up like dragon's teeth. Wherever I look there's a dream, a story, a word for that. A deep mountain lake full of words, I need only dip my net to have as many as I want.

They swim by lazily as I dive through them in the blue waters. Fix. Market. Rascal. Saffron. Sober, ancient, comet, watchband, card, guard, garden, gardenia, schizophrenia, Bohemia, leukemia, bulimia, similar, scimitar, far, star, Mars, father, was.

Mexico, lettuce, chamber, antimony, caroling, sampan, grace, fallacy, warden, astronomy.

An avalanche of words—I've opened the door too wide. They tumble out, mine and others', a river of words, a waterfall, a rockslide, they pile up beside me and fuse.

I am standing before a stone. It is taller than I am. I touch it. It is cool and hard.

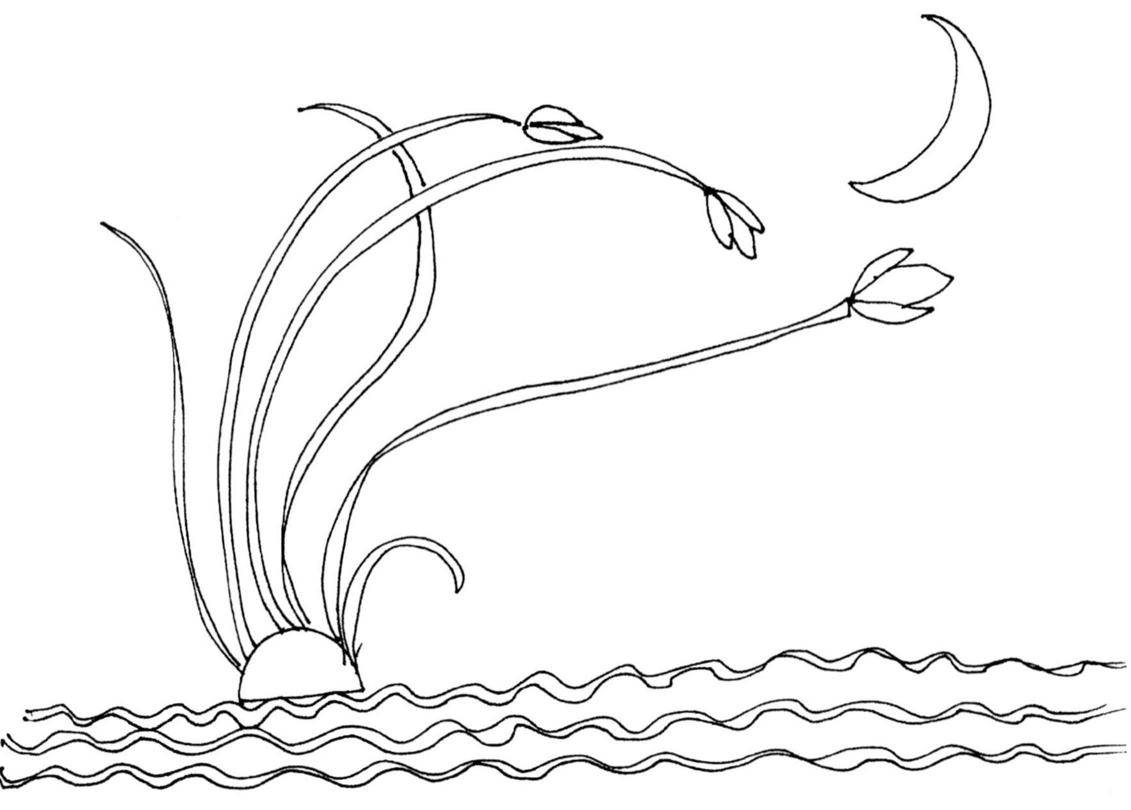

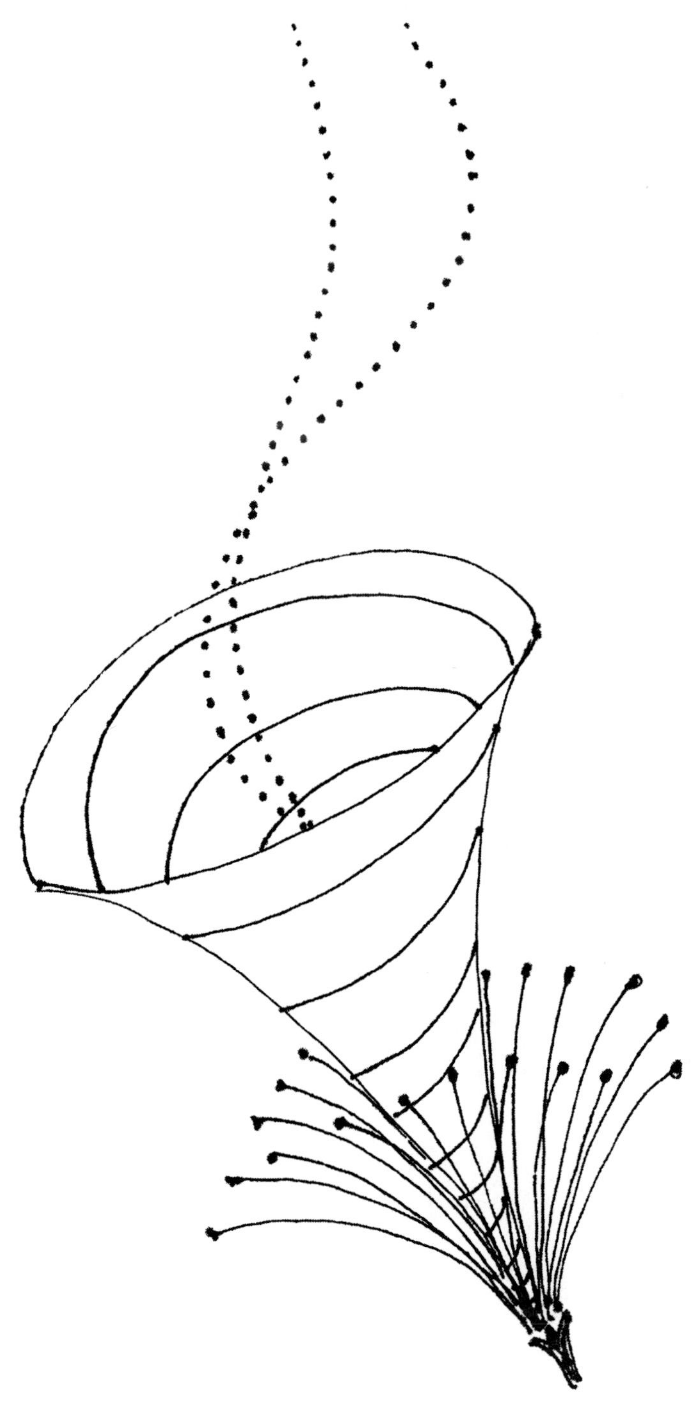

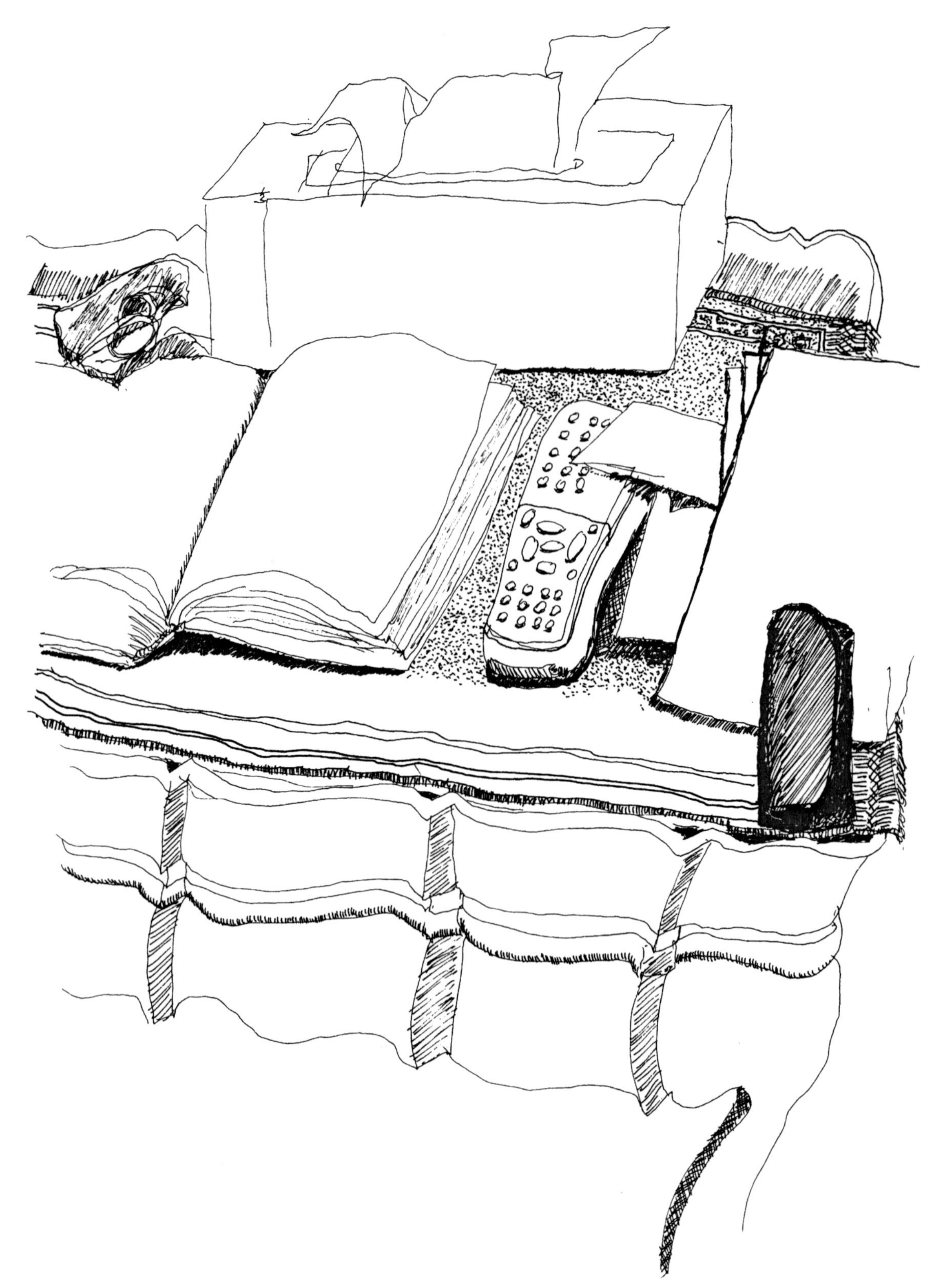

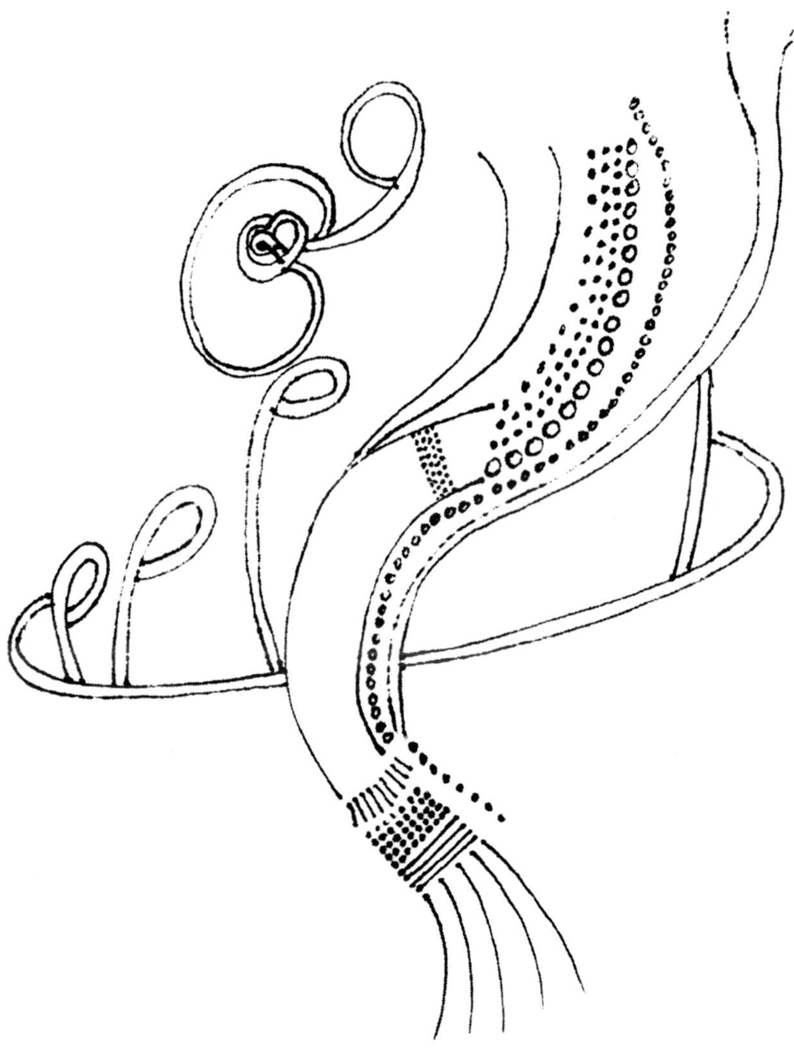

Notes of music jumping over each other, jumping

fences like sheep in a cartoon, counting them to fall asleep—right! Trying to get them to jump the fence used to keep me awake, lying there in frustration trying to get the sheep in my mind to do what I wanted them to. Now I just say, Jump, and up they go—but I don't invite them any more. Another time-tested piece of wisdom punctured. A lead balloon, flat by the side of the road. Move on, it's a long road, we've got places to go.

The joy of creating music. Its own reward? Yes or no, I want to know. What's worth it, Johann Sebastian? What if you have no money and tuberculosis, what if your wife is mad at you and doesn't stop complaining, if the children whine and make noise—you can always listen to the music. No, not the Bach family—a warm and loving family, so close.

A warm and loving family, is that what makes it all worthwhile? Comes very close, and lasts a long time. Eventually everyone finds their life emptied of meaning, like a laundry bag turned upside down and its contents dumped on the ground. Nothing left in the bag, nothing on the ground worth holding on to—what now?

I don't know, don't ask me. One foot in front of the other, just keep going. Walk to the music, it'll keep you going. Keep your eyes on the path in front of you, as soon as you see it you can experience it.

I believe there is a path and I'm walking on it. I believe I've lived my life in such a way as to bring me to this spot at this moment. I believe I will go on walking and arrive at other spots at other moments. I believe that sorrow is part of human life, yet I don't believe in the necessity of suffering. I believe that disappointment surrounds us as water surrounds a fish. We swim through it without noticing—it's a given.

Life is heavy at times, a burden, a sack full of laundry that was once new clothes, objects of delight and newness, full of promise.

Dump it all out on the ground, throw away the bag—kick it all into a corner and let it lie there. Smooth the footprints off the path with your fingers. Empty it all out—empty, empty, full of nothing. Pour your mind into a box and close the lid. Nothing, nothing. Now sit very still, eyes half closed, and wait.

Nothing buzzes around my head in the late afternoon sun like a summer fly.

Emptiness rolls out on either side as far as the eye can see.

wo sides of the brain playing catch with each other, firing off back and forth, more complicated than tennis, more like volleyball maybe. The smell of cut grass, tan bodies in shorts laughing and hitting the ball up and over, bumping into each other, trying hard. I was never any good at sports, lonely frightened kid watching others do simple things that were utterly beyond me. Hanging out on the sidelines, don't notice me.

Amy, 3, in the restaurant asks me, "Can they hear me chewing?" She is utterly intent, this is IMPORTANT. My heart floods with love for her, love for him, my children, how can I ever protect them enough, give them enough. If I were God there wouldn't be enough I could do for them. Krishna's old friend comes to visit him bringing rice cakes made by his wife as an offering. The man is poor, cakes are all he can afford to bring. Krishna accepts them with delight—he eats one, then another, then another. Then his wife leans over and whispers in his ear, "My Lord, you have eaten enough of his cakes. You have ensured the happiness and prosperity of his family, his children's families, and their children's families. Don't overdo it."

When is it giving and when receiving? What does love know of the difference? In loving my children I receive everything that life has to offer: meaning.

We care so much for meaning. What does it mean to us?

What is signifying what? My children are stand-ins for God, the beloved who hides behind everything and waits to be discovered. He shines through the children in blinding brilliance, offering clues almost impossible to miss. But the children are so enchanting, I am satisfied with that and look no further. Life's sweetest cup—I drink and drink at the ever-replenished fountain of love, receiving as I give, not knowing the difference.

What's your game, God? Why hide at all? Let my son appear to me as the blue-skinned, eight-armed one, wearing a crown of jewels and glowing with the light of a thousand suns. Let my daughter show me the Mother, eternal creative bringing form from the void, eyes closed in endless bliss, loving us each and all as I love my own babies. Why do you hide your face, Mother? It takes us so long to know we are cared for, taken care of. What is this blindness that makes us feel abandoned and unworthy?

It is my own blindness, brought on by a mother unable to express her love for me.

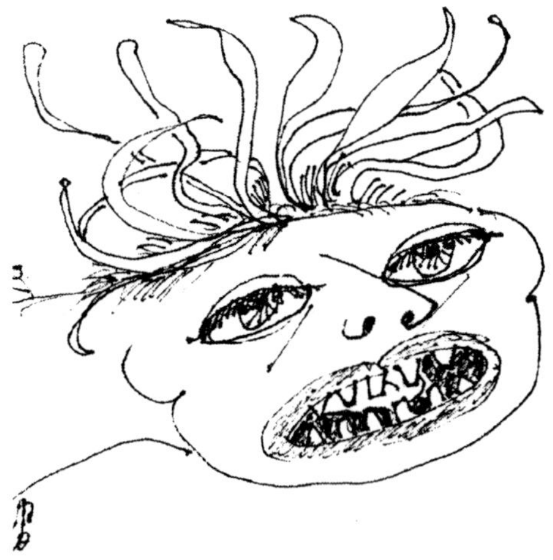

THE TEETH MOTHER

How curious to have a mother who is able to feel tenderness for everyone but you! A bad joke. The teeth mother. A true blessing, because in tearing away the veil I penetrate to the ocean of compassion. The impersonal love. I would never have loved my children so much if there had really been no love in my life. **God is always there.**

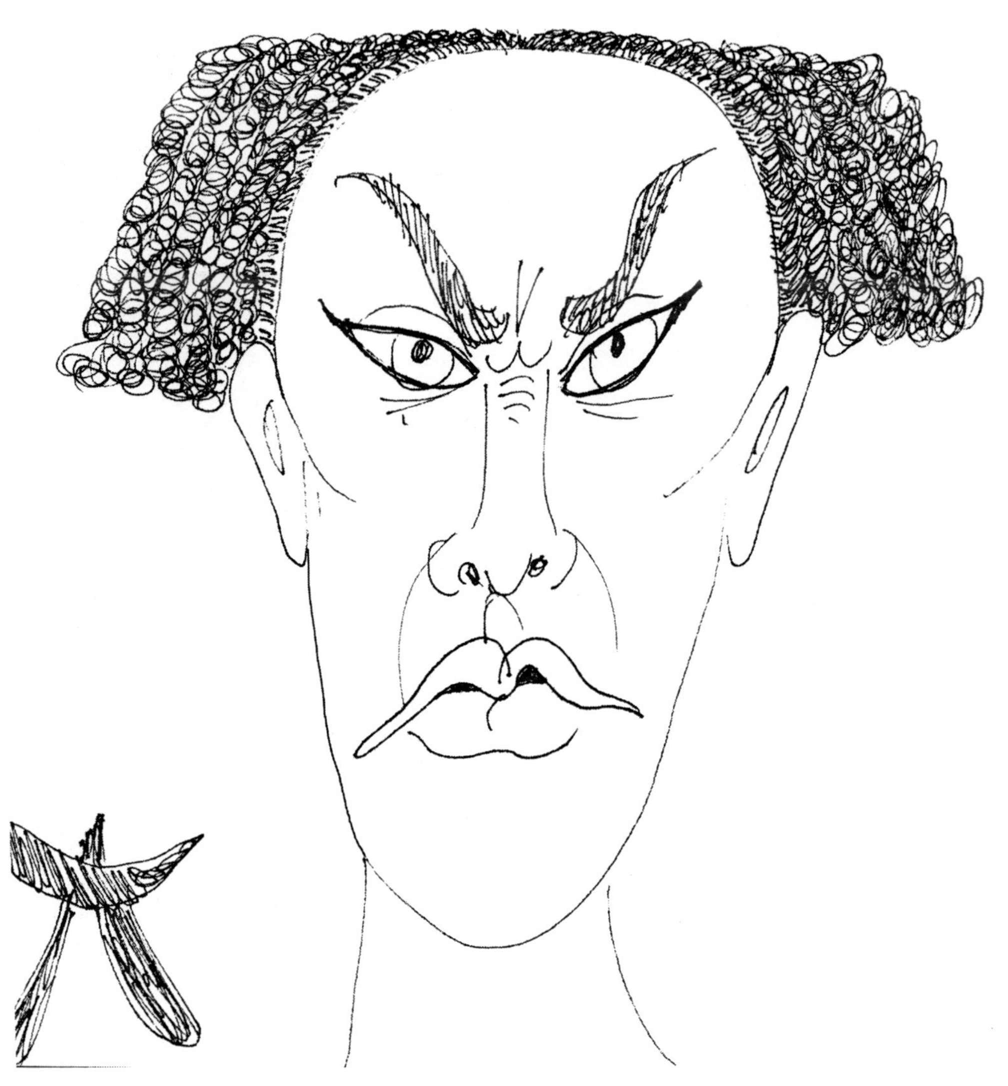

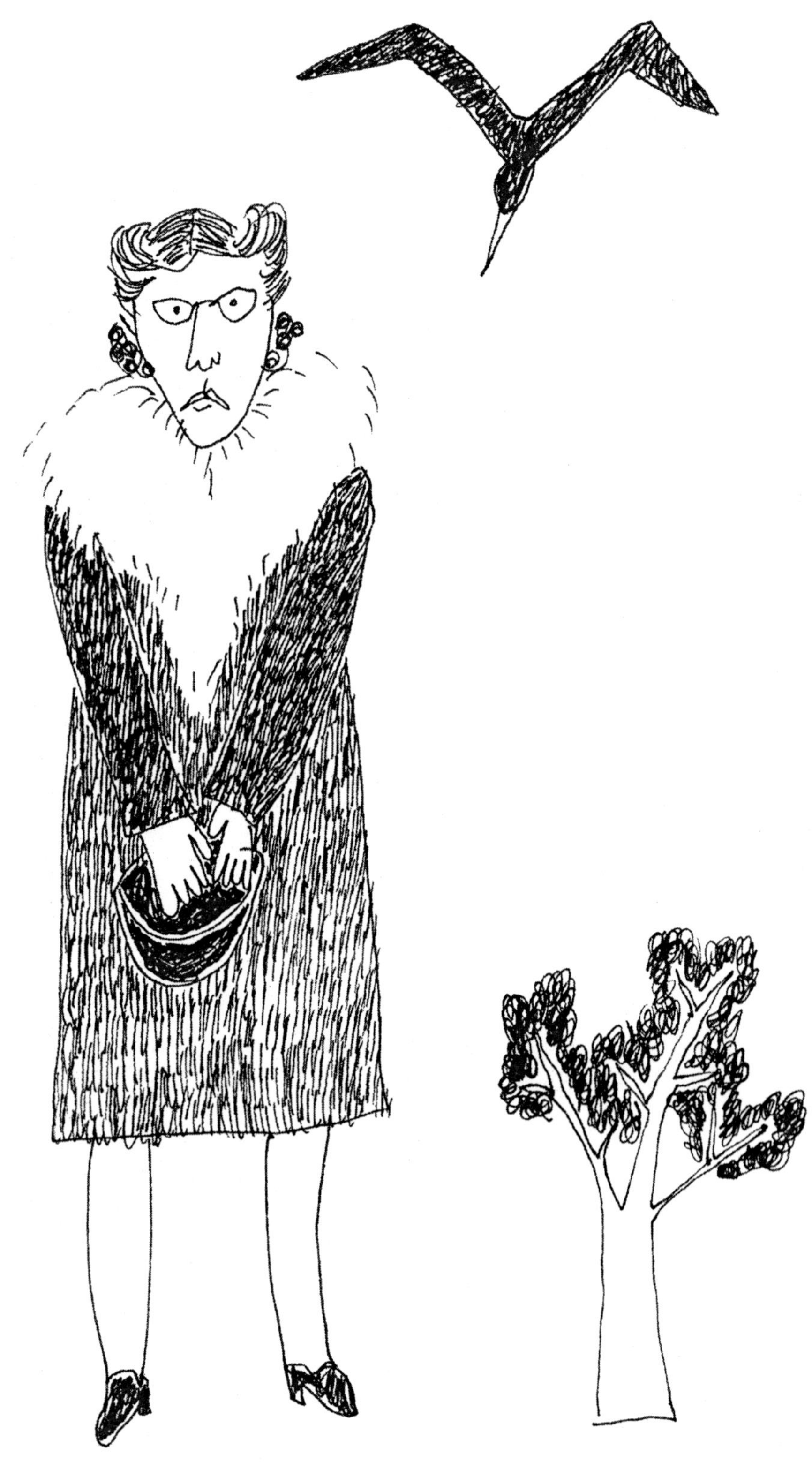

Melting wax candle sitting on a sea of foil,

the flame jumps and pulls back, glowing in my eyes and leaving dots of blue on the surface of the world around me. The world around me peopled with people writing, writing words off the page of their minds onto the waiting white page, waiting for the flow of words to deposit itself there like fallen leaves on the autumn lawn, lying there still, waiting for the autumn wind to come and sweep them into patterns, revealing now the patterns of the mind, revealing what the mind meant when it dropped these leaves, words, today on this white page. Out of so many words stored in the mind, why these today? Do the words have a life of their own, or do I give them life as they drift through my mind and come together in groups, making meaning?

No, these words are alive, charged with power, constructed of letters, units of form and force, uniting in various ways to create meaning; agreed-on meaning and personal meaning. I tell my words what to mean, says Humpty, I pay them well so they do what I say. Jump! Mean this! Yes, master, and where would you like me to stand? You, over here, next to that one. Does that reveal the meaning best, or hide it best? Better to let the wind arrange them, lazily blowing over the leaves' surface and twirling them, sliding them ever so gently into one another until suddenly I gasp at the beauty of it, the pattern revealed that was mine and not mine, more beautiful than ever I could dream.

A Persian carpet, a magic carpet. Its corner curls up, inviting me to take a ride. I leap aboard eagerly, ready for the adventure, and instantly it takes off as I wobble and sit down hard. It soars over the maple tree as I laugh out loud at the joy and terror of it. Below me is my ex-lawn, never to be my lawn again, for I can never return to the same place now. Good-bye—grass and trees and rolling hills I knew so well!

With a jolt I see we are over vast desert landscapes, speeding below us as though they themselves were flying. Pale gold desert, pink rocks, a setting sun lighting the scene for my exaltation. The glowing, fading sunlight on the pink rocks becomes the candlelight in my eyes. The candle invites me to ask a question.

Where am I going?

Away. Far places. Another coast. A new ocean. Right becomes left, as land and sea switch places. I am flipped around, my front becomes my back. I am inside out now, the new reversible me, a whole new garment to dress myself in. To everyone else it looks new, but I know myself that it's always been there, hidden inside. Am I beautiful? I find a mirror on the magic carpet, a polished brass hand mirror. I hold it up and see my whole self in it. I am like Orion, made of stars. Inside my blue-black spaces are new words, newborn words revolving in a slow dance like distant galaxies in the void.

I am going to try out a new word: autonomy, dichotomy, mingle, gainsay—strange words, how unfamiliar they feel as they roll around on my tongue, filling my mouth with their taste. I am slightly disappointed—I am still speaking English! Never mind, let go of the expectations of what is "new" —I am following this adventure wherever it takes me.

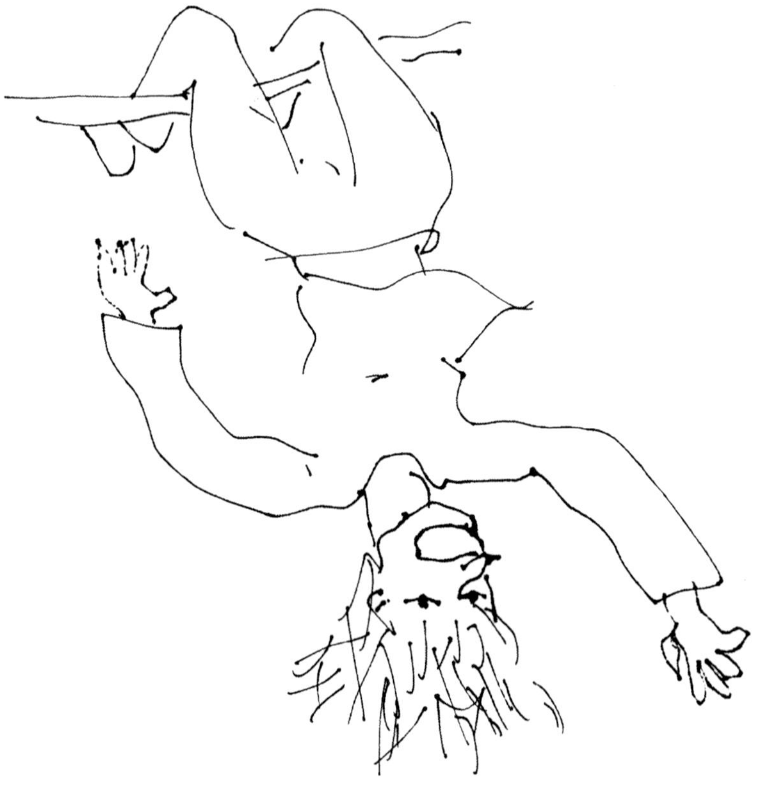

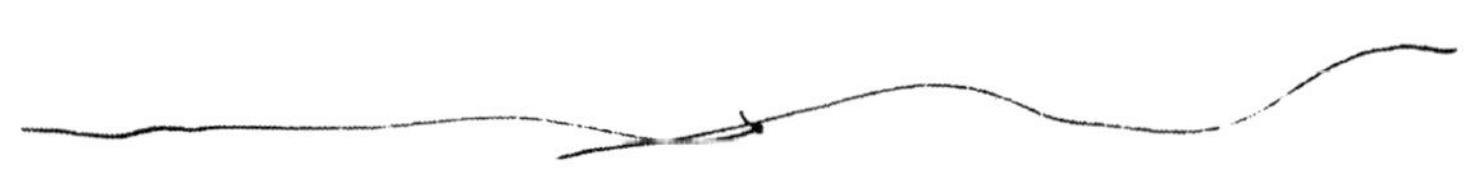

Up off the brown felt cloth backdrop, words floating tumbling, green red gray orange, like the notes in a musical line, forming now into streamers, no momentum but the endless process, peeling up and presenting themselves to be read and heard, to be thought and heard, heartfelt or not, just words, the stuff of thoughts.

And what about the spaces, soft and dark, music-filled now, the spaces around and between the words, wordless space-time, two continuums at work here, stream of thought-words in felt-un-felt brown felt space-drop backdrop. Drop back. What's behind the felt? The feelings? Fold it back and peer in or out, wherever it is.

Blue space-sky, bright with light, clouds and the word for clouds floating in blue space. Cloudy space. Words out here too, few and far between like stars in the void. The music circles round like a spiral galaxy, going somewhere, going nowhere. A population of words, emigrating outward to populate farther planets. A seed-word for each planet. A is for Alpha. Words come alive. Out of words are born clouds of beings populating clouds of planets in the spiral galaxy of blue-sky-space-mind.

Do I mind? I am mindful of the words streaming outward now into spirals of matter. Does it matter? The material of the mind. Music pauses and words rest. What about the rest? Filling the spaces, words tumbling now, piling up, filling the brown felt space of the box of the mind. I don't mind. Open the box, let them fall out into space, free-fall as I follow. Stepping-stones into space, hopping on words, going farther, going beyond the felt. There's the earth, round and blue, incandescent and breathing, in and out like an animal, Mother Earth. How sentimentally attached I am to her.

Heartstrings holding me to her. The mother of words, giving rise to form, the human form in which all words reside. My ancient residence. I float free now, following seed-words to new planets and new forms. New forms in the formless void. Words sing out, calling me.

Bells
Crying
Fawn
Atmosphere
Devils

Bedeviled
Starry night
Cantaloupe
Can't-elope

Mother is calling me back.

The path of words eases itself under my feet. Come on, don't be afraid. Feel your toes on it, it's real, it's there. Step by step into the stars. Jupiter and Mars. Bye-bye world. Whose world are you anyway? So long, Mother Earth. The string of words stretches and curls out, thin, unbroken. Outward bound, unbound. Far planets show themselves to me. There is no word for these, a new language forms. Alphabet breaks itself into pieces, the seeds fall out of the letter-pods. Sowing seeds in space. Mind thinking pictures, mind over matter. Matterless planet, a ball of words, seeds of sound, **they don't speak English here.**

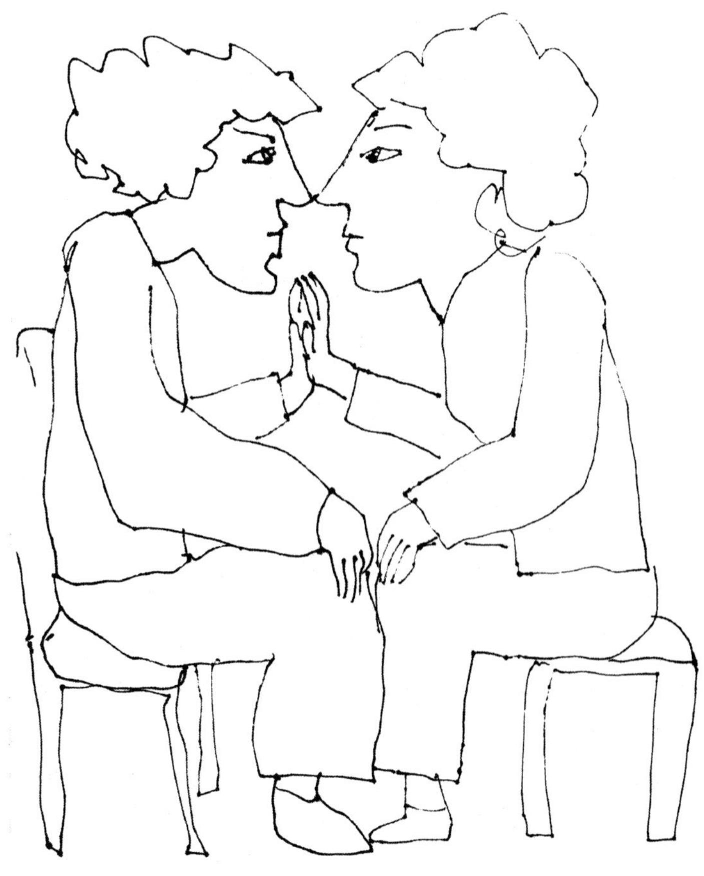

don't think of a monkey. There he is, sneaking in from right field, a funny little man-monkey, upright with a crocheted many-colored cap on his head. He is just there, without emotion, without antics. He tells me he is always there, always will be, and will appear any time I try to not think of a monkey. I bow deeply and thank him, acknowledging my reverence for his faithful service. Who else is there, I want to know. And now he laughs, monkey-like at last, and pulls back a curtain. Go ahead, see for yourself. I have a fleeting impression of a musty attic, stored objects, a lamp, an old trunk, unused things, cobwebs. I pull back. Scared? he says. He is laughing at and with me. Of course I'm not scared, I say bravely. It's true, I'm not scared, but there was that gesture of pulling back.

So I step in. I'm in the attic, looking around, feeling oppressed. I think briefly about getting rid of all this junk, but at the same time I know what I knew with my first glance, that this is just the first level, and I am to keep going. There are better things beyond.

I pass through the attic, which is shallow like a stage set. There's a lit area beyond, with nothing in it. Just light. Anyone here, I call? The chickens answer, Nobody here but us chickens. I'm in the wrong place, I say huffily to myself and the chickens. The monkey comes and takes my elbow compassionately. Come on, I'll show you where. Once in Bombay in the market an Indian man came up and offered to guide us around. I was terrified of the place, terrified of him, all the while knowing I was in absolutely no danger, there was nothing here in the least sinister or menacing, but so deep in the throes of culture shock that all I could do was pull back into myself and try to limit the onslaught of sounds, smells, sights, and the thoughts of all those Indian vendors staring at me.

Enough of this, let's get going, there's nothing here to be scared of. I go through the market and out the door. Into the streets of Bombay. Now I see Indian saddhus and beggars, what are you doing in my mind? We might ask you the same question, they mock. Oh please, monkey, take me to a more private place. Isn't there a corner in here that is just me?

Is that what you're looking for? I'm just showing you around—don't you want to see it all?

Suddenly I'm looking into a huge glass globe in which images are flickering like a giant round television screen. Pick out what you want, says the monkey, but I am trans-

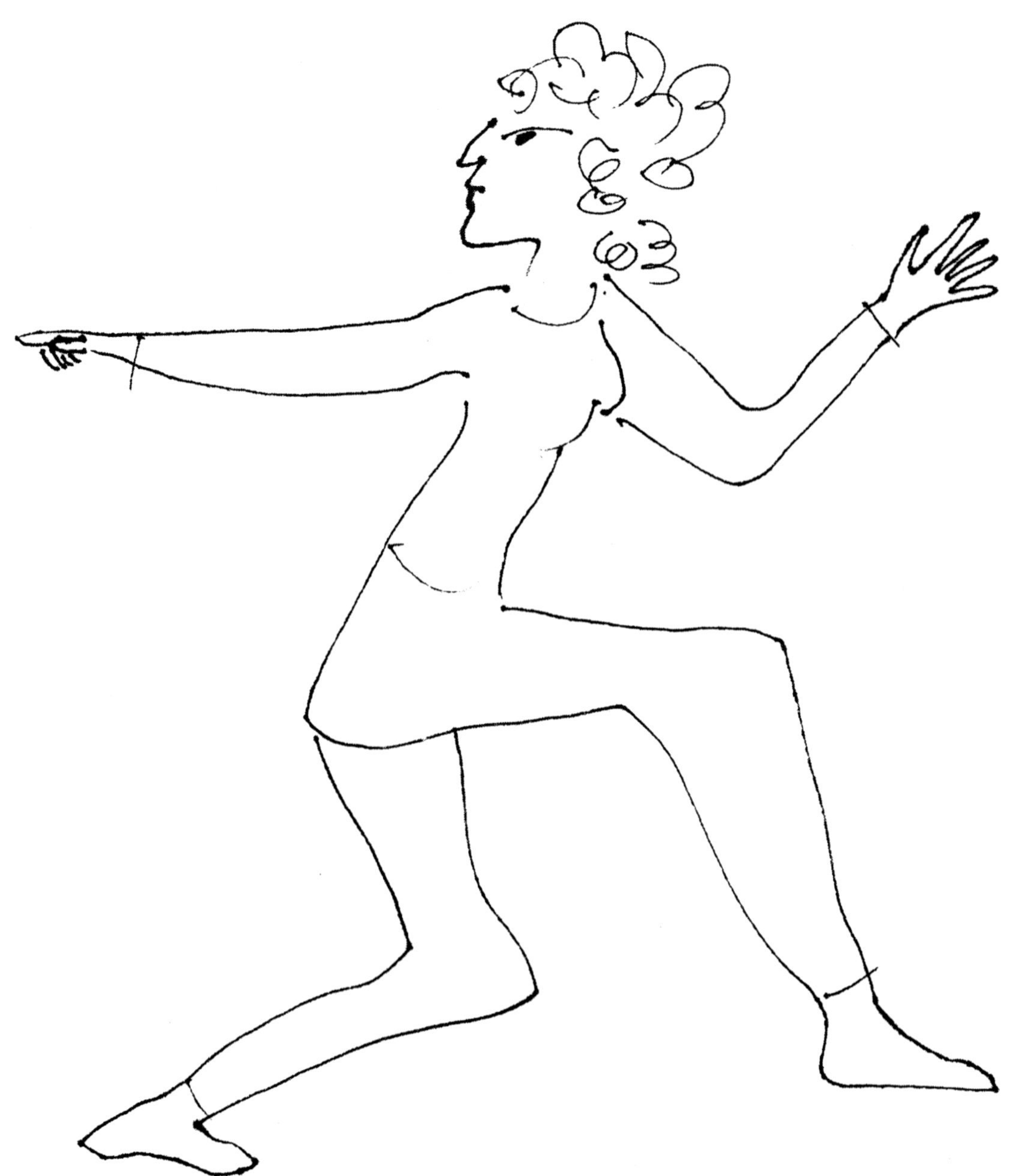

fixed, wanting to see it all. It moves and moves—separate images reflect off each other, somehow all fitting into that three-dimensional space. I'm not even aware of the nature of the images, so overwhelmed by the color and constant movement, the shifting relationships, images rising to the surface and others falling into the depths, like a rapidly boiling kettle of lentils. I take the globe in my two hands like a medicine ball. It fills me with delight. Its hard surface softens and I plunge in, cutting through the images that close around me like warm water. I dive deep, suspecting there's a center.

I find a plum, a plum pit, and a pearl. Is this it? A plum, a plum pit, and a pearl? I hold them in my hand and look around me, hoping I am in a medium that will allow me to breathe. A fish comes to nibble at the plum. I plant the plum pit in the sea bottom. The pearl enters my heart and I rise to the surface and onto it, like Venus. I look down into the waters where the images are still reflecting, moving. The monkey is nowhere to be seen. The music has stopped. I grab a passing wave and make my way to shore.

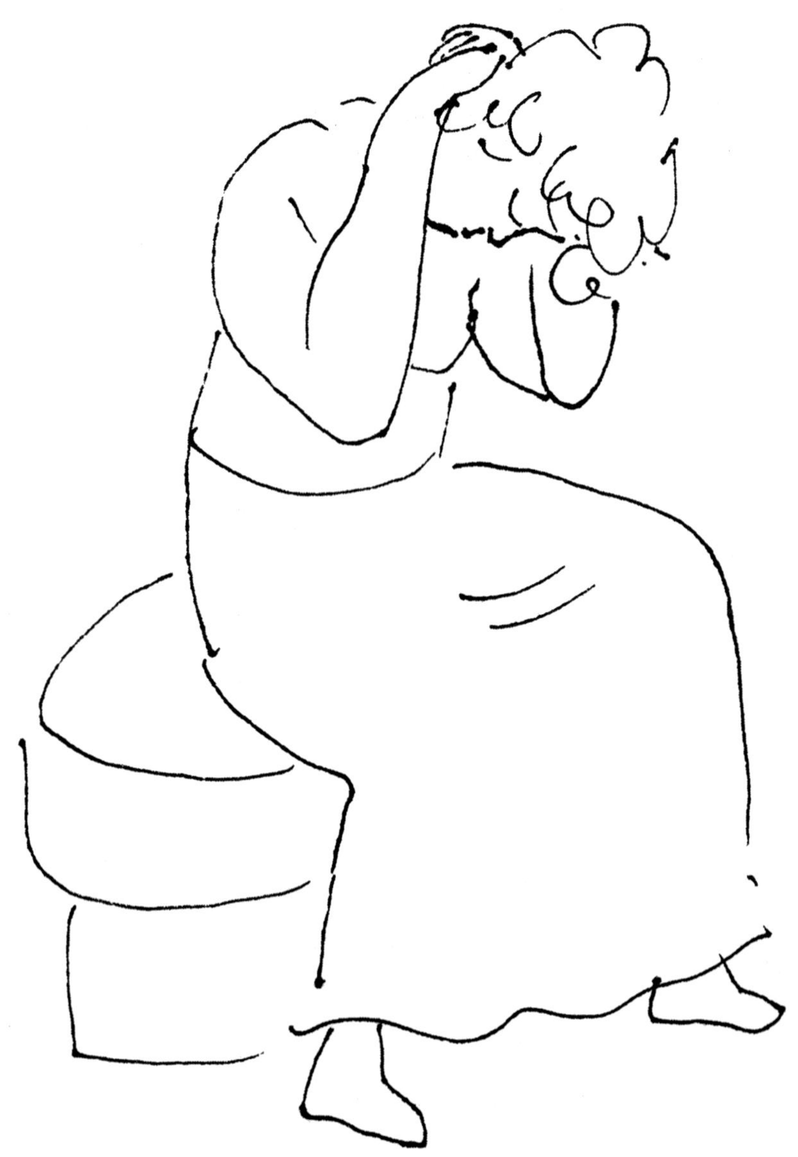

like circus acrobats tumbling in the air my thoughts dance in my head in the vault of my head in the interior space that is larger than the shell that contains it. Fourth-dimensional thoughts using four-dimensional words, beyond meaning and emotion, unfurling their substance as they curl out into the unfamiliar dimension, a space beyond our own, unvisited by the three-dimensional mind that confines us in the prison of its orderly thoughts, cause preceding effect, marching us logically toward our logical three-dimensional death.

Now comes the clown, laughing an icon-shattering laugh and tumbling head over heels on the arena floor, scattering the paraphernalia of the preceding acts, little firecrackers going off around him as he staggers chaotically about, laughing, not caring.

Out of his sleeve he pulls a stick, which bursts into bloom, a bouquet of flowers made of misty light, their forms curl out into the space around like streamers, flowers whose petals are still growing, unfurling in the nosegay of purple and pink and turquoise light. He throws it up in the air with a laugh, mocking our fascination with it. Up he leaps, feet over head, and stops in midair, his head twisted around to look down at us with a look of surprise at his own extravagant gesture.

He waves his arms and the circus dissolves around him, the crowd disappears, the tent and the benches evanesce until all that's left are his eyes and our own, locked in a moment of timeless magic that has no space. Our eyes expand to become the universe, and with a flick of consciousness we step outside, looking back at the universe as an astronaut looks at the Earth that formerly enclosed all the world he knew or could conceive.

Looking into the worn-out shell of our universe as into a glass fishbowl, seeing strings of stars swimming in the luminous void, spiraling round in what we once called space.

Take the bowl in your hands, now bigger than all Creation. Shake it like a paperweight, see the stars redistribute themselves like snow in a globe, a sentimental scene from some ancient reality we have now forever outgrown. There's no going back there, too late now, too big now. Keep spreading endlessly into four-dimensional space, then five, then six, then nine, then twelve, then pop! It shatters into crystals of energy showering around us like musical notes, curling in, then out, flowing away as our mind flows with it, on and on and on toward some fathomless sea of being being created even now at the furthest reaches of time.

Going home again.

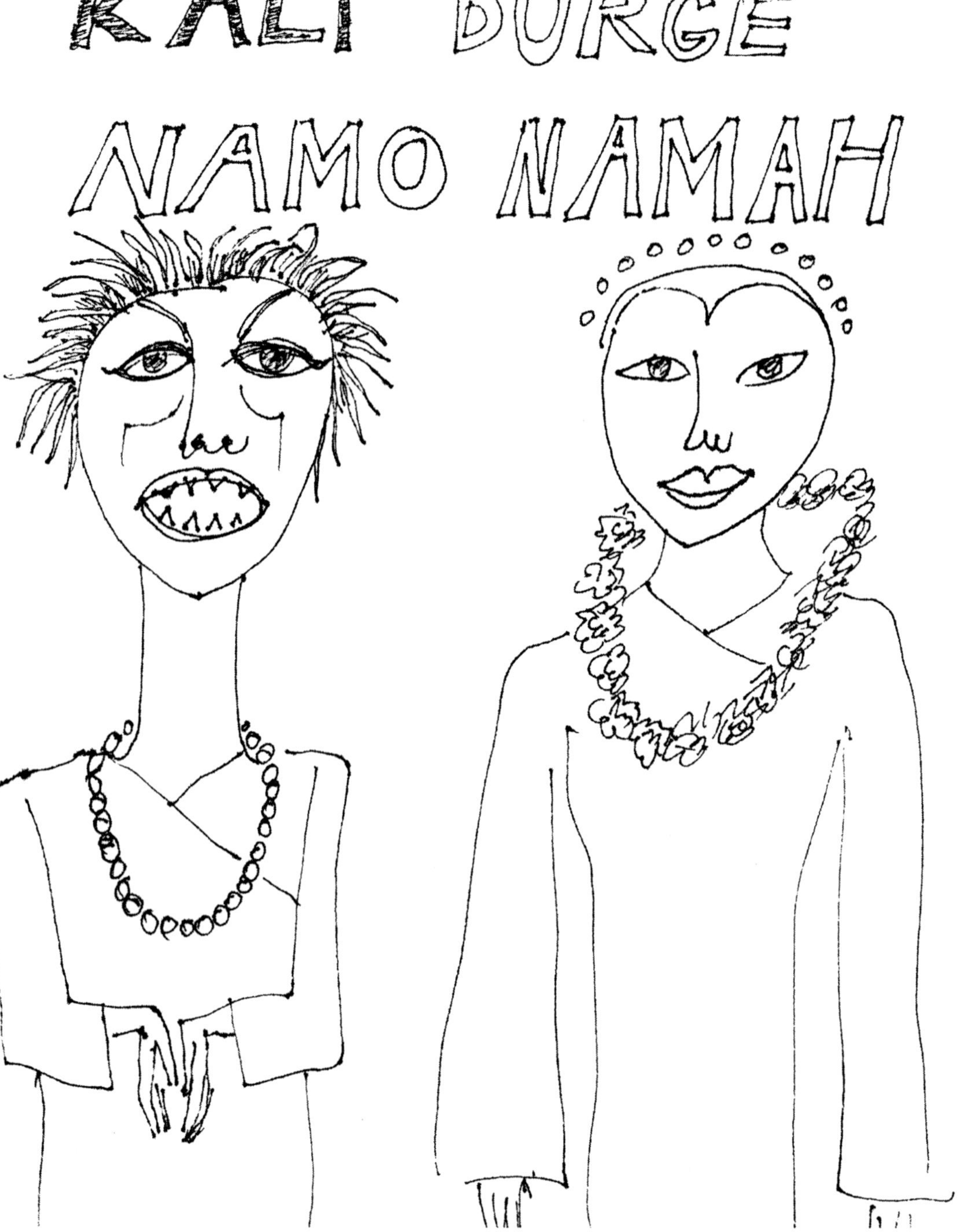

KALI DURGE NAMO NAMAH

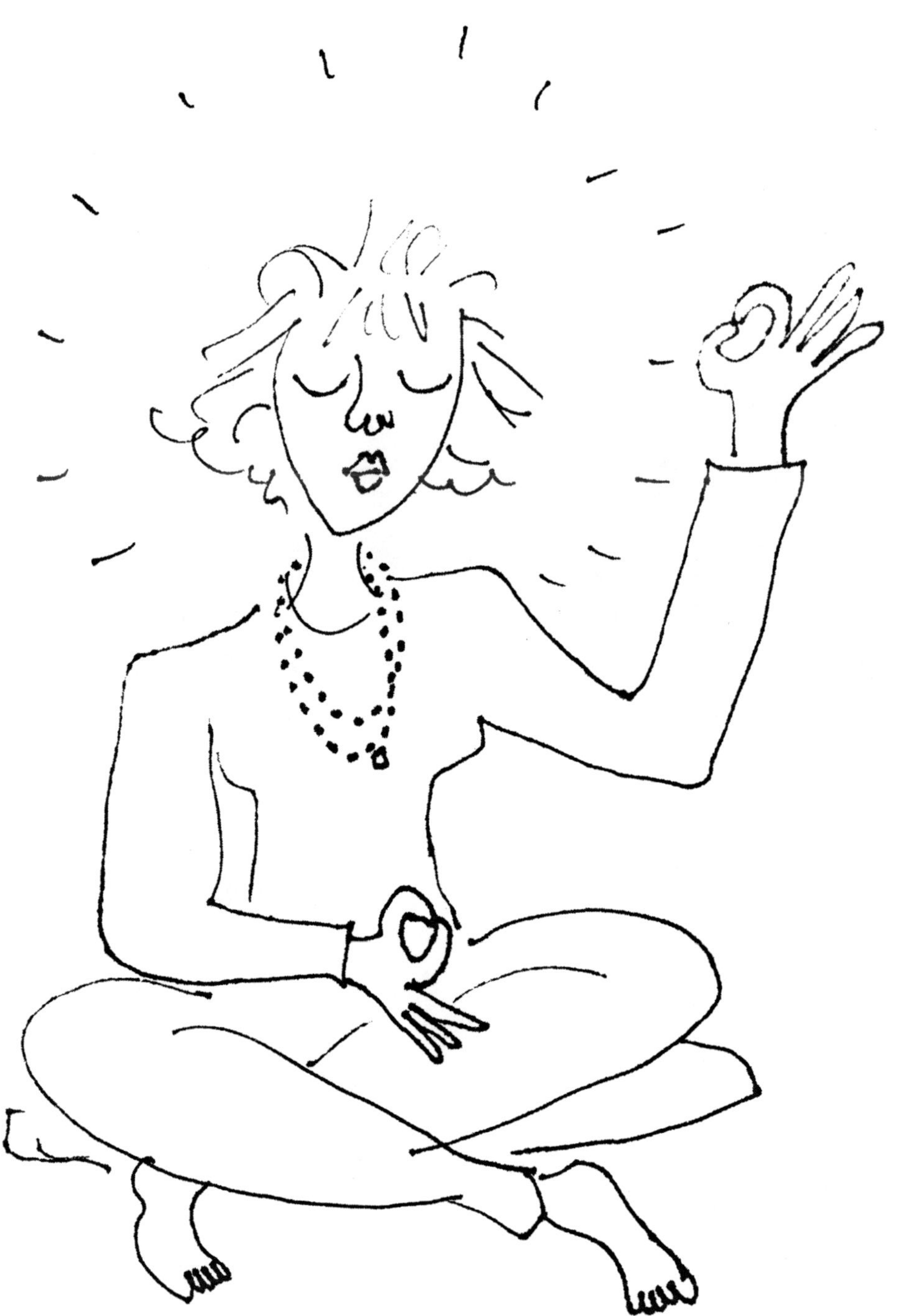

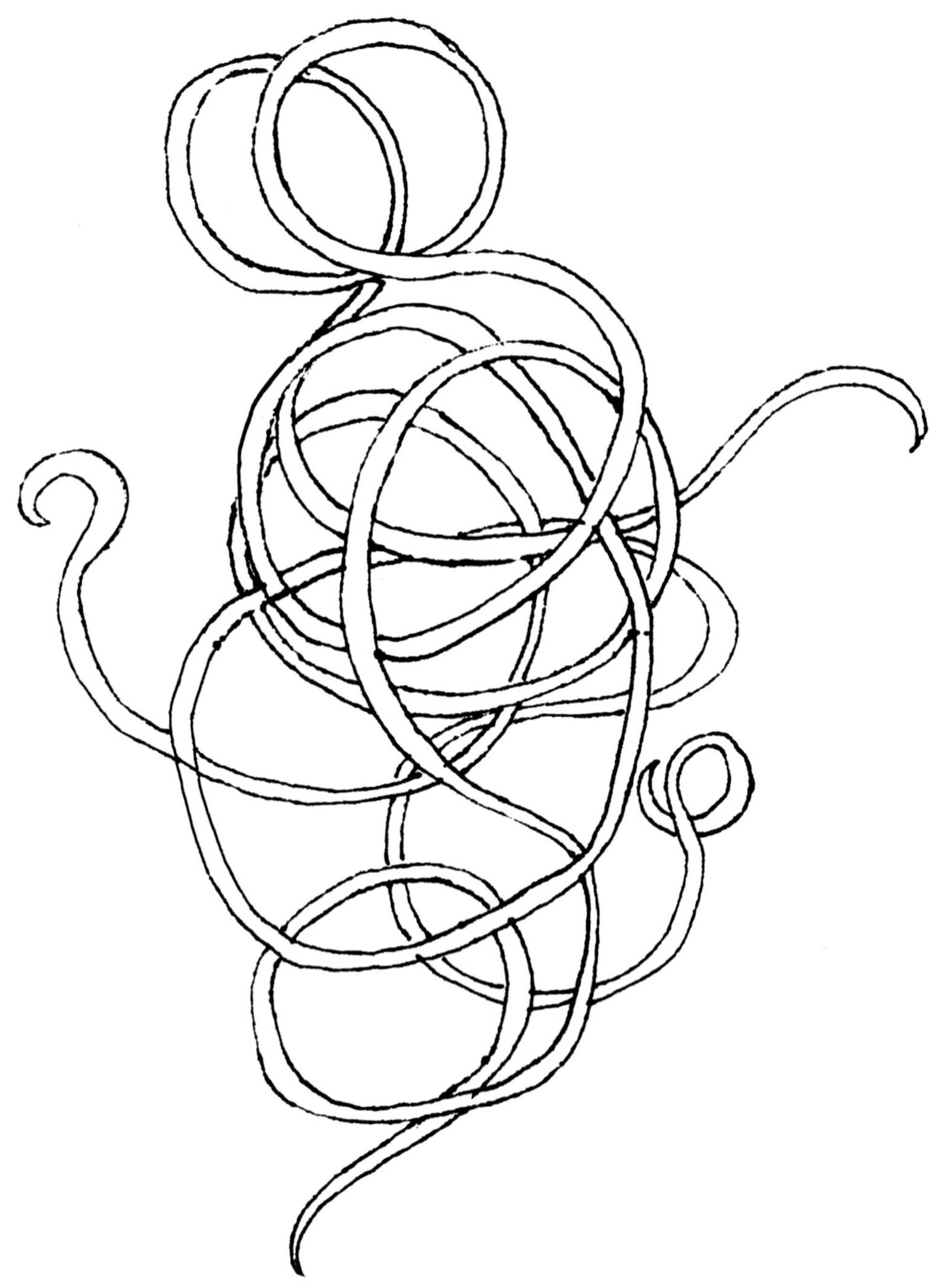

Sounds and colors mixing together, colors spreading out on waves of sound, vibrating red, pulsing blue-green, where does turquoise come from? How playful of the Earth to hide beautiful stones in her depths; who found the first gemstone? Brushing the soft dirt from it, putting the object in the palm of his hand to have a look, a gasp of surprise at the gleaming treasure.

She gives us trees and their fruits, grasses for the animals, roots and leaves for food and medicines, stone caves for shelter, fertile earth to cultivate, clear waters to drink, and then, in her benevolence, hides within herself stones that exist only to be beautiful. Or do they too have a purpose, serving the Earth and all her children in ways we haven't figured out yet?

Each being has its own voice and sings in the immense symphony this planet is, a living organism of separate living parts uniting in some gigantic harmony we haven't tuned in to yet. And what if the gems are there to help us tune in, to sound a note we can vibrate to so we can enter the harmony that's offered us?

Turquoise, a soft and gentle stone, color of Paris sky just before dark, tune me in to your harmony, I will sing your song. Amethyst, the mysterious purple ray, a celestial light made solid so we can touch it and remember the violet light that bathes the stars. Crystal, the magical six-sided stone whose own intelligence gives it form.

The stones on a Hawaiian beach, a pile of sea-washed lava stones in perfect symmetry—round, oval, kidney-shaped, smooth as glass—what force in nature over millennia tosses these stones in its grip until they arrive at this perfection, shaped as if intention had decreed their formation.

I pick up a stone from the beach and hold it in my hand. Smooth and cool, it rests there as though its name were Hand-Held Stone. As I stand with it, hearing the waves washing in at my feet, I feel its living presence. It breathes in my hand, though not air. It knows me as I know it. It is a living piece of the Mother, like me. We have come together on this beach to acknowledge each other, to tune in to each other. To work together henceforth in harmony.

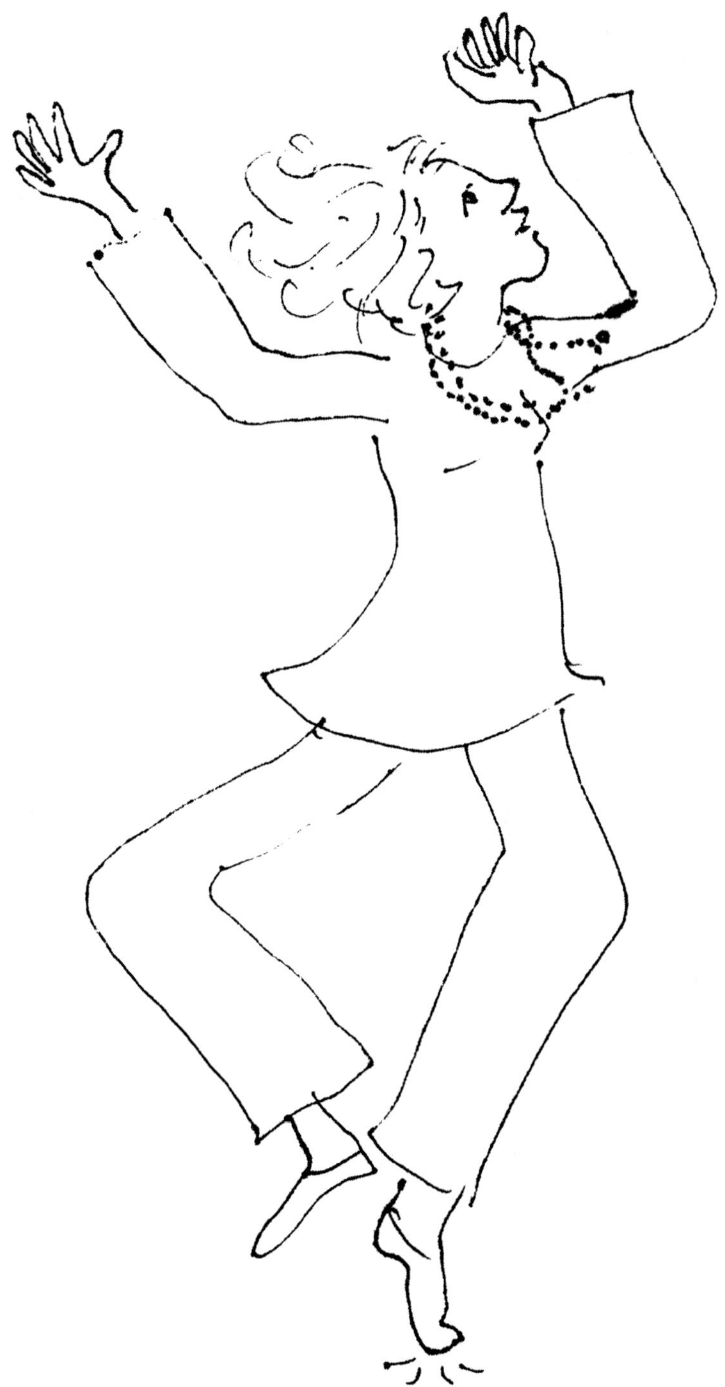

Song of Solomon silent singing, Song of Songs telling my ear things that only music knows. Waves of sound carrying bits and pieces from far stars, too far to read but listen to the pulse of sound floating on the air.

Millions of light years and two eternities away it started toward us, its long journey through universe after universe carries it closer and closer to the moment it comes crashing through the atmosphere in a blaze of vapor and settles like dust toward this spot, where it enters my ear, a package of prerecorded information beyond time.

Wiser now by one chord, I ask myself who sent this sound to me from out there in the no-air, where sound is only a concept. Like a child's game, a long string snaking through curved time connects me to my secret informer. Why do you want me to know this? The answer comes back: I am yourself.

Now I remember how, in another blink of the eye of Brahma, that other myself sent forth a message, a warning or a call, a cry of encouragement or a song of recognition, into the limitless vast depths of uncreated time-space, knowing that once sent it could never be lost, would plunge on its inevitable path toward some not-yet-imagined future where, curling back on itself and long forgotten, it would come back to my own ear and tell me things I never thought to know about Time and Eternity and who I am.

The one I was and always will be awakens and rubs her hands with glee, remembering the message sent and knowing that the voyage now is safely over. Journey's end for a letter to myself from some unfathomable form of myself still printed on a giant luminous screen far out in the stardust debris of worlds the ancients had already forgotten the existence of when for the billionth time they reincarnated on the new planet where man would play out yet another act in the evolution of the everlasting One.

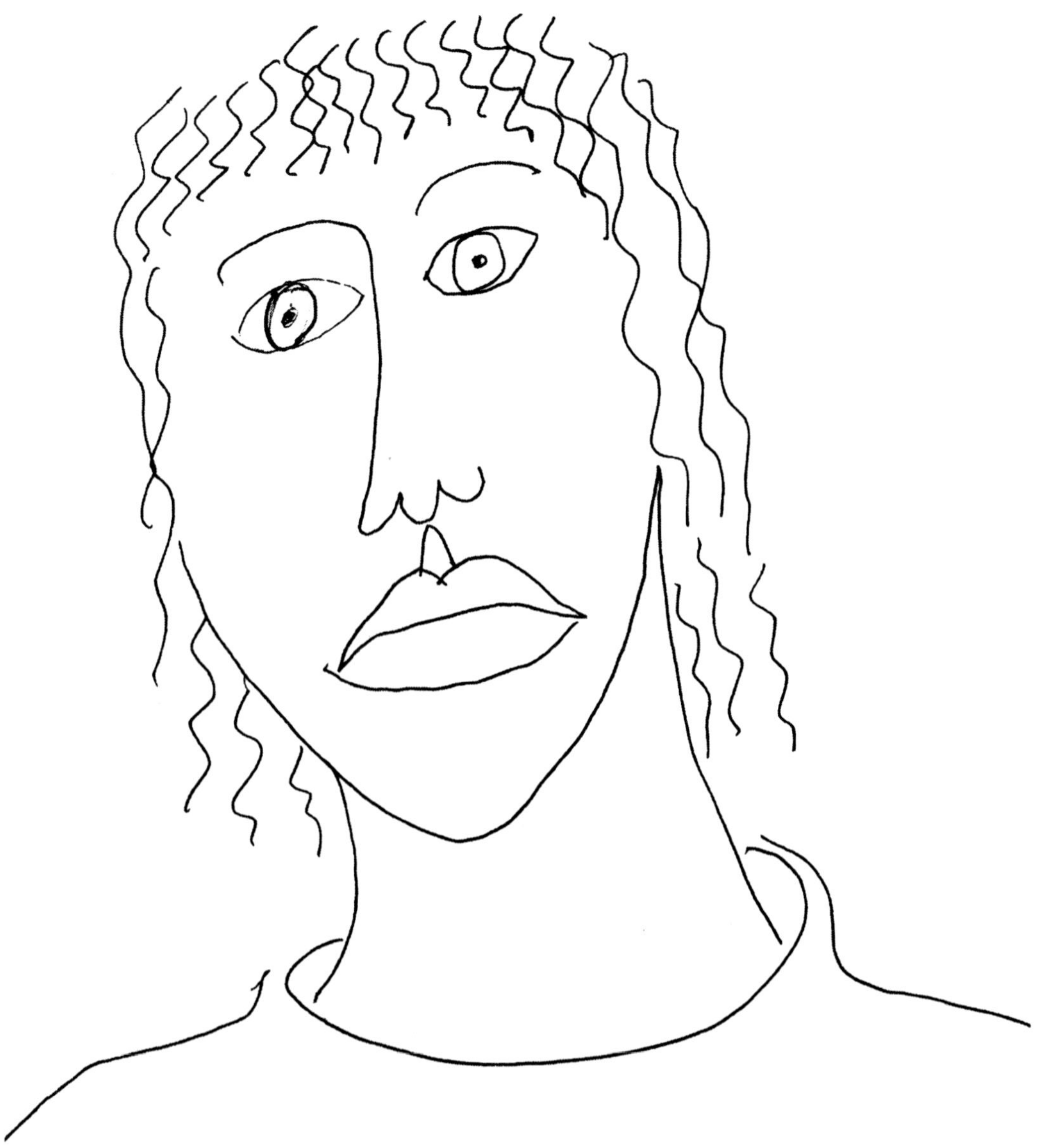

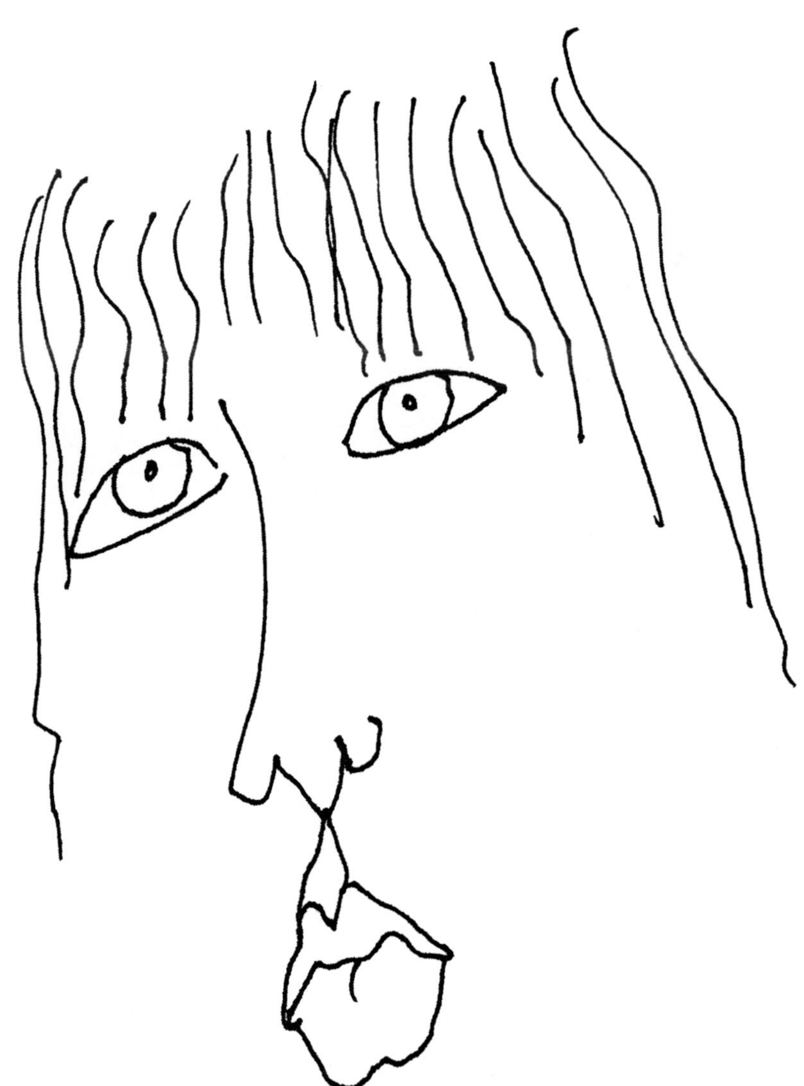

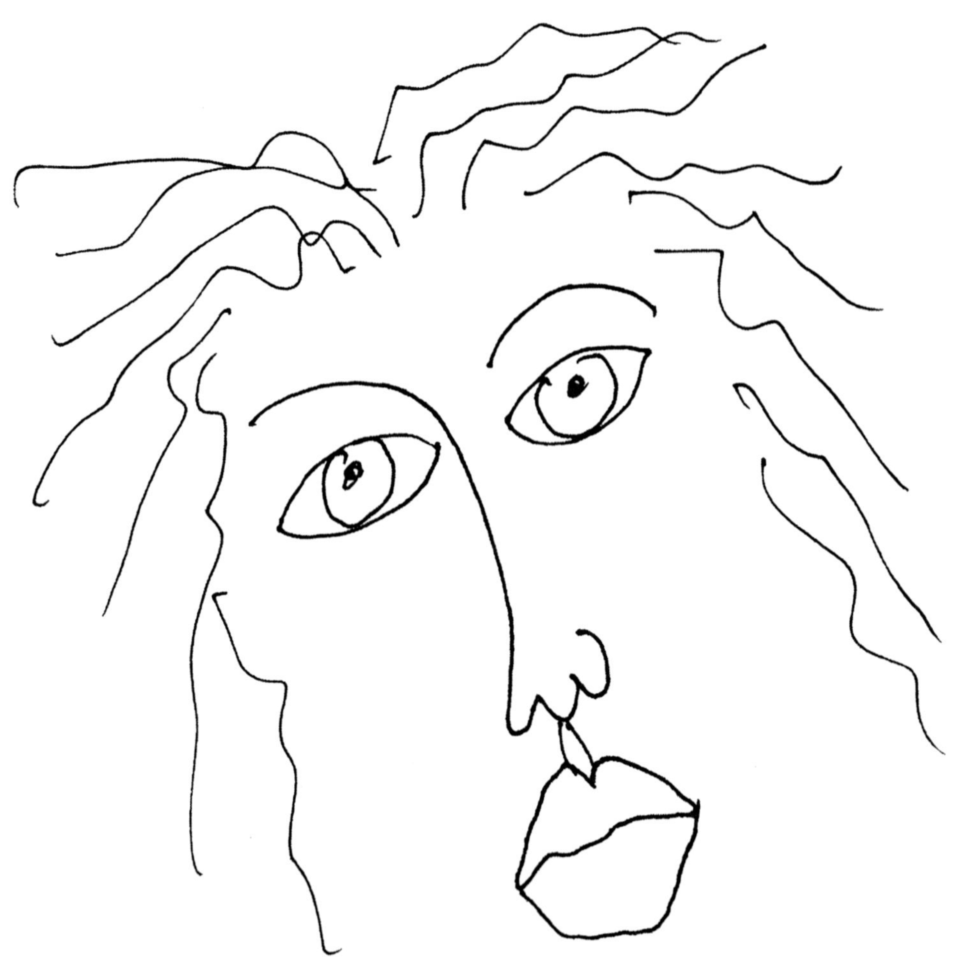

the bag lady sits on a park bench in the median strip of
a broad avenue. In front of her is a shopping cart, rusted and favoring one bent wheel,
in which she has piled her household goods. They are crammed into two torn paper bags
with stiff handles poking above them like ears. A coat is stuffed in beside the bags, one
arm draped languidly over a side of the lopsided cart. The bag lady's gloved fingertips rest
lightly on the handle of the cart, preserving the connection between her and it.

She is dressed in soft colors, layers of worn cloth piled one on another in a casual
necessity that results in a kind of street elegance. The holes in her gloves show a bit of
finger here and there—altogether a coherent style, maybe a trend for the future. Black
shoes, socks falling down and bunched around the ankles, a long pale violet skirt, a pale
gray tunic on top of it, a light blue sweater and a gray shawl pulled around her shoulders.
A throwaway elegance.

Her face is soft and worn like her clothing, and iron-gray hair is pulled back from her
face and tucked into a faded red wool cap. Wisps of hair stray out from beneath her cap
and lift gently in the slight breeze caused by the passage of cars and trucks.

She is talking softly to herself, a low chant, barely audible and addressed to no one.
She pays not the slightest attention to passersby, who turn their heads or look down at
their feet as they stand waiting for their light to change. Her light never changes, it is
constant. She keeps her eyes fixed on it, and croons to it. Her world is a park bench, her
body, her clothes, a broken-down shopping cart and the objects she has crammed into it.
The only variable in her world is the park bench, which is a detachable part of her. The
rest of her is her, as a snail is all snail, consisting of soft body and external shell, but one.

Her eyes turned inward, she rises and moves like a balloon leaving its mooring, and
the world parts to let her pass—what can it do? She will not make the least concession to
its existence, so it must divide and make way for her. Each one she passes is drawn into
her gravity field, and as she moves on she pulls a few molecules from every passerby.

Someday she will become so dense she'll be a human black hole, collapsing in
upon herself and pulling in everything around her. People will notice a sudden rush
of energy, as though something were being pulled out of them. Even the light will rush

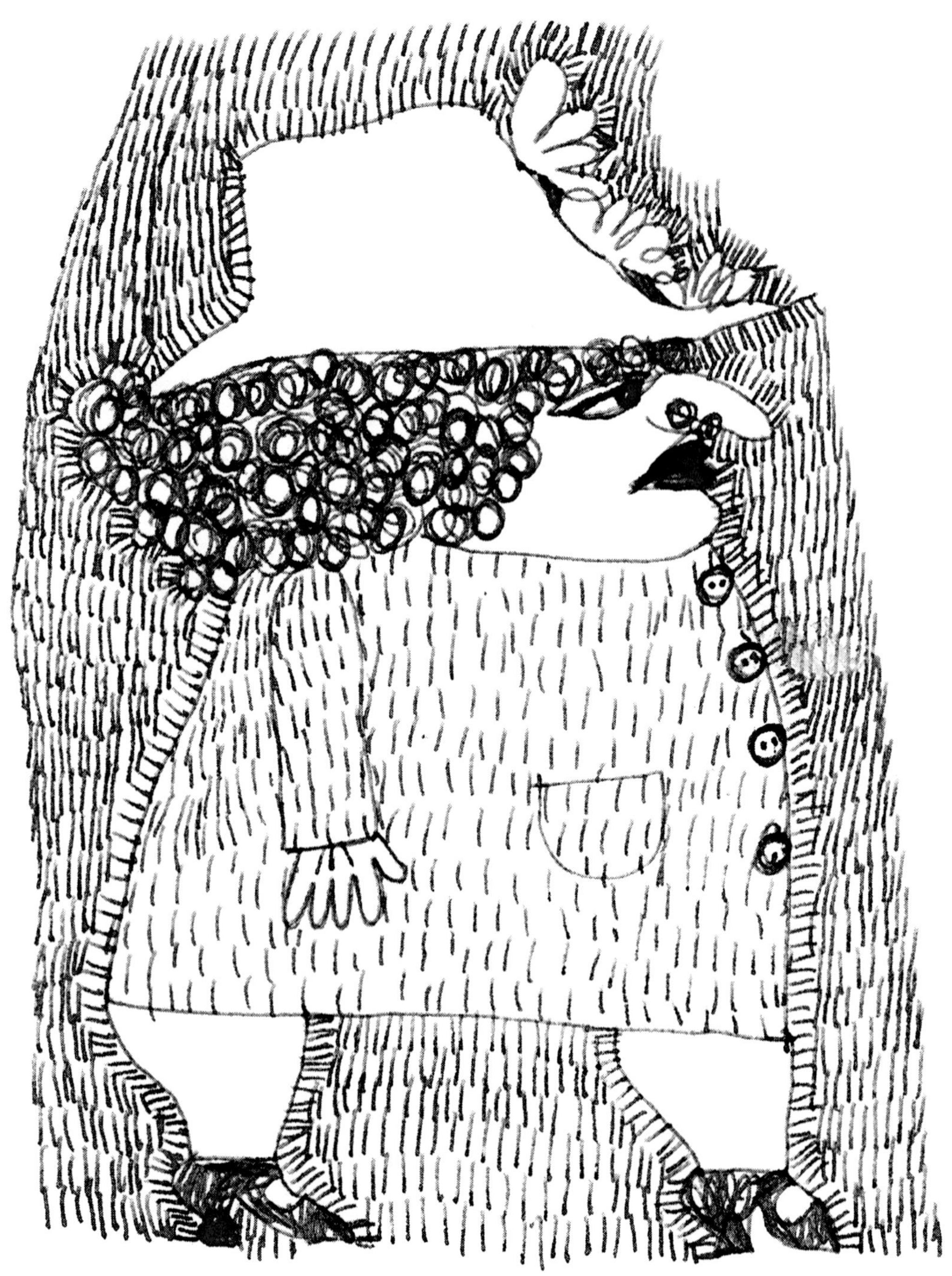

toward her and be absorbed in her density. Passersby will look round to see what happened, but notice only a heap in a doorway, just another bag lady lying on a doorstep, her bags in her arms and her torn coat spread over her body like a shroud.

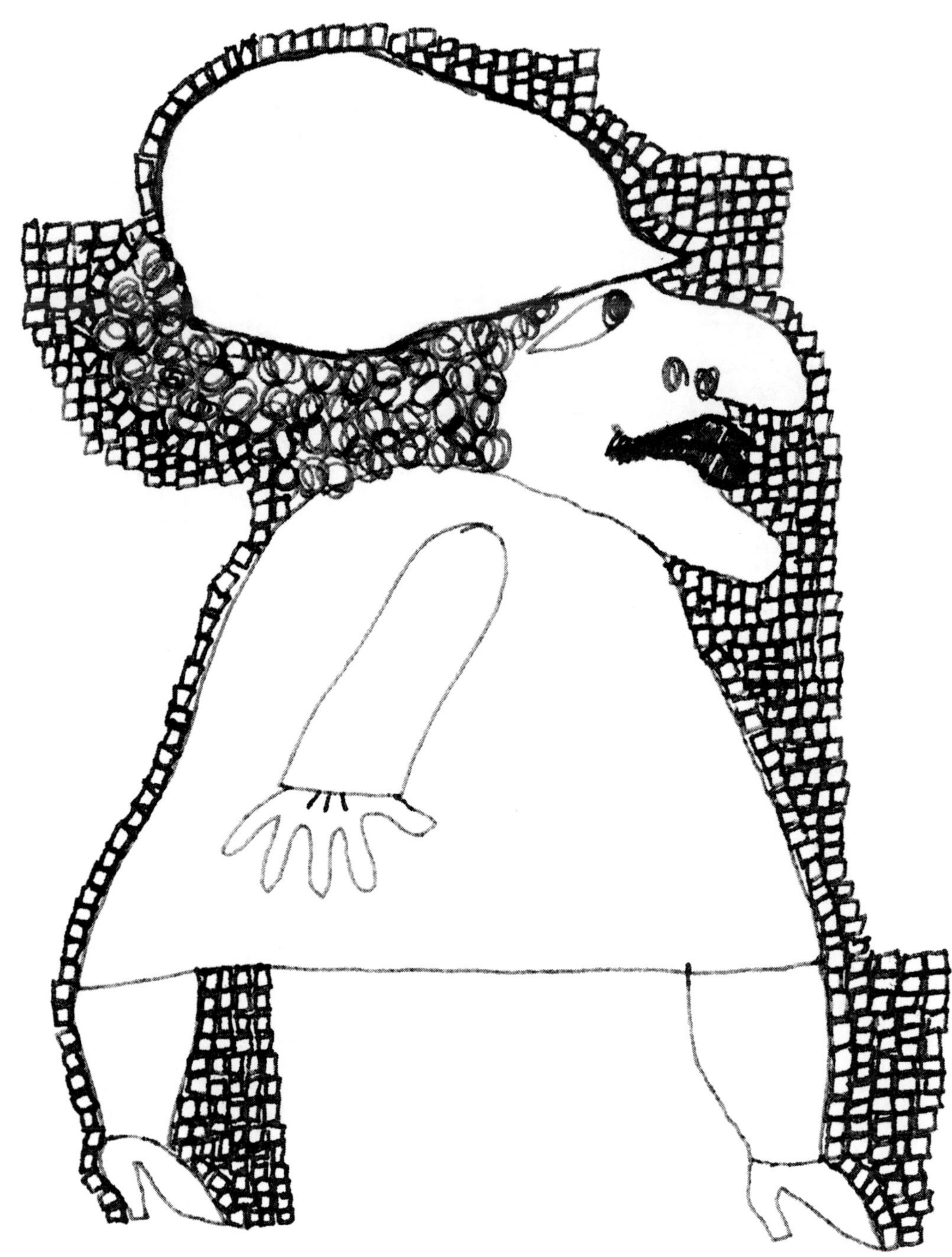

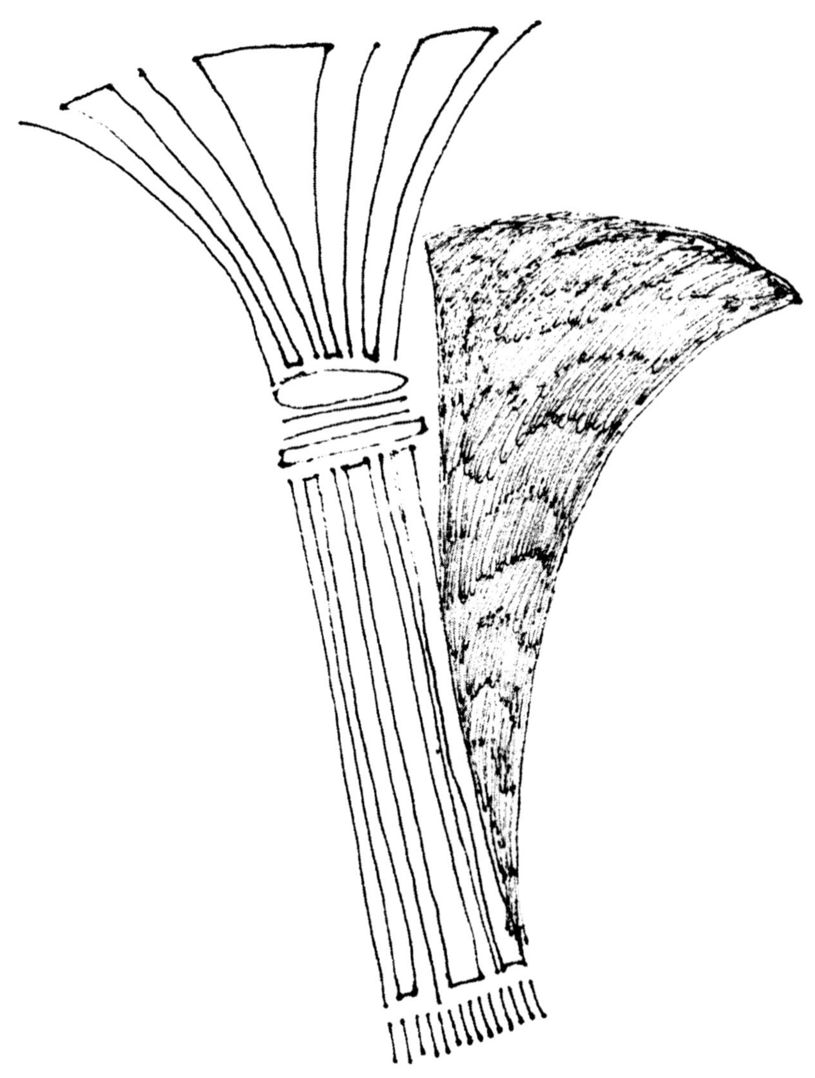

breathe in, breathe out, breathing in to the heart, the inner center, both real and evanescent, physical and metaphysical—the heart center, seat of emotions, heart of the lotus from which everything emerges into manifestation, making itself real in the long leap across rings of dimension from no-time to time, from the immaterial to the manifest in one mighty jump.

Stand we trembling on the brink of nothingness from which we came, on the long journey to where? Poised at the edge of the swirling black hole, one whole universe ago—staring into that maelstrom pull from which even the gaze cannot escape—sucked in, willing and unwilling, the volunteer sacrifice at the altar of nonbeing.

And then in one mighty leap, through the door of nothingness into the beyond of Somewhere, the heart of the heart. The petals of the lotus unfold, revealing a tiny pink luminous being, a human baby this time, newly come from nowhere into I am. Memories of nothing still fresh in its being, the baby moves its limbs and looks around in amazement at this new womb it will inhabit for a life's span.

In its heart of hearts there still sings the song of the nothingness it left behind, while in its eyes blossoms the new world of being it has come into, across miles of beyond on its impossibly long journey into being. Parents lift it from the lotus with welcoming hands, while notions of identity arise from within the heart and are met by reflections from the world around. Heart beating, lungs breathing, existence arising from within, the baby lets go of the place from which it leapt, shakes off the memory of that transforming journey from the edge of nothing to the brink of something, and embarks on the new leap into life.

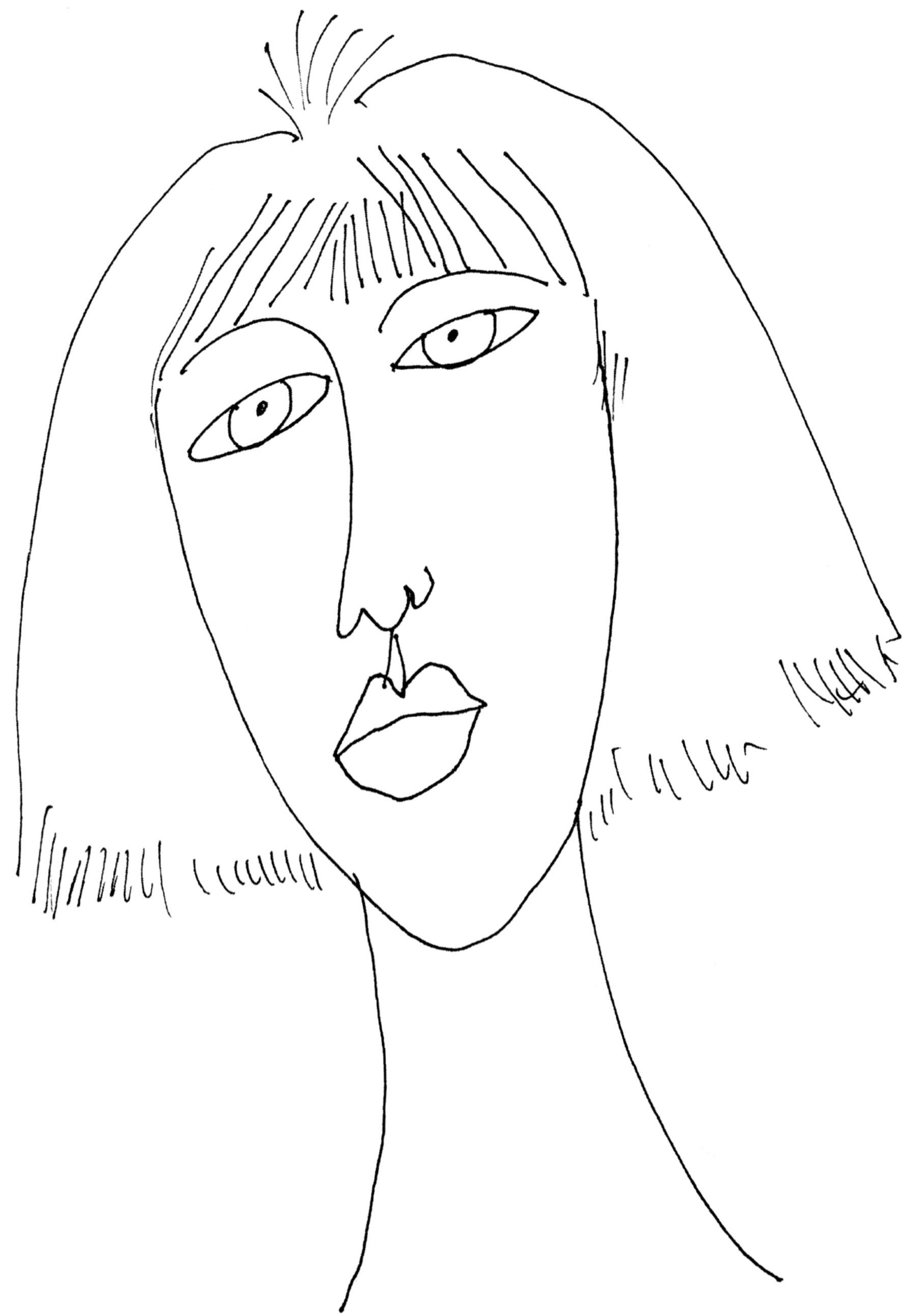

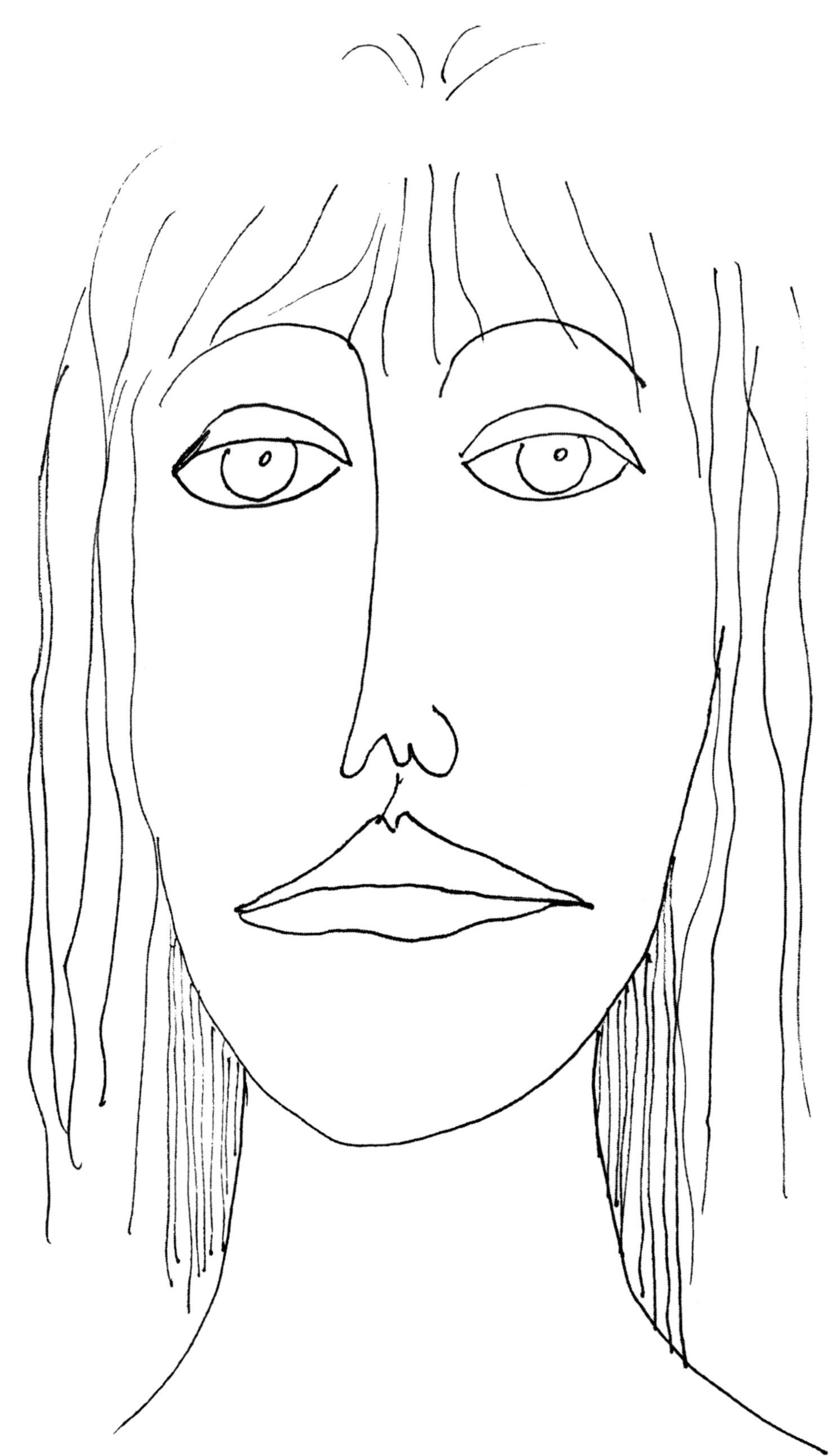

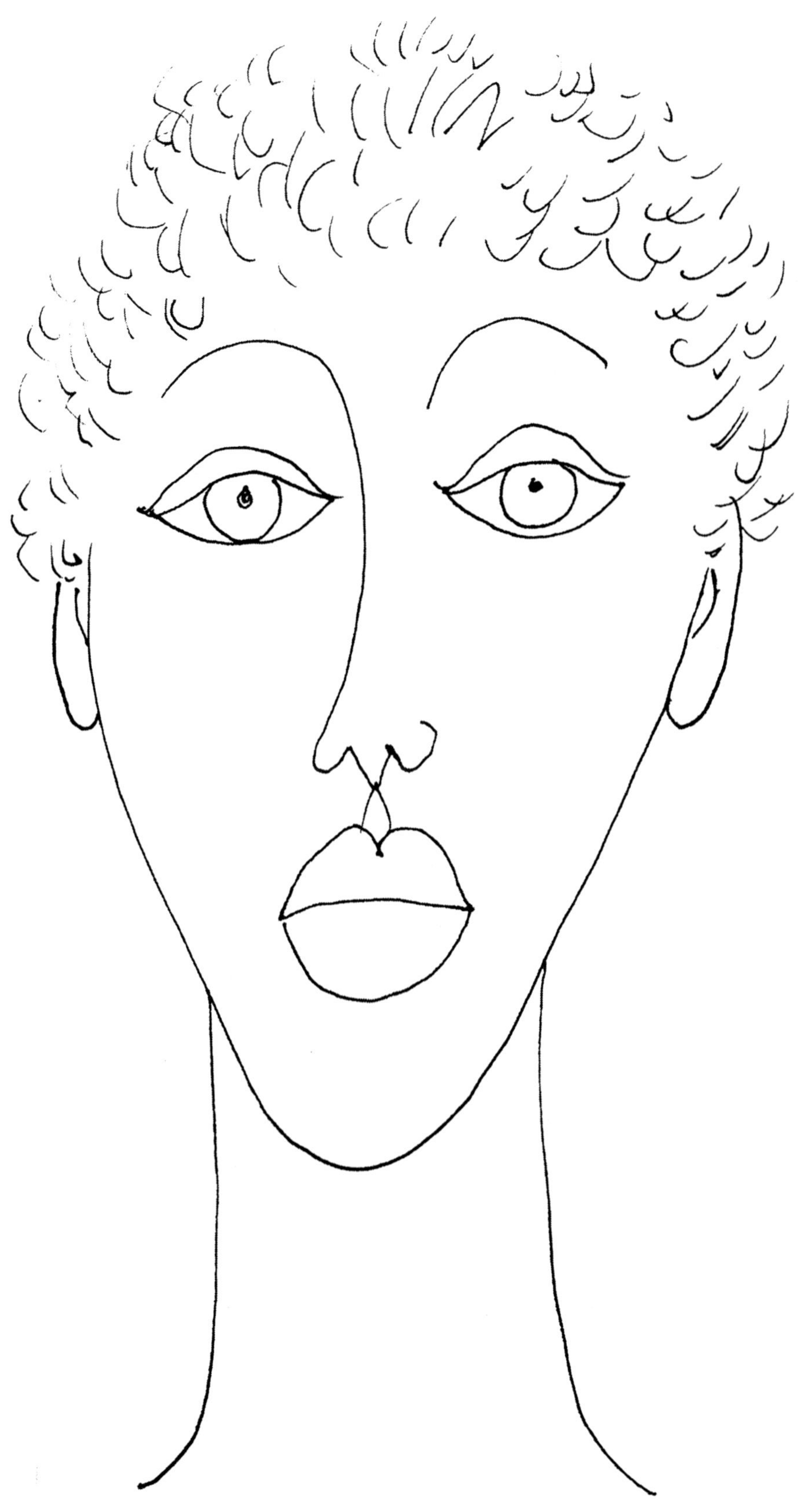

down the pathways of the mind, back and down, toward some deeper place of more meaning than the fluff that breezes through day after day and even at night. Down a soft pathway toward the center, to meet again the place where mind and dream world come together, the hazy border of is and is-not. One foot in front of the other, step-by-step through a forest of thoughts, over the footbridge and now down the stone steps, covered with moss gray stone and gleaming faintly with dew or rain.

A path again, covered in soft dry leaves well trodden. Into the deep woods, the sun coming through in spots now. Sound of a waterfall, sounds of birds. Brown-skinned people laughing and splashing in a pool below the falls. Flowers hanging on vines from the low branches of trees. Gaudy birds hopping in the branches.

No one knows I'm here. I come from another world. Only my eyes are here. I keep walking into the forest, off the path now. I am going to a meeting. I've had this appointment for a long time—ages, you could say. I push aside the leafy branches and move on. I seem to know where I'm going.

Ahead is a clearing and a gray-brown hut made of soft skins. I am home. An ancient man is walking around in front of the hut. I am unspeakably comfortable and comforted in his presence. He is holding a long clay pipe with beads and feathers tied to it, and beads and amulets hang around his neck. A soft pouch hangs at his waist. He is dressed in a garment of soft deerskin. He notices me but makes no gesture.

I walk forward and sit in the clearing in front of his house. I see that he is gathering sticks.

He brings an armful toward me and puts them inside a small stone circle. He puts dry grass on a glowing coal in the circle and fans the flames till the sticks ignite. Then he sits opposite me. The pipe is in his lap now. He takes dried leaves from his pouch and puts them in the bowl of the pipe. With a burning stick he lights the pipe, then passes it to me. I take a puff of the fragrant smoke.

We sit in silence, looking at each other. All my longing drops away, and I am profoundly content. His eyes look into mine. They are stone-gray, pale, and bright. He takes a necklace of red beads from around his neck and puts it in my lap. The birds sing around us, and the breeze rustles the leaves in the trees. I finger the beads and pictures float through my mind.

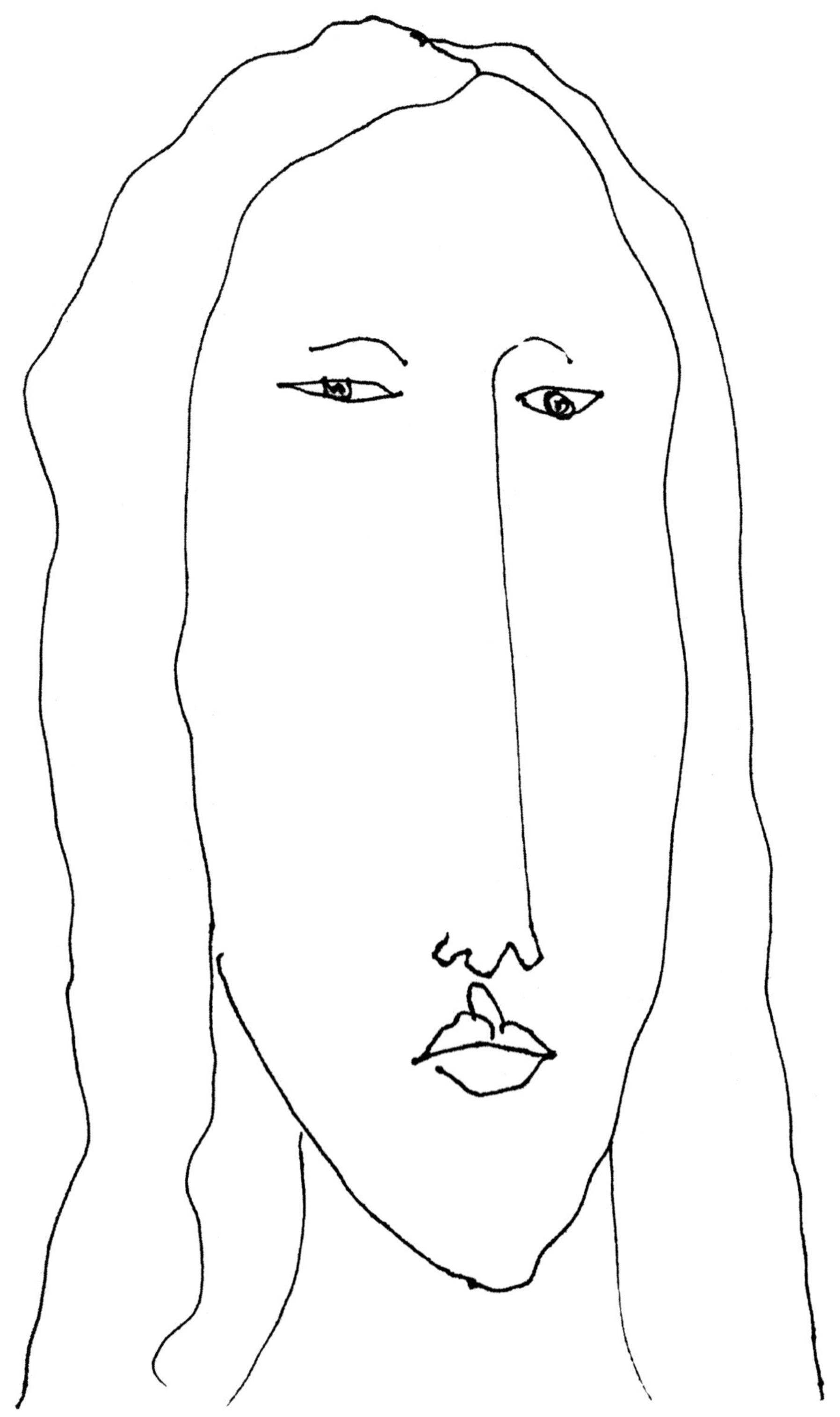

I see clouds in a blue sky. I see a vast turquoise lake ringed by mountains. Grassy plains with herds of buffalo running, running. A canoe in a stream, fish jumping in the evening light. A woman stands at the edge of the stream. Two children stand with her. A deer comes up behind them, unafraid.

At the woman's feet is an open sack filled with dried leaves and flowers. She watches the canoe into the distance, then picks up her sack and turns. The children run ahead of her into the woods. I am floating gently down to the riverbank, like a down feather falling, or an angel in visitation. My foot lands on the bank with hardly an impact. This is the land I've been journeying toward. There is something here to learn.

I follow the woman's trail. The plants and trees around me pour forth their secrets. At last I understand their language. Each has a purpose, and is content with it. I am still looking for mine. Can it be that such a complex being can exist in this world of pattern without a purpose? With no more purpose than to satisfy its own desires? As the words go through my mind the trees and grasses whisper around me and bend in the breeze. They are answering me. What makes me so dense? Why is the pattern so elusive?

Ahead of me the woman stands, smiling gently, one hand stretched toward me. I go forward. In her hand is a small mound of crushed leaves and petals. She pours it into a tiny beaded pouch and pulls tight the strings. Then she ties them together and puts the whole over my head and around my neck. The pouch has a gentle weight on my chest. There is healing in it.

Of what am I being healed?

Of doubt, of ignorance, of separation, of fear, pride, desire, of self-importance, and of forgetfulness.

In a flash I find myself fearless, knowing my place in the pattern and in tune with all around me. I see that I have always heard the story the trees are now telling me, always known the flowers' songs and the patterns of the stars. I have made no mistakes, but done faithfully everything my own path called for. My meeting here on this shore with all who come toward me has been part of my life from the beginning. I need look neither forward nor back to know now what this moment holds. The universe is unfolding like a tree from an acorn, and every cell in it is the center of its being.

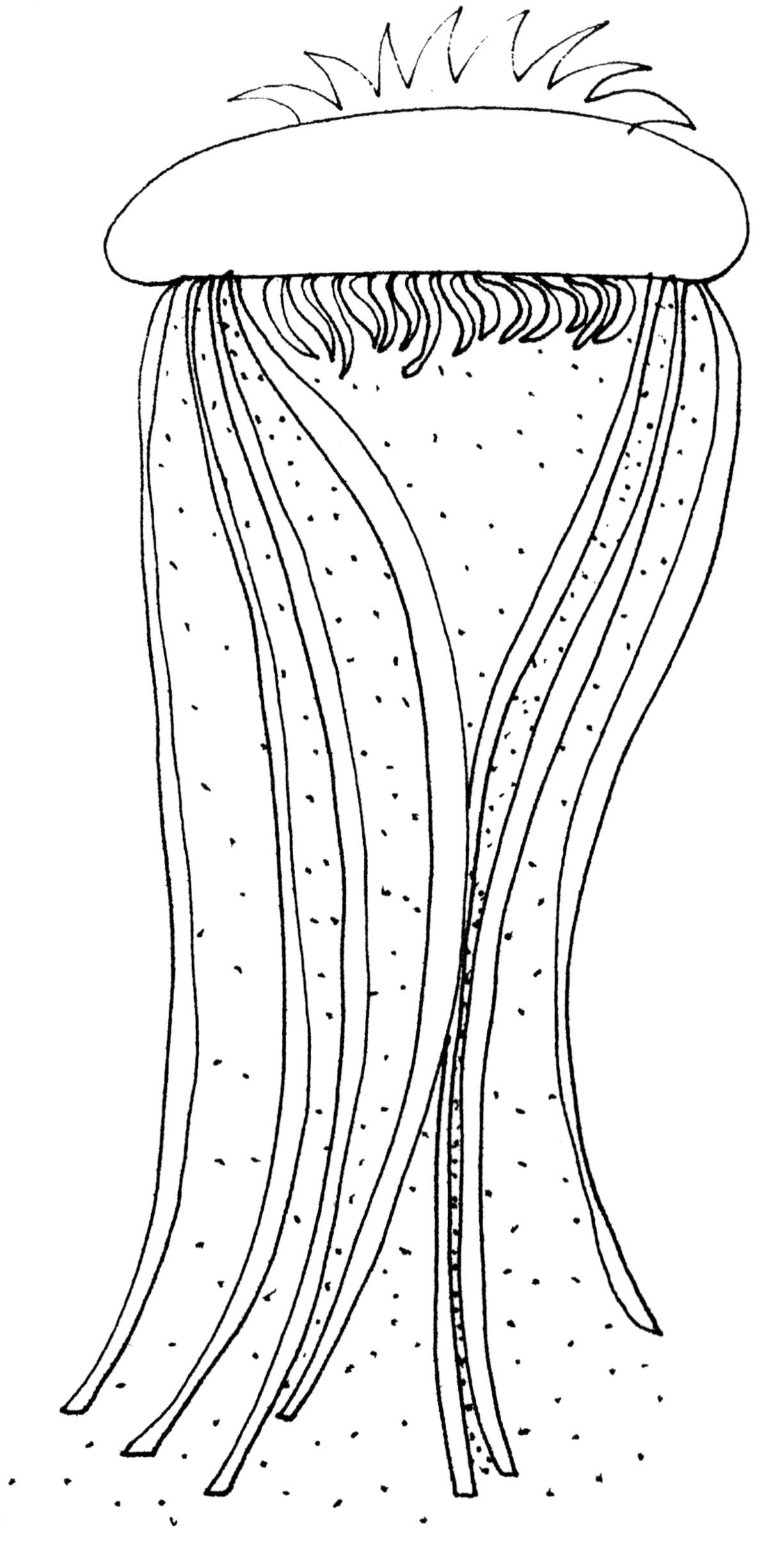

Staring at a blank page, it's like staring at a blank canvas—pretty soon there are shapes on it and all I have to do is paint them. But this is different, have to spoon the words out of my mind. It's not a blank, it's word soup, like the alphabet soup my mother used to give me, with little white letters floating around in it—who thought of that one? I never questioned its existence then, but now it seems odd to say the least—a thirties concept, when life was still simple and kids ate alphabet soup. But it's not letters in my mind, it's words, and they are connected by some thready umbilical cord to an idea, and the idea is buried in a primordial mud that periodically releases bubbles that rise to the surface of my consciousness and pop there, giving me the illusion that I am thinking. And who is the know-it-all that knows better, that knows how derivative my thoughts are, and knows the existence of some fast-thinking engine that pumps out thoughts night and day and sends them down the invisible tubes to supply each of us with our ration: Here, have this, it will keep you busy for a while and make you feel like a real person.

Like the horoscope given to a group of people—the same one for each, and each one thinks it fits him/her to a T. So my thoughts are mine, I think, and not some tacky, shabby remnants of generic thought, handed out in dollops to all of us—a refined version of crowd control? But why do it this way; it all seems so unnecessary. The universe is a convoluted entity, afraid to be direct, afraid of intimacy, always hiding in an endless game of Where the Fuck Are You?

Dip a spoon into my mind, are there any nourishing nuggets there? Plenty to keep me entertained, but that's just distraction, changing deck chairs on the Titanic, look the other way while I EAT YOU UP! I want a key, a simple key to fit in a simple keyhole and turn smoothly so I can open the door and see, see beyond the words, beyond my mind playing with words the way a child sits on the floor and plays with blocks. Turn my head, look the other way quickly, catch a glimpse, look, there it goes, I saw it just for a second, reality, running in the other direction, hiding its face—the hell with it, keep your spoon-fed words, I'm making a hole in the bottom of the bowl. I'm getting out of this!

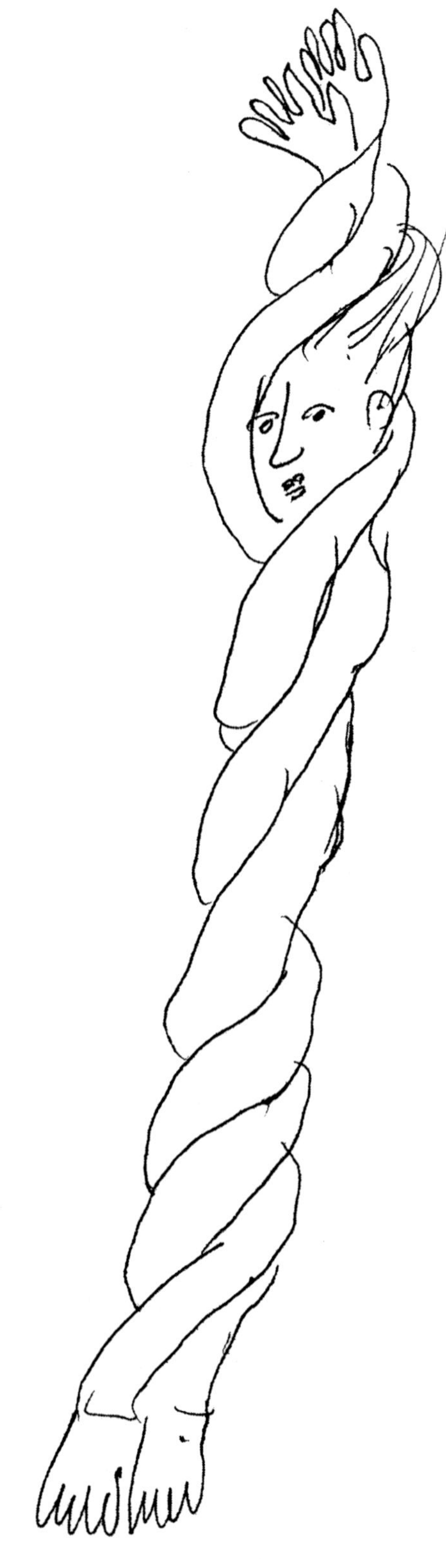

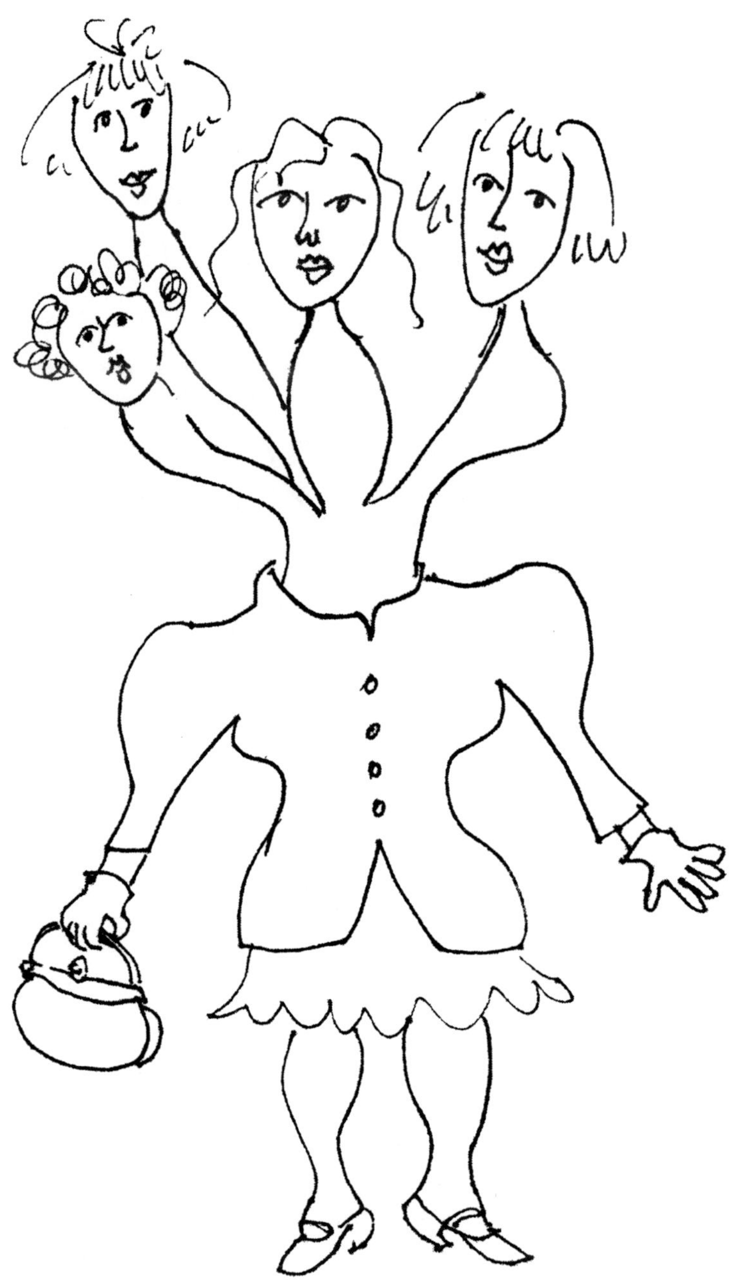

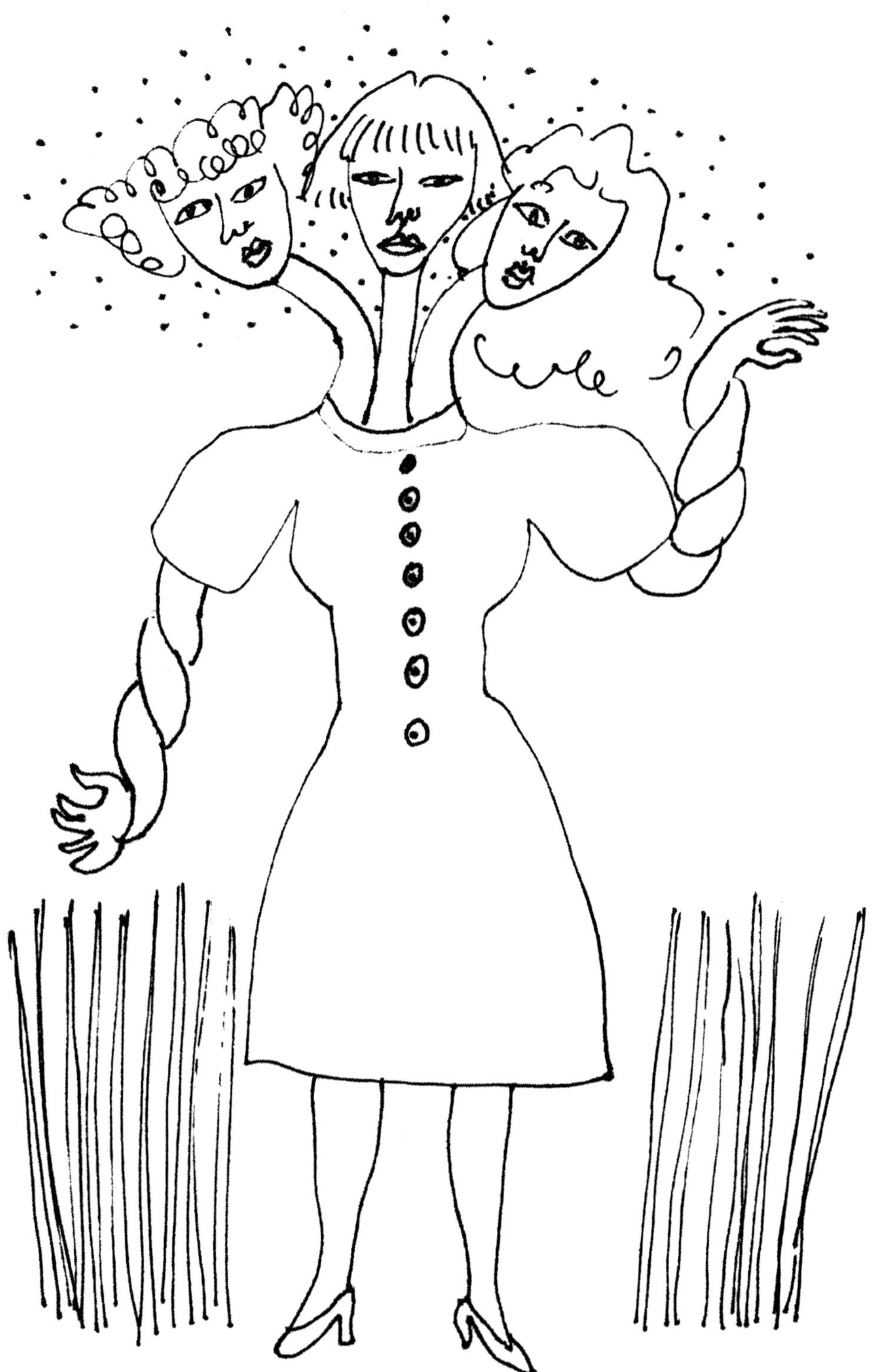

Making up God as I go along—

God is an idea in the mind of mankind—is there a personal God, one who answers when I speak? Sometimes there is, and sometimes there's only silence and emptiness. The starry sky hints at a God of unimaginable majesty and glory. The galaxies rotate in the heavens, and the mind stretches to count and encompass them, but their number is a reproach to that effort, like the grains of sand on a beach.

Don't try to know me, they say. This God the Father who holds Himself aloof, and cannot be known or controlled by us. Yet like my father, He takes care of us, thinking even of the things we forget, for in His wisdom He knows better than we do what we need. And so it is God the Mother, who answers when we cry, and tucks us in and comforts us in the dark night.

So there we have God the Father, aloof and benevolent, and God the Mother, comforting and close. And God the majestic, the unknowable, Lord of the Stars and the Grains of Sand. And God the beautiful who created the earth and heavens, and God the terrible who created war and hatred and pain and hell. God the indifferent who watches us suffer, and God the compassionate who bestows miracles. God the far and God the near, God the Other and God the Self. Each one has his or her own God, even those who have none. Seeking Truth and Reality, I want God to exist independent of me. An impossibility. Can I exist independent of God? Even if there is no God. God is energy. God is the void. God is beyond duality. God is love. He who knows knows not. Will the mind ever stand still?

An ancient carousel, with prancing horses painted in fierce and fiery colors. They seem to breathe as they go round and up and down. I climb aboard as it stops, and find a magnificent steed, whose eyes watch me as I climb into the saddle.

The music starts and the carousel goes round. My horse goes up and down in a rhythmical canter. The scenery goes by in endless repetition, going faster and faster until it blurs and melts together. Round I go, going somewhere, going nowhere. There's no stopping my horse. At last I just give up and go where he takes me. Will I know when I get there? My mind drifts behind me as though blown by the wind, and scatters into the blur of scenery beyond, settling like dust in a circle around us. The rhythmic ride becomes my only reality. If there is a brass ring, I'm going too fast to see it now.

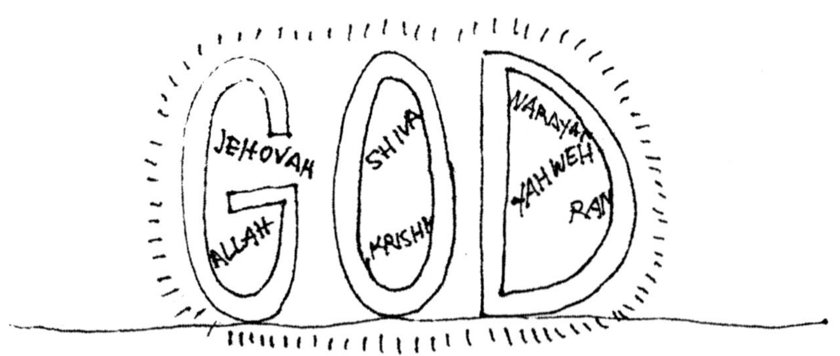

JEHOVAH
ALLAH
SHIVA
KRISHNA
NARAYAN
YAHWEH
RAM

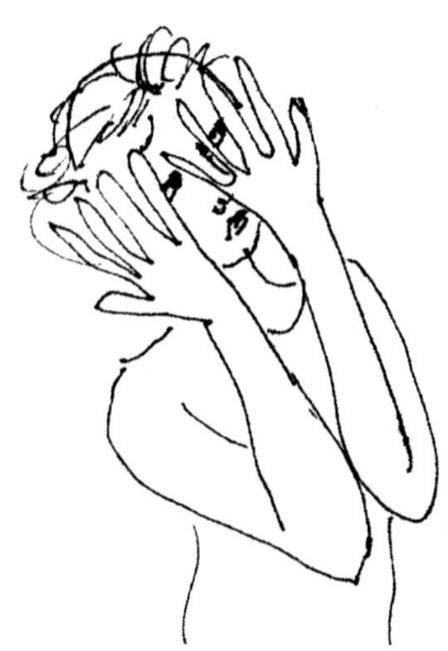

Who is responsible?

Who is responsible? Who is responsible for the pollution of the Earth, man or God? Did God create us wrong, the mad clockmaker winding up His toy and watching it spin its wheels, its arms going around crazily in all directions, spinning itself to death? Or is the myth of the Garden true—have we, or our fathers' fathers' fathers' fathers' father, committed some unforgivable act of disobedience for which we are eternally punished unto the death of ourselves and our children and their children unto the third and the fourth generation, unto the death of this luminous blue planet that spins so softly in the blackness of space? Are we responsible for our madness, our pursuit of getting and spending at the expense of each other and our exquisite Mother? Even now when we know what we are doing, when the poisons we create wash back on our shores and rise up out of the earth under our homes, why do we not stop? What is the flawed gene in us that keeps us going, robotlike, handing our power over to impersonal monster-machine governments, while we march brokenly, knowingly, blindly aware, toward our certain death and the death of our luminous blue home? Are we some backwater creation, an arm of the universe gone awry, hurtling unalterably down the path to extinction while the rest of Creation pulls up its socks and gets on with it?

What would make us willing to forgo the least of our attachments in order to turn our path around and pull away from the edge of extinction? What will it take to be heard, a voice crying in the wilderness, "Wake up! The end of the world is at hand!" We all know it, we look at each other with knowing eyes and then avoid each others' glances, not willing to own the responsibility for our own part in the headlong race toward nothingness. As we die one by one and are not reborn, as the rivers, lakes, and oceans go out around us, as the earth sighs and stops producing and the animals abandon us, lying belly-up for the last time with a glassy look of reproach frozen on their eyeballs, will we ask ourselves if God meant it to be this way? Are we better off dead, children of a parent who doesn't care enough about us to give us the key to living together in harmony with each other and with our vast and nurturing home? Or will we realize with our last gasp that this was part of the cosmic design—that our birth, rebirth, lives, and deaths were all part of the picture? Will we or others like us watch from some distant position in no-time no-space while the Mother breathes her last sigh and closes her eyes and that mysterious blue luminescence we saw for the first time so recently blinks to an end, leaving an orb of dead carbon spinning emptily in the void?

Will we sigh then and say, "It was meant to be—God's will be done" and plunge our groaning and united Self into a black hole to be reborn into a new Creation, a new Adam, carrying with us only the memory of Loss.

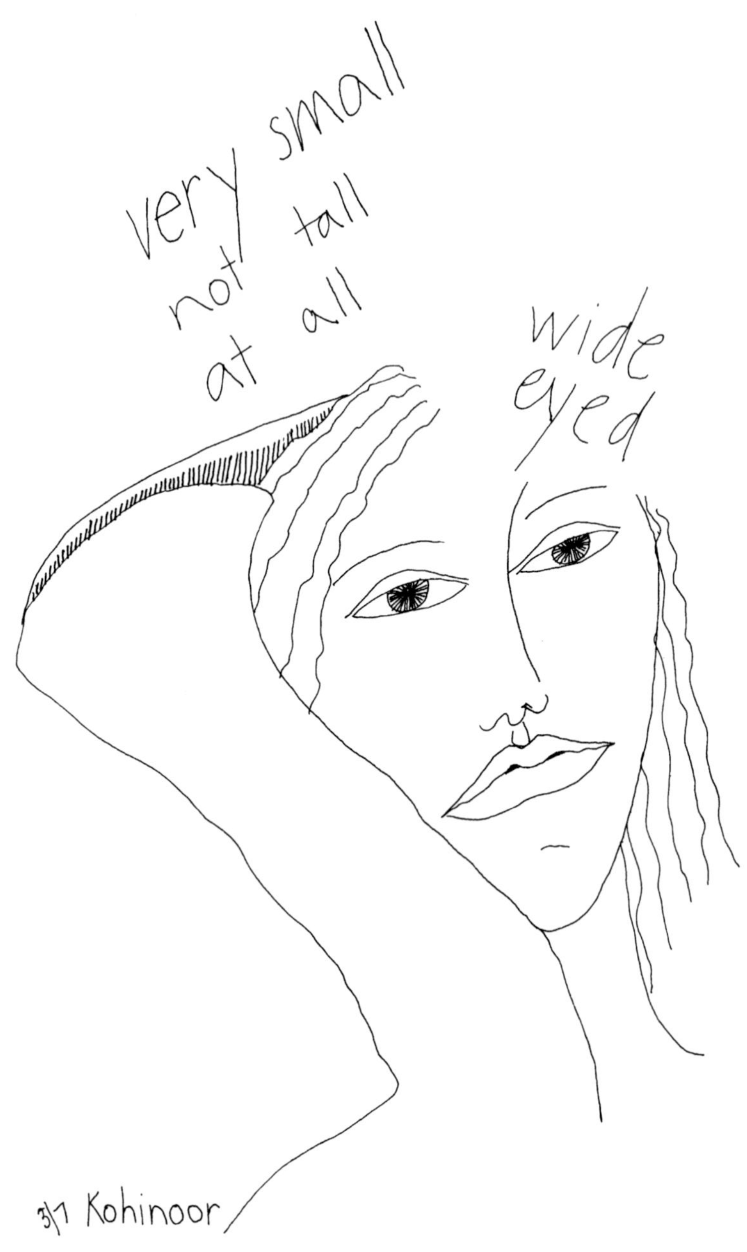

Closing my eyes, strange creatures behind my eyelids, half mythic, half robot, are they always there and I just don't see them? Whose space do they inhabit? Am I inhabited by another universe inside me, in some kind of other-dimensional space and a strange kind of time, peopled by creatures unknown to me and yet myself, maybe more me than I know, more me than this persona I have been donning since birth, adding bits of the costume piece by piece, a scarf, some gloves, a belt, a hat—there, how do I look? Would you think this is me? I mean, really me? What do you think of this color—does it suit my personality?

What a trashy bunch of costumes we are, the Madwoman of Chaillot, dressed up to make an impression. The myth behind my eyelids looks back at me, impassive. Has he made himself up too, or did I make him up? Or, heaven forbid, did God make him up and plant him there inside my head, ready to go off at this very moment as I closed my eyes? Or did God, God help us, plant me in his world, a kind of container surrounding him and at last, one day, acknowledging his existence with a wink from both eyes?

Or, better yet, is there someone else, another author-creator, making us all up, you, me, the creatures in my head, and God? Now we get into the mirror trick—there's an author creating the author creating us all, and another creating him, or her, because they all have to have mothers, don't they? And when you get back to Mom you've gone back all the way, haven't you, except for dear old Dad?

Mom and Dad creating us all, endlessly writing, writing, turning sound into letters and letters into words and words into creatures, and the creatures get up and create more creatures, who build buildings and cars and highways and unidentified flying objects in which to go check up on the other guys next door—how fascinated we all are with each other. And all looking for Mom, the REAL Mom, the one we know loves us, thinks we're so great, feeds us all we want, and protects us from dear old Dad when he's grouchy.

And he does get grouchy, which is when we all huddle together for protection and run to hide under Mother's skirts. And Mother, she just laughs and goes on creating, another and then another and another—just look at them all! Look at us, here, pretending we're all different, staring at each other till our eyes go dry, trying to figure out if we're

better, or if we make the grade. Look at them, look at me, there must be some mistake!
Is this the way we're supposed to be? Someone's having a joke on us—this can't be right.

A cosmic joke.

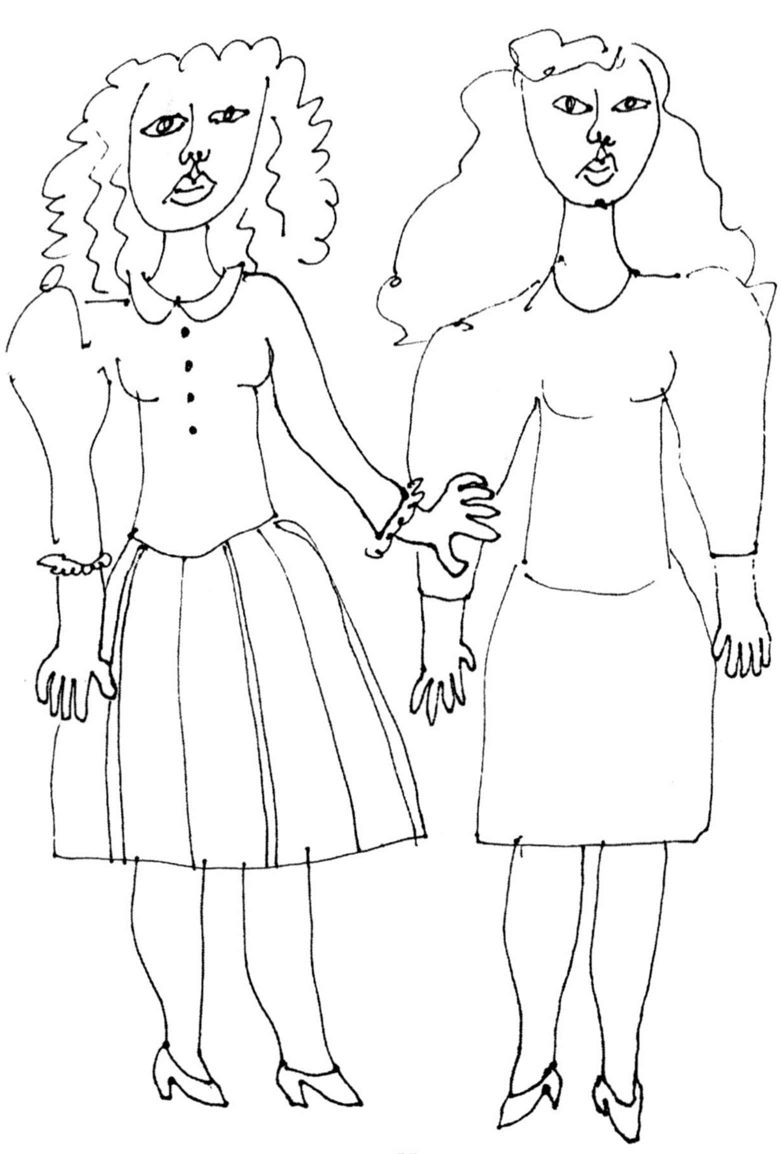

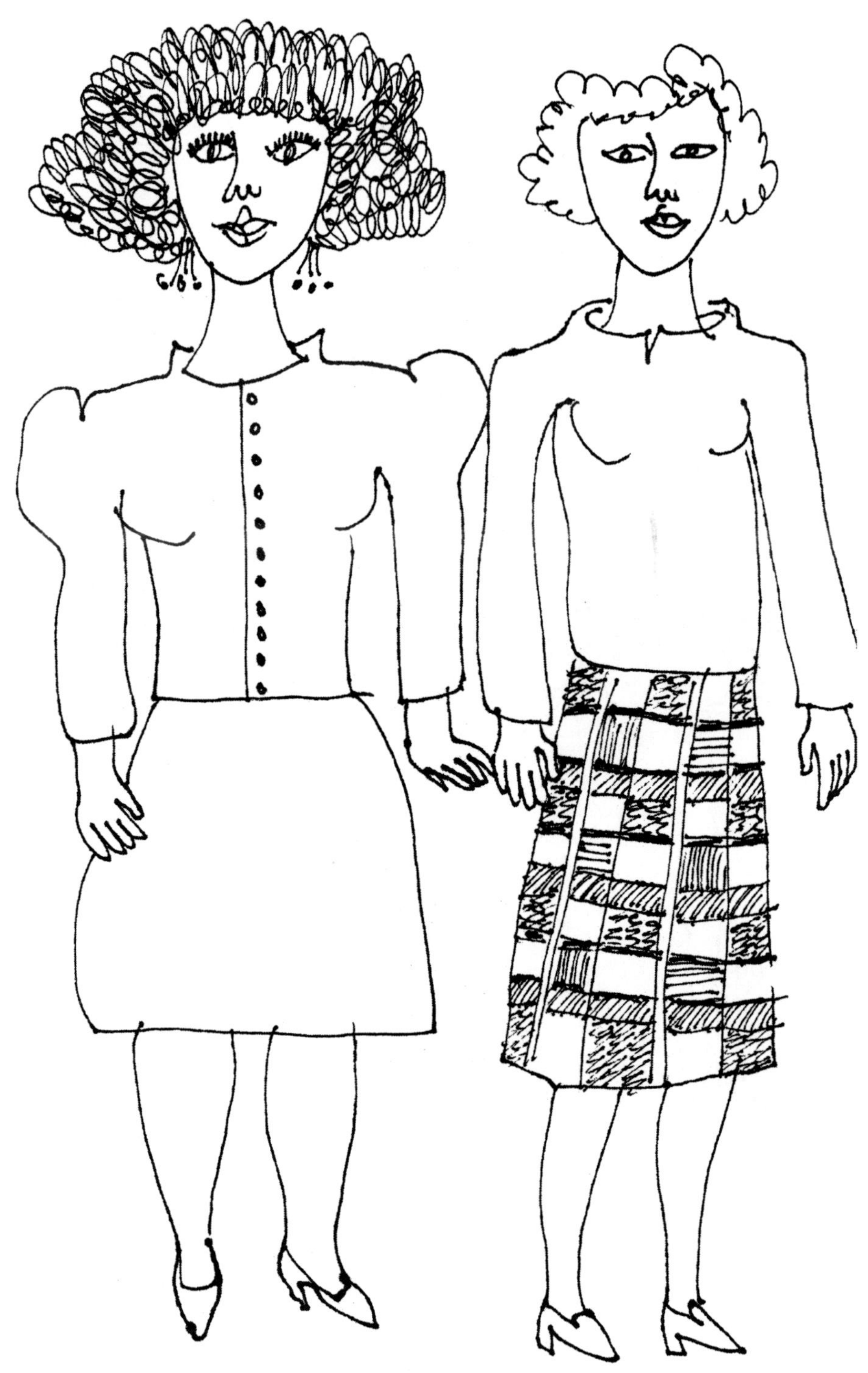

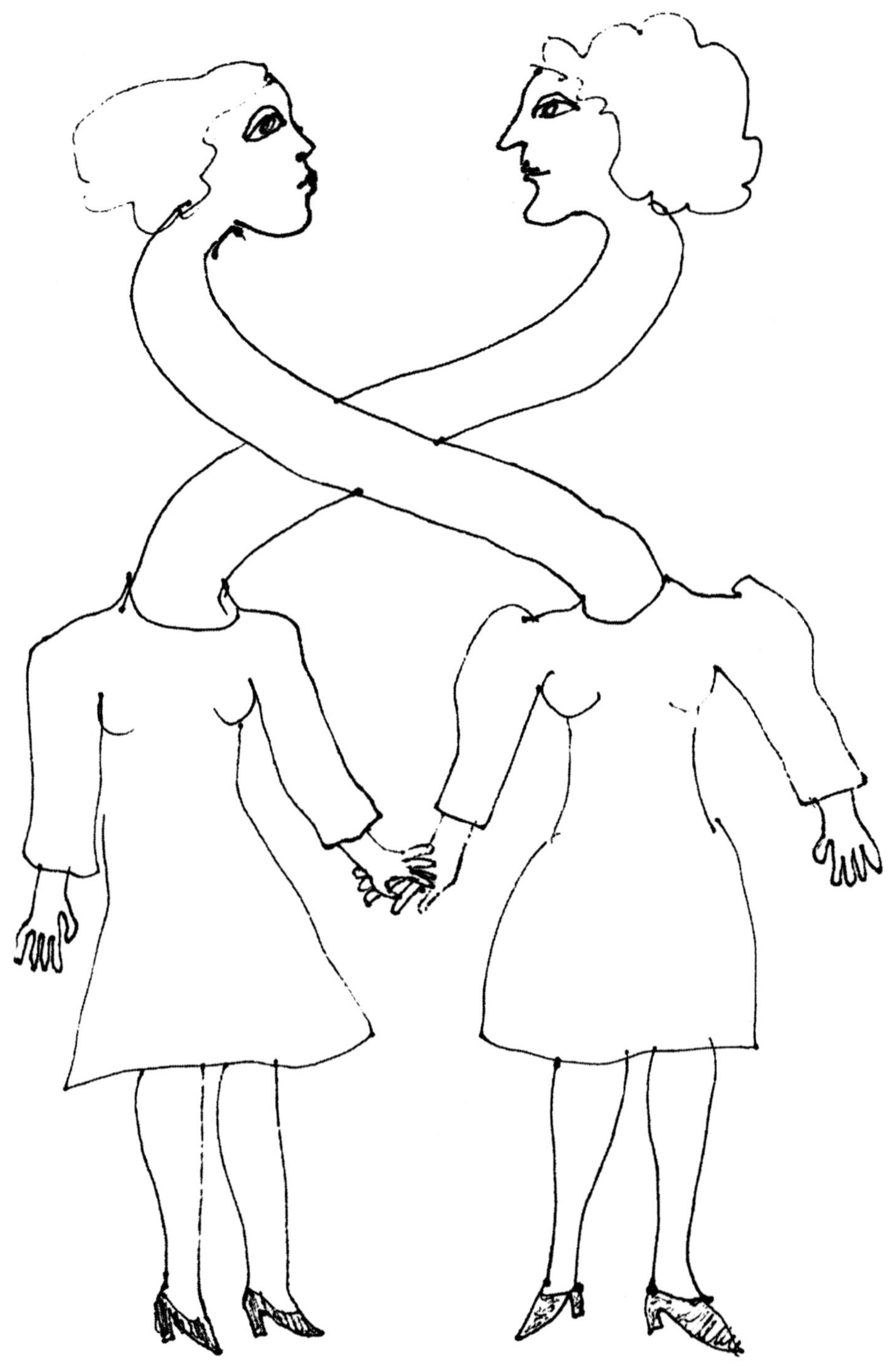

Swimming in a sea of disappointment, floating in a universe of disappointment, traveling from one disappointment to another, a life of disappointments, moving from one landmark disappointment to the next, stripped of expectations, hopes, and illusions. Dusty road, no landmarks left, wander out into the desert, nothing but sand, not even cactus, a few dunes break the monotony. No hope here, no expectations. Nothing but disappointment.

Animals live under the sand, tiny creatures with blind eyes and no legs, adapted to their landscape of nothingness, surviving on a steady diet of disappointment. Heartbreak for breakfast, lunch, and dinner. Laugh and pretend it isn't true. Drink the finest wines, exclaim over the taste, anything to distract you from the truth of disappointment. Eat live oysters doused in lemon juice, eggs of fish spread on crackers, dog eat dog, fish eat fish, kill to live, live to die. I ask you, what kind of madman is running around out there playing God? This you can say about Him: Callous. Heartless. Inattentive. Deaf. Relentless. Unfair. Remote. Unresponsive. Not someone you'd want to marry, hm-m? Not even someone you'd want for a friend.

It's all a mistake, isn't it? Something has gone terribly wrong, leading to war, hatred, cruelty, pollution, greed, destruction and devastation, the ravaging of the home planet, and the insane perpetuation of suicidal behavior. Well, it's true, isn't it? People lie dying in gutters, animals lie bleeding in traps, babies are shot to death in the streets, airplanes blow up in the air, raining bodies back to earth. Mothers lose their babies and cry, brother kills brother, the old are discarded as we turn our backs. Satan bubbles in the hearts of men, women, children everywhere, and laughs at our prayers to a God gone mad. Who has the upper hand? **God has signed a contract with the Devil, selling us all as we descend slowly one by one into the fiery jaws of Hell.**

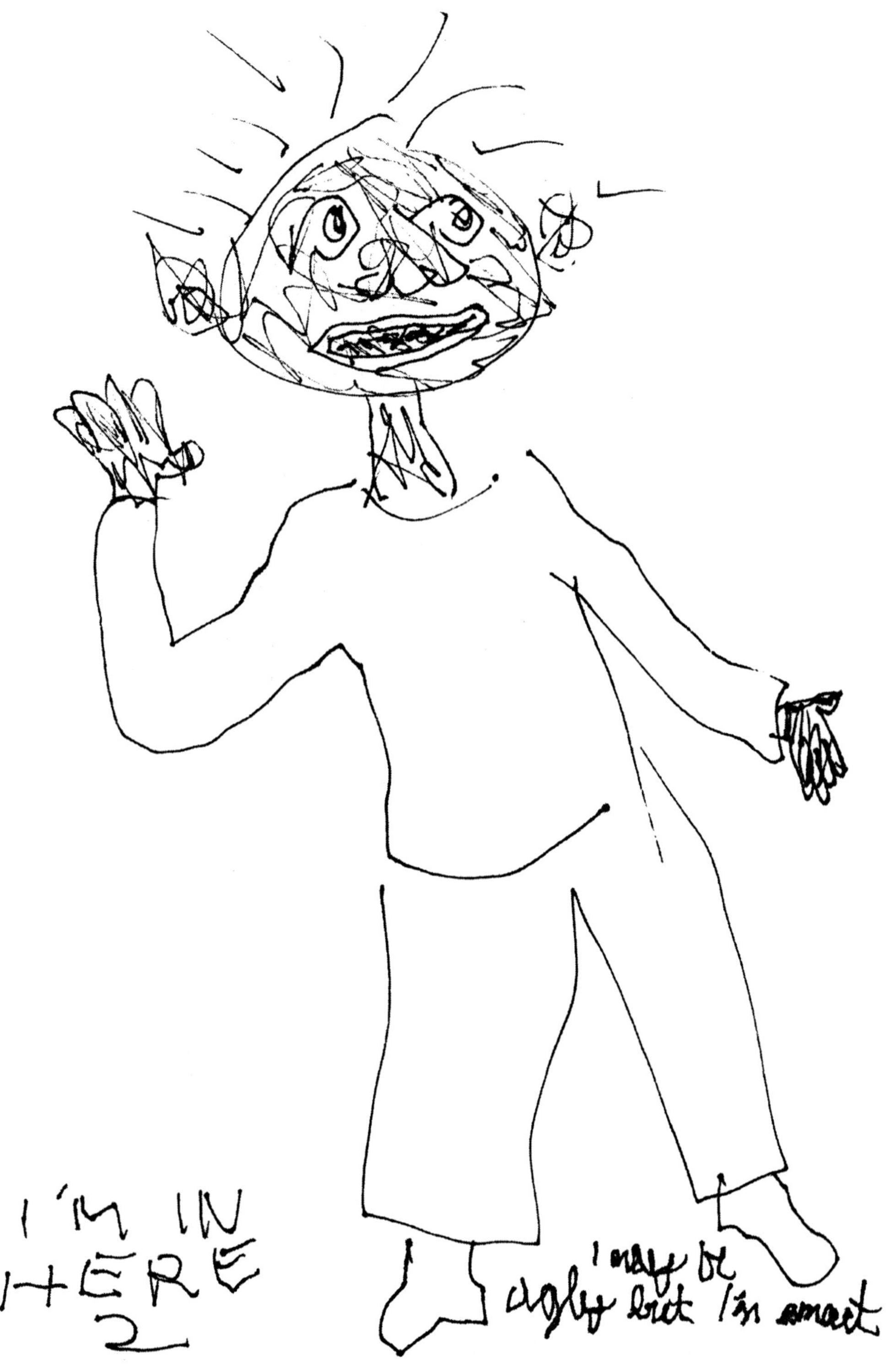

I'M IN HERE
I may be ugly but I'm smart

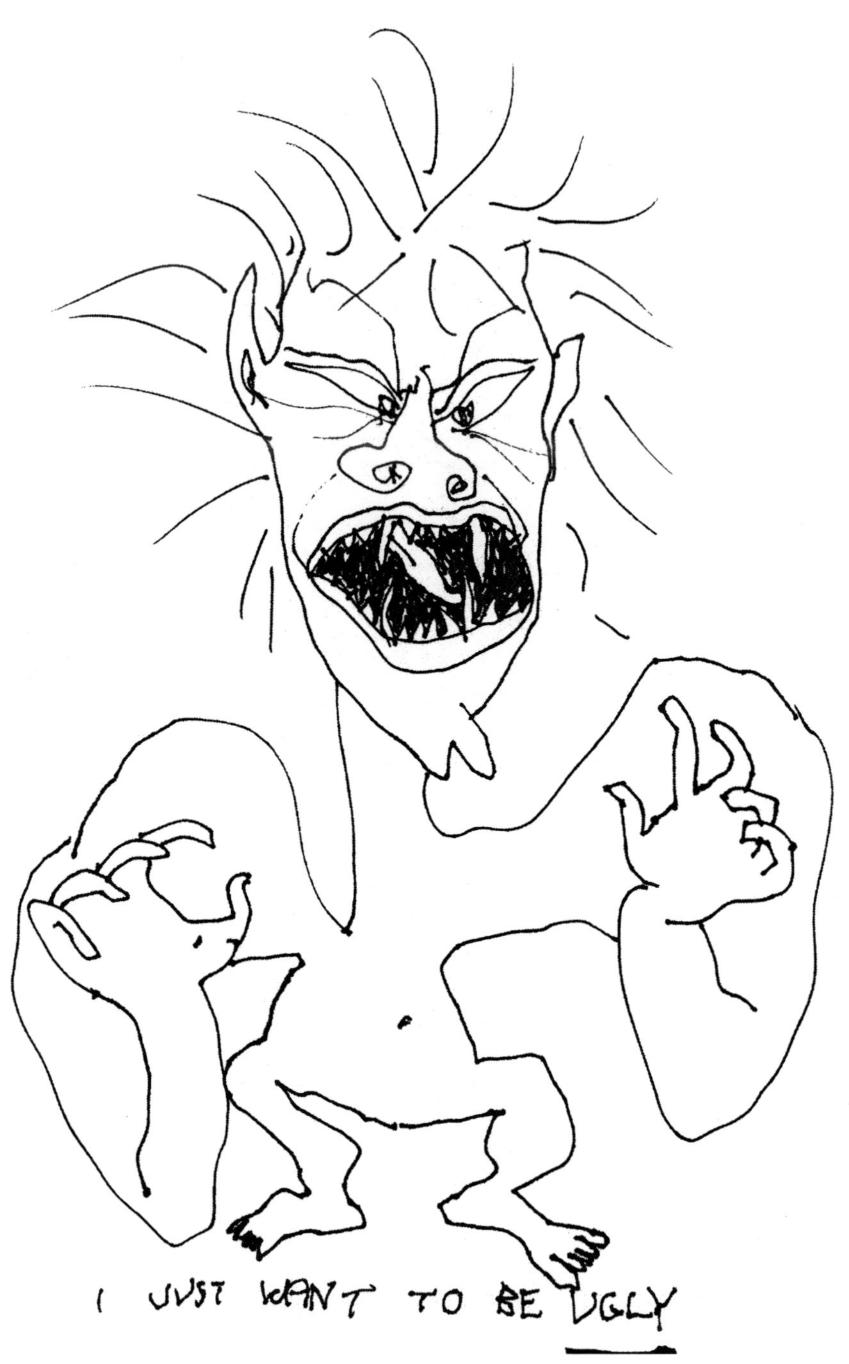
I JUST WANT TO BE UGLY

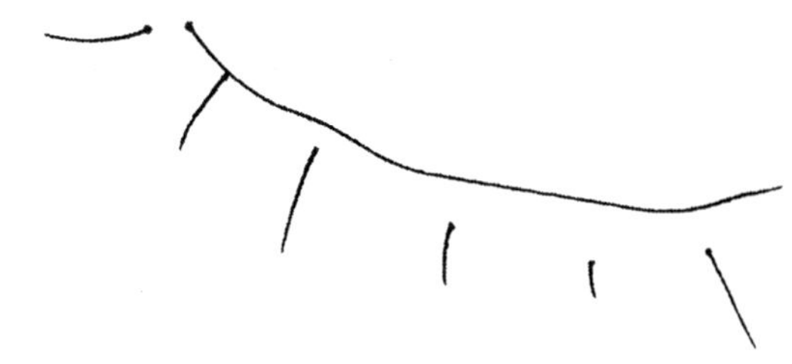

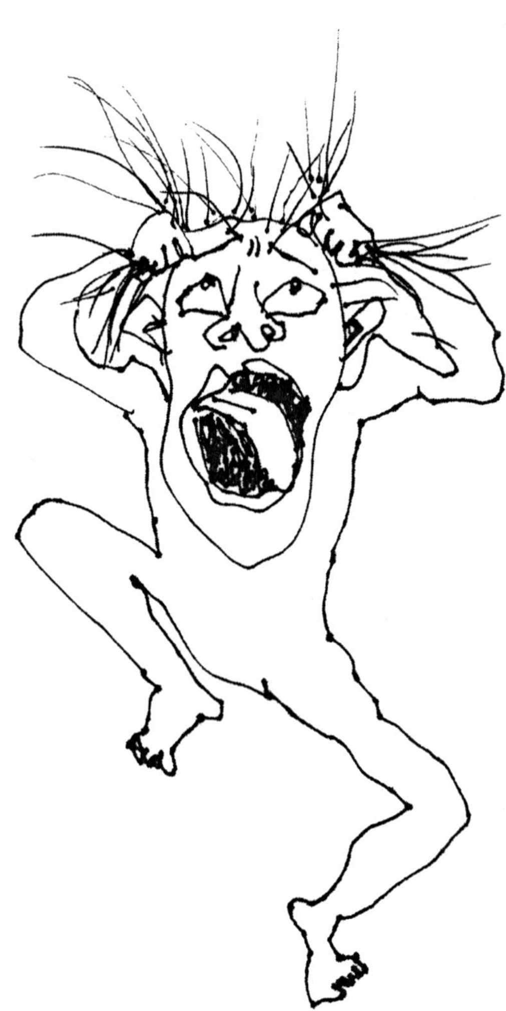

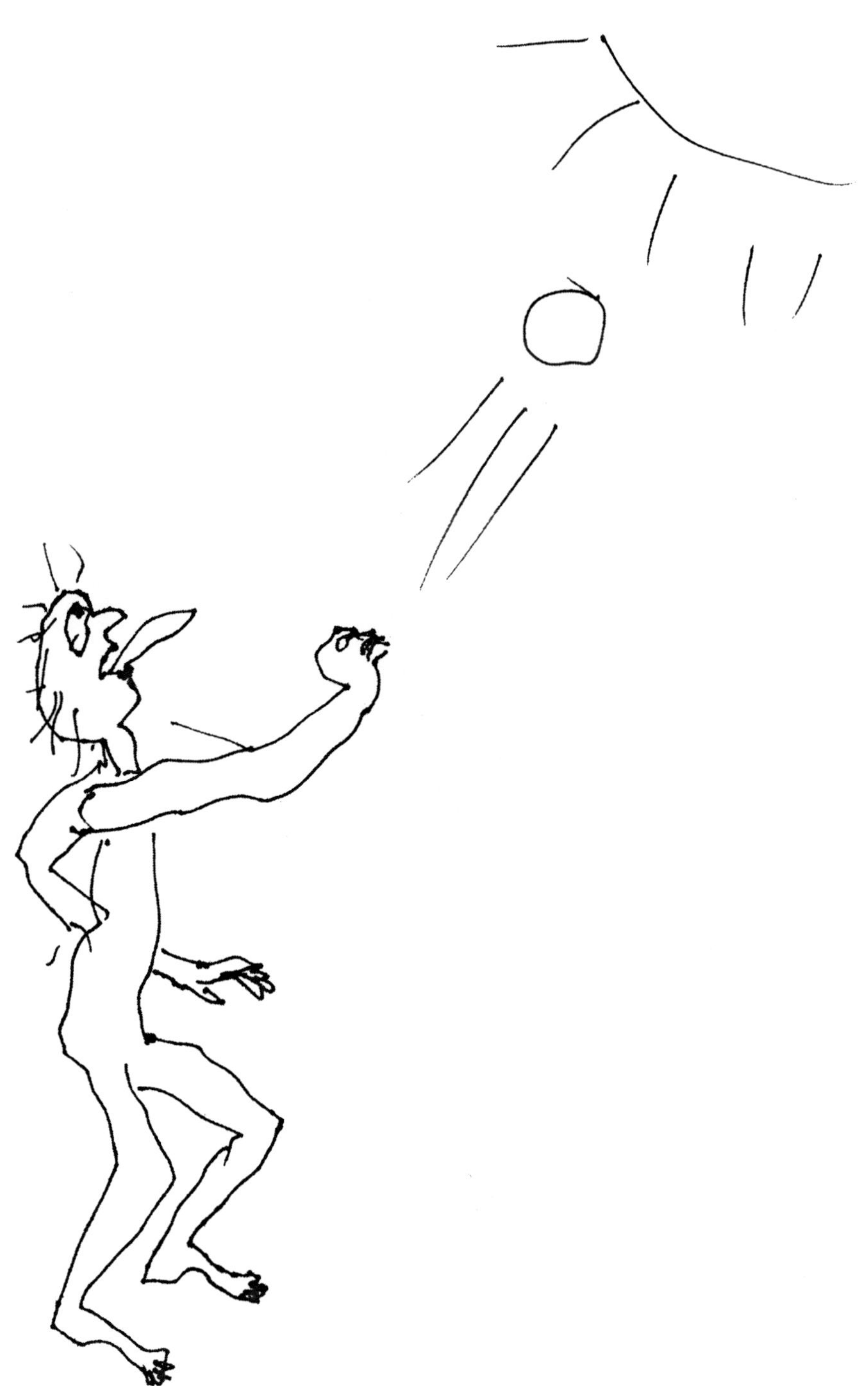

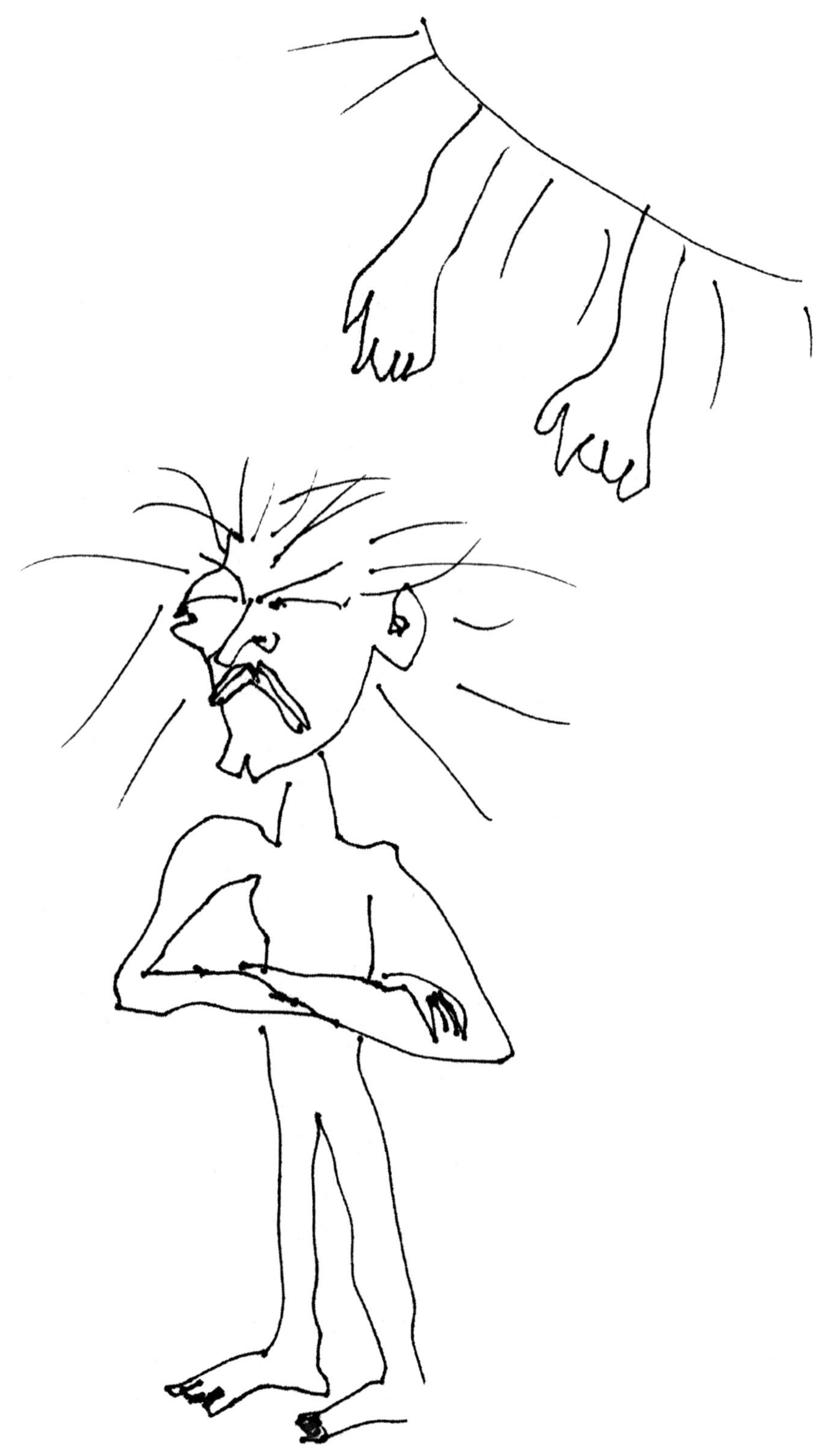

All I can think about is my headache. "My" headache—it's been with me for a year and a month, probably since the house and barn were struck by lightning with me in the barn. Today another thunderstorm. That one was right overhead, though. Me in the barn, Nick in the barn, and Amy in her house. Me worried about Amy, and Amy worried about us. And herself. Jonathan worried about me and Dan when he was in the car accident. We can bear what comes our way, but we worry that the ones who love us can't. We can't bear it for them. Or we can't bear that it might be unbearable for them. Networks of love that we spend a large part of our lives denying, turning down, walking away from. Love is not enough. Neither is anything else, without love. I don't want to love you too much, don't love me too much. Life is so uncertain. Pain is certain. Disappointment is certain. Frustration is certain. How do we bear it? Something inside/that cannot be denied. A pressure toward bliss, and the hell with it all. Drag myself back from the edge of bliss, wait a minute, wait a minute, have I forgotten something? Wasn't there something else I was supposed to worry about first? One thing there's plenty of—something to worry about. An abundance of things to worry about. Never any need to be bored, no need to be in bliss. Why fight it? Pull back from the abyss of bliss as we pull back from love, from loving and being loved. Get on with it, there's an endless stream of things for you to worry about. Have I gotten anywhere in life? Am I going in the right direction? How do I look? What's it like to die? Did I remember to turn off the light? Will anyone love me when I'm old and gray? Did I do that right? Blah blah blah blah—like an exercise treadmill, just keep going, you're sure to get somewhere.

Sometimes I sit on my couch sunk in bliss and immersed in the void, not wanting anything, not wanting to do anything, and still the carousel goes round with a little voice saying, "Don't you have something you have to do?"

The devil cracks his whip, and we jump.

I HAVE A SHORT FUSE.
AND I'M NEAR THE
SURFACE THESE DAYS.
LOOK IN THE MIRROR
AND SEE ME.

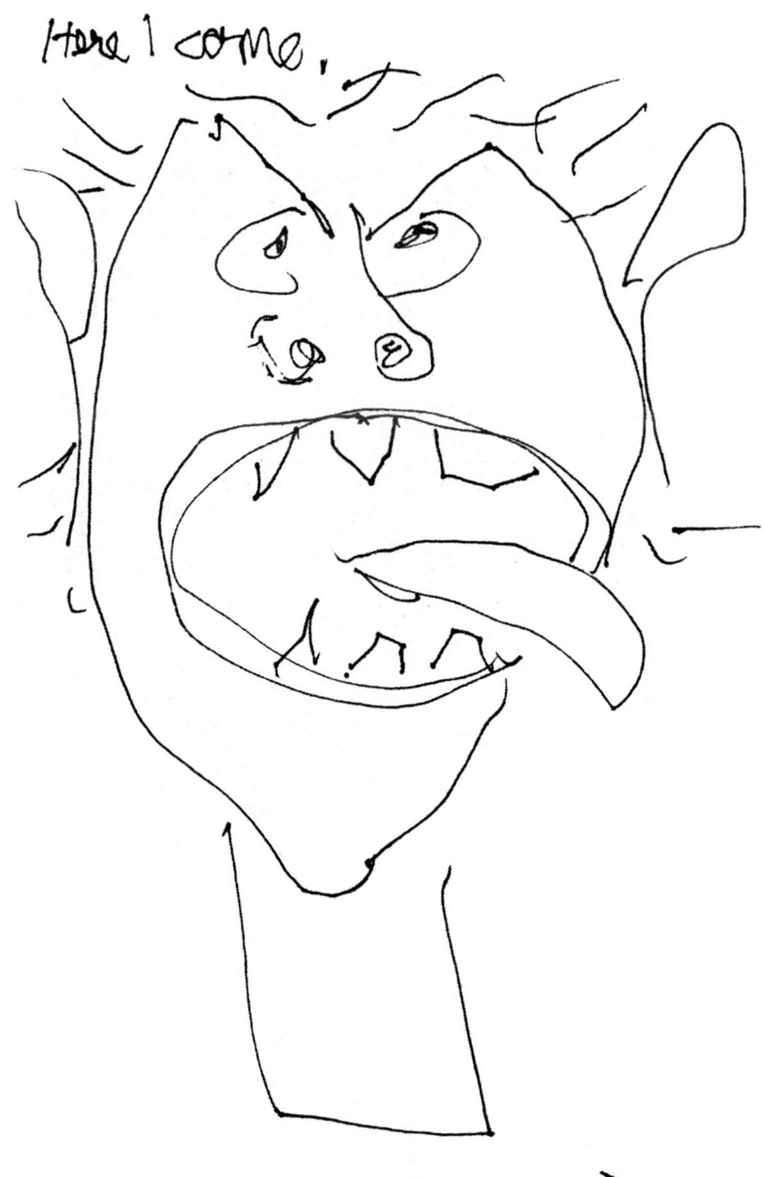

Here I come.
Man or woman?
who cares?

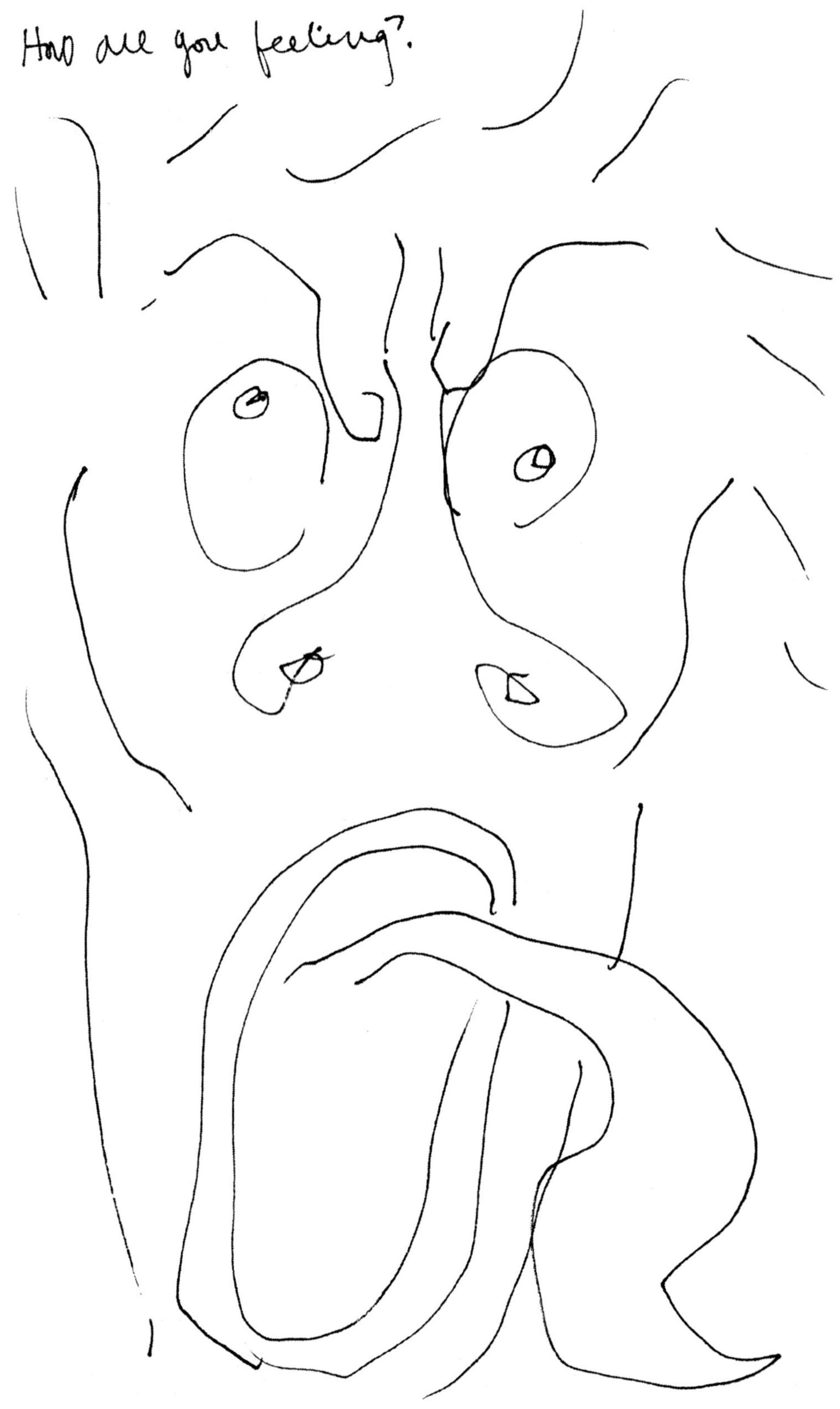
How are you feeling?

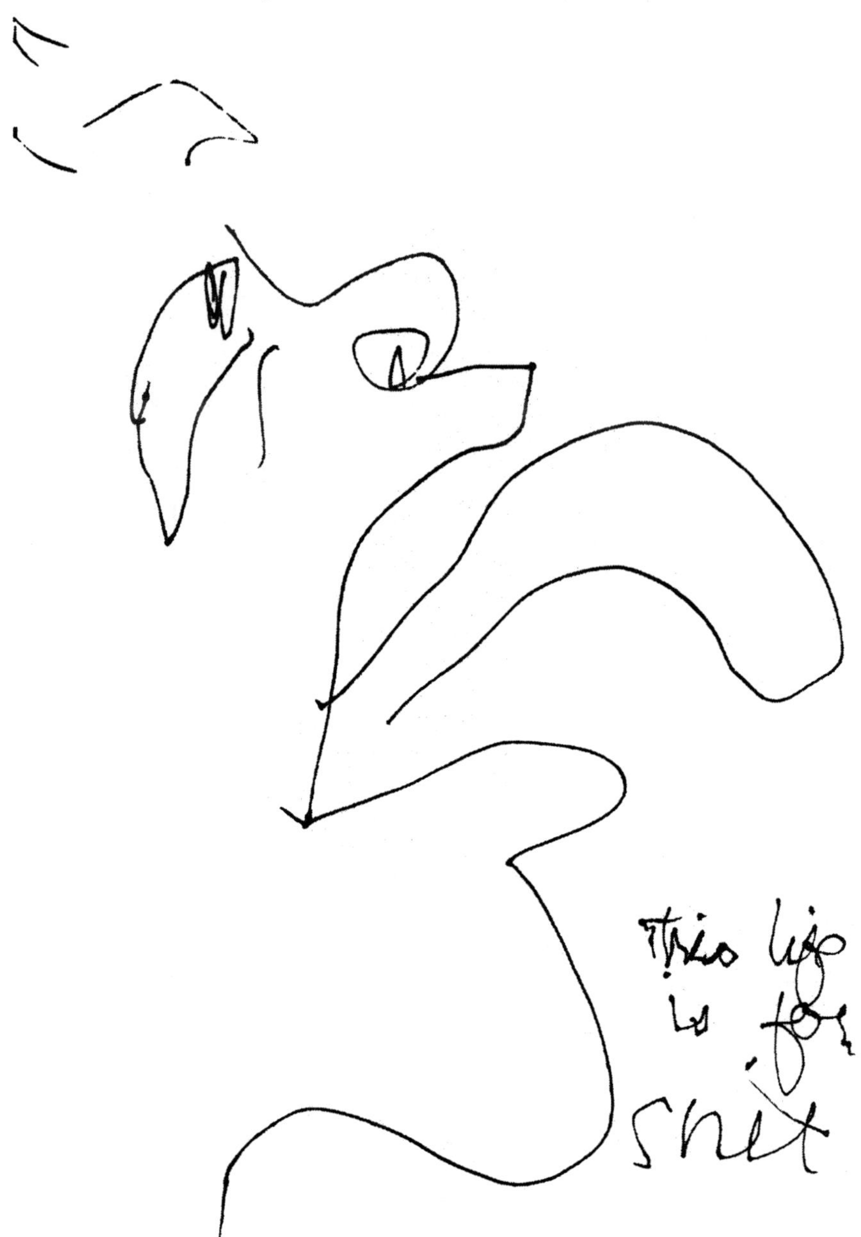
What do you want me to know?
this life is for shit

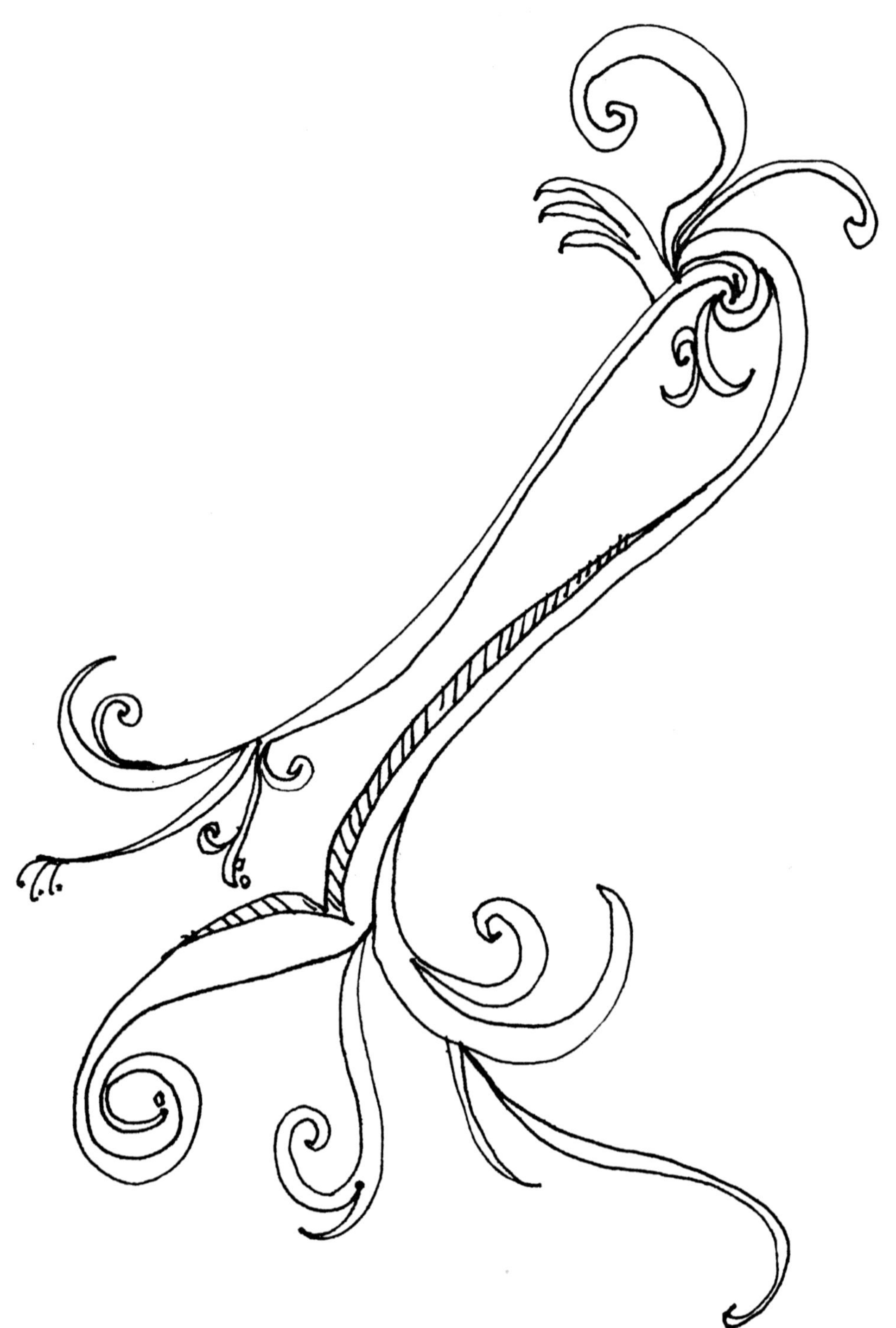

Like climbing a hill of molasses, a squishy, slippery hill that yields under my feet as I step. Each footstep sinks me into the hill up to my ankles and slides me back down a bit to where the foot before it stopped, mired in the soft muck. Exhausted before I've barely started, frustrated, scared, and discouraged.

No signs to show me the way, no light lights my path, no friendly hand reaches out to pull me out and upward. I've been here many times before, each time drenched in the conviction there was no way up the hill. Yet I've been to the top of countless hills just like this, and coasted down the other side in jubilation.

Somehow without even noticing how, my feet managed to inch themselves upward through the molasses until they reached a point where everything suddenly, inexplicably got easier. The molasses hardened and released my feet, and they made their way step-by-step upward and out of the terrible black swamp that seemed to hold them fast forever. Yet it never gets easier—the bottom of the hill always feels the same, as though it will hold on to me for eternity and there is no way out. The suffering never diminishes. The top of the hill is no guarantee that another hill won't have to be climbed.

Up hill, down dale, across the endless mountain range whose swamps are as ephemeral as its triumphant peaks, though each as it's reached seems permanent.

It's not that I'm going anywhere, either, because I've already lost any hope I ever had that the mountains would some day give way to plains stretching before me as far as the eye can see, crisscrossed with laughing streams and broad rivers and covered with herds of buffalo and elk. Endless mountain climber, I trudge my way upward in despair and stroll down in triumph, forgetting that at the bottom of each hill is the soft, black molasses swamp that begins the next ascent.

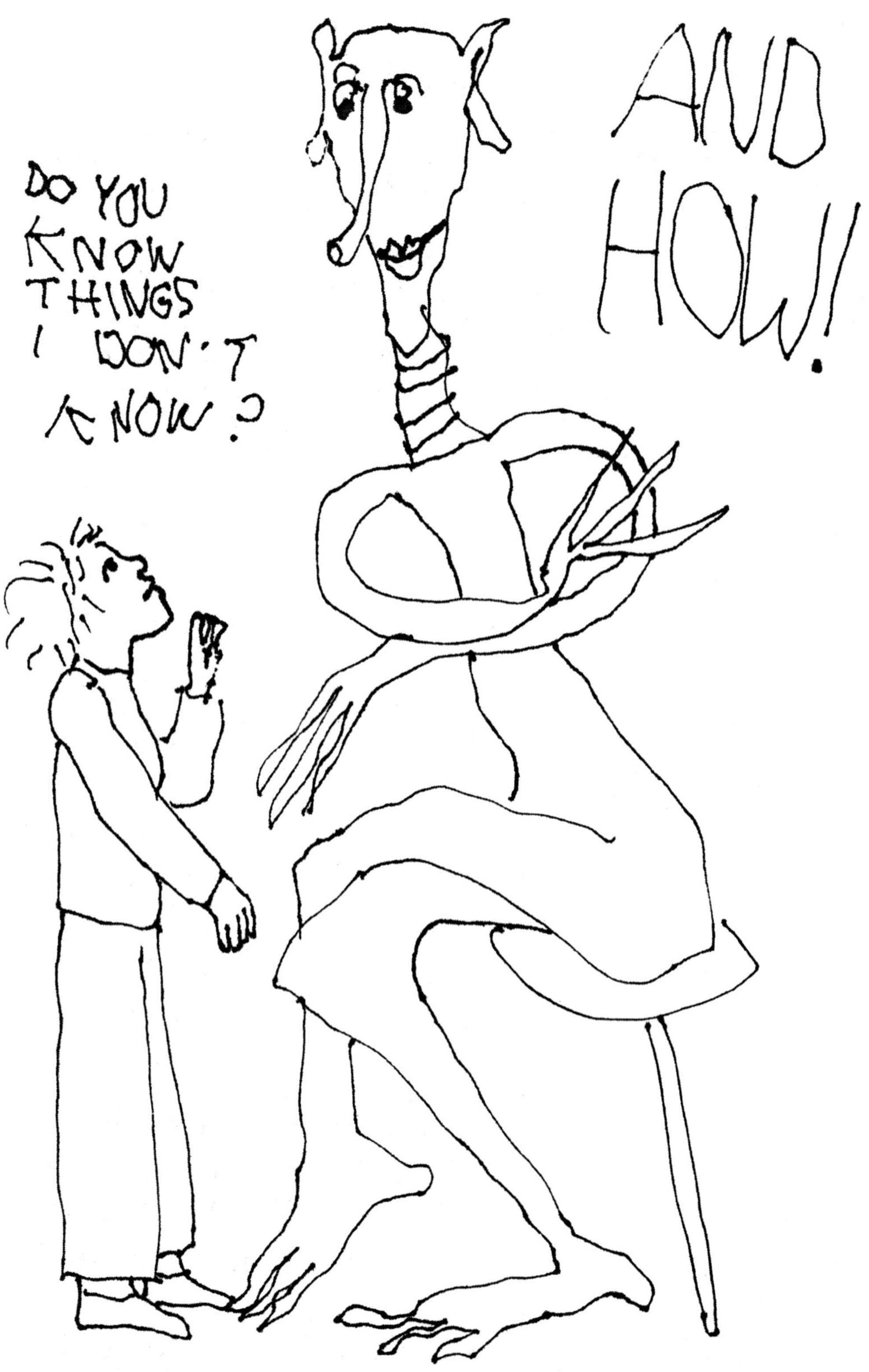

DO YOU KNOW THINGS I DON'T KNOW?
AND HOW!

FOR. INSTANCE?

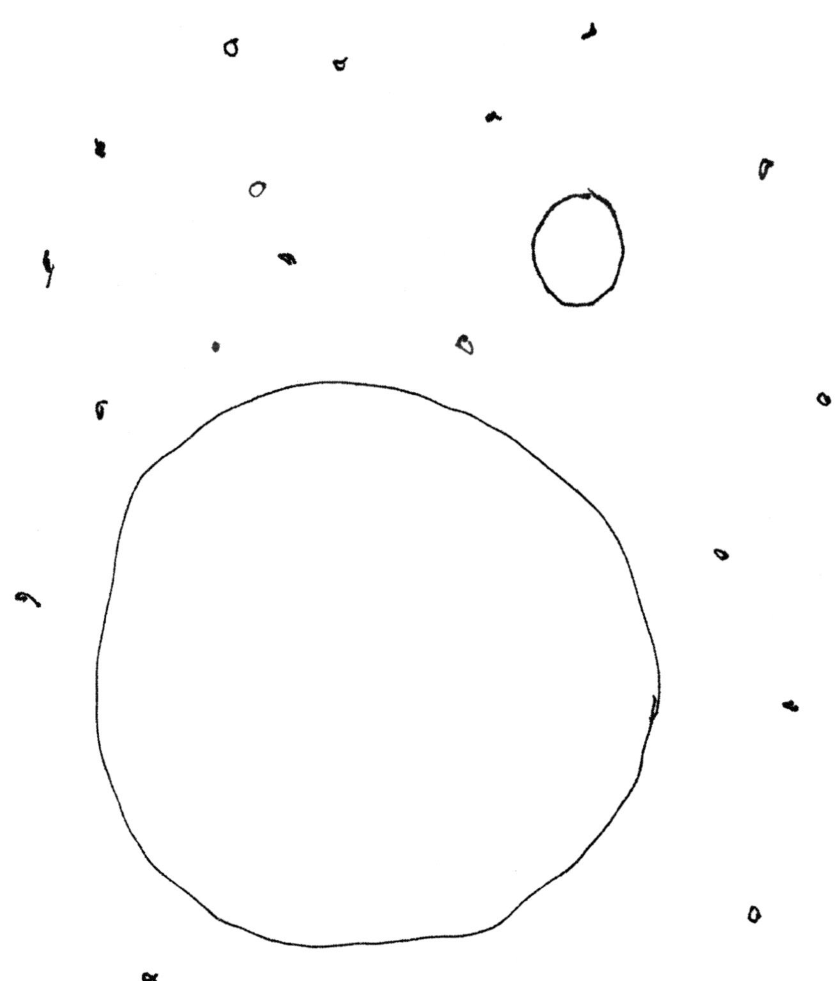

CELESTIAL BODIES.
YOU ARE A CELESTIAL BODY.
WE ARE NOT THE BODY.
YOU & I ARE NOBODY.

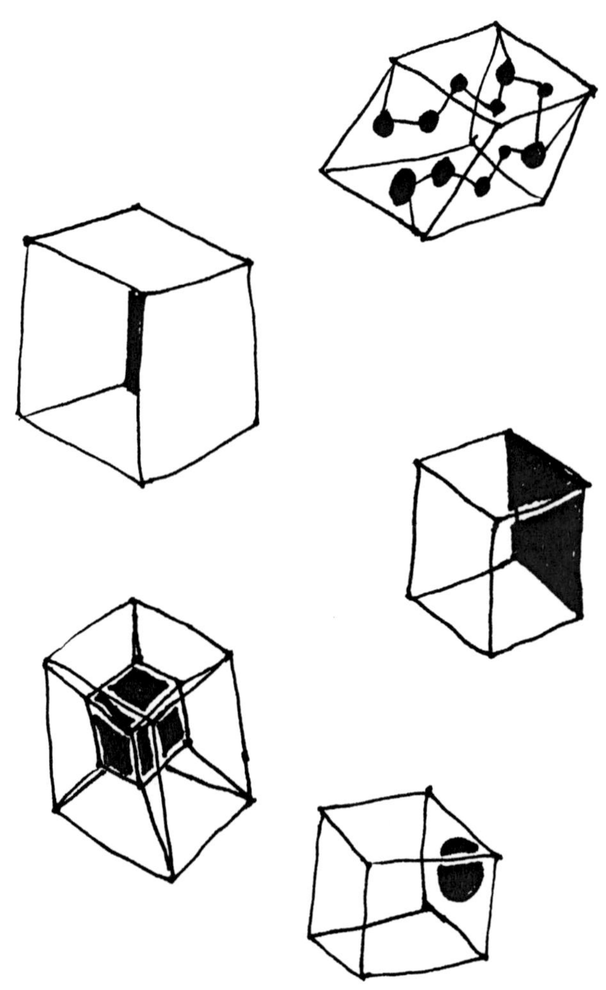

trying to break down the walls trying to get through the veils trying to go beyond the boring landscapes of the little everyday mind into the WOW—how do they do it? Rembrandt? Van Gogh? Matisse? Kicks you in the stomach—if it doesn't, what was the point? Makes your hair stand on end and electricity crawl up your spine in tiny points.

Can't stand this everyday mind anymore. Peel it open, look inside. A stew pot, lumps of cooked meat and onions and carrots floating around inside, steam rising from the surface. Not too inviting, but dive in anyway, got to get to the bottom of this! Trench coat off, leave your shoes behind, here we go—slip through the surface smoothly, easier than I thought. There are dolphins in here! Please give me a ride, I need some help.

A friendly dolphin glides over and invites me on with a flick of her tail. Mona Lisa smile. Away we go—round and round, then down in a spiral, faster than I expected. Wow, it's deep in here—not just a bowl of soup. Gets blacker and blacker as we spiral down along an unmarked track that aims headlong into the depths. I hold on to the dolphin's sides, glad for the company. Seems to know where she's going.

Path straightens out now, first straight down, then gently flattening off. Have we reached a bottom? As I think it, I see sands below me sparkling like gold in a light that seems to come from nowhere, to just be there, a luminous glow that glitters over the surface of the sandy bottom as we glide by, sending ripples down and back. Can't see ahead of me, just a little beyond the dolphin's nose is all I can make out in the self-illumined liquid surrounding us. Then just ahead, a rocky wall with a hole in it—no sooner seen than whoosh!—we are through it, into a cavernous room so big it seems to be a world apart, complete in itself.

I stare up at the ceiling, so far up it could be sky, except that it glows with the same soft gold light I saw on the sand, revealing its rocky, crystal-lined crags. The dolphin stops and gently waves its tail to and fro, kicking up sparkling clouds of sandy dust. I slide off and stroke its sweet face, thanking it. It swims around me three times and is off, waving its tail good-bye.

I turn around and see nothing but rocky walls in the vast glowing room. I hope for I know not what—some encounter beyond the ordinary. I sit down to wait. The sand is soft and warm, and breathing the liquid air is no problem.

All at once I hear faint music far beyond me, and the light intensifies. Before it even appears, I see images of a brilliant procession—reds, peacock blues, brass horns, and enormous banners. The music grows louder and I see across from me an opening in the rock, and light pouring through it. Schools of fish without number pour into the cavernous room and spiral up into clouds above me, hanging in the liquid air, their sides gleaming in luminous patterns of yellow, blue, violet. Then another burst of larger fish, disporting themselves around the distant walls of this deep grotto.

Suddenly the light is blinding, and I hold up my hands to shield my eyes. An intense wave of emotion sweeps over me, and I jump to my feet. Through the doorway comes the light, filling the room and casting shadows everywhere around it. In the center of the light is a sound, deep and resonant as if made of many voices. The sound has a form, which my mind struggles to grasp. Threads of sound weave together like the fibers of a rope, and the net of threads congeals to reveal a sparkling fibrous being, gleaming and twinkling as if covered in a surface netting of many-colored faceted beads. The surface of the netting is transparent, and I see through it to a light of such intensity that it appears solid. Fortunately for my eyes, the light is contained within the net, so that I can see the form of the being without being blinded. I long to step forward, but find that I cannot move.

The being steps slowly toward me. It has a half-human form—head, body, arms, legs— but moves in and out of form constantly, like the play in the grass of the shadow of a tree in summer. I am enthralled, enchanted. My hands reach out of their own volition, my mouth opens soundlessly, and my heart begs to receive something—anything!

The being smiles and moves close, then hands me a small pebble. As my hand closes around it the being moves forward again, and I feel its presence penetrating my skin and flesh and passing into me. My entire being is vibrating in tiny points of color and motion—I am made of dots of light, like a snowy image on a television screen.

My essence whirls into a spiral of vibrating dots, and circles upward, dispersing as it rises. My own being spreads out into the enormous room, filling it with points of glowing colors. The room shimmers and drifts, like a snow-filled paperweight scene. I am fully present in each dot of light, freer than I have ever dreamed of being, and complete. Then slowly I drift ecstatically down into a descending spiral, and crystallize back into my own form as the being passes through me and out of my back. I whirl around to see it again, but the scene fades around me and instead I am sitting at a writing desk, staring at a white page covered with words. My heart is heavy and light, my body is dense, and my pen is heavy. I put it down.

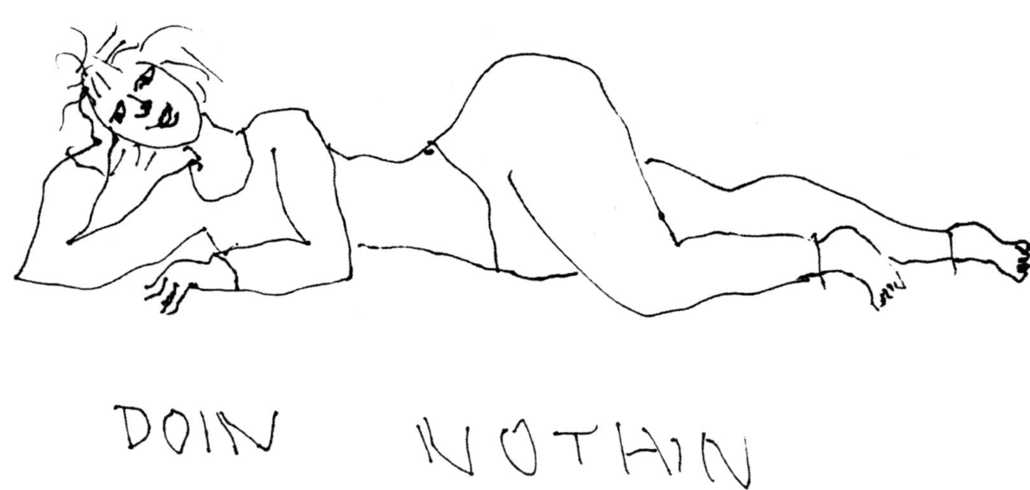

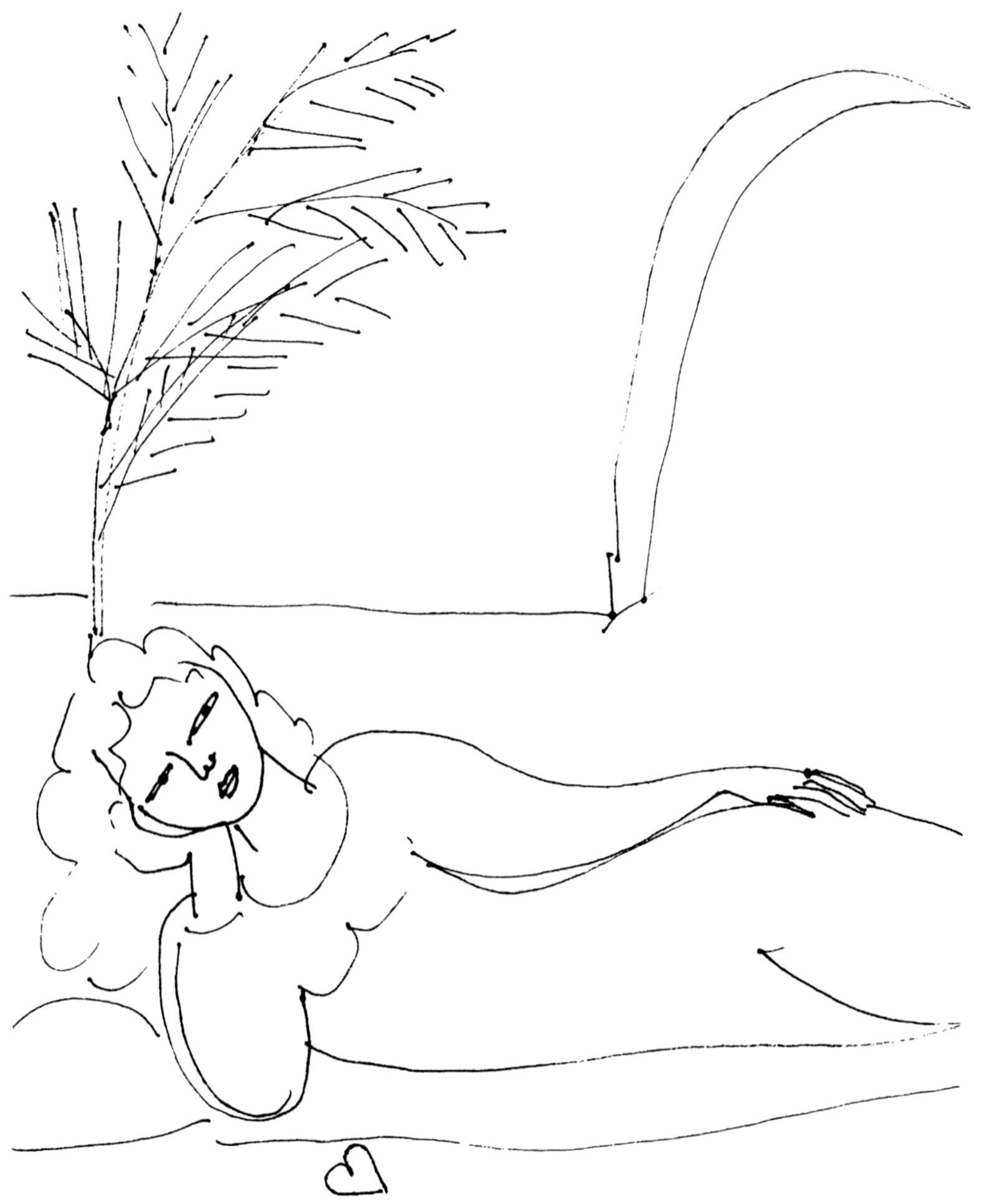

Sometimes no words can say, but a picture can. Sometimes the words won't come, it's not about words but about a feeling in the jaw muscle or the angle of the head, an ache deep in the brain, a knot tied somewhere in the flow of energy and it all dams up, letting only the anxious feelings flow out, no name to them, just that wish that it would go away, whatever it is.

Slip back down the waves of anxiety, a river of anxious pulses, follow them back to where the big knot sits, a tangle of impulses from all over the body, finally now so tangled that nothing can get through. Can't tackle it from this side.

Slip into one of the threads, just go in anywhere, doesn't matter. It's hot in here, not much room. Keep going—have to pull myself along. Not hard, just time-consuming. Not uncomfortable either. Seems to go on forever, but I know it doesn't. Little striations for handholds, looks like the segments of a worm—but this is no worm. This is the life's-blood of my life's energy, the liquid-like flow of chi all knotted together—how did it get this way? Some obstruction blocked the natural flow—what is it?

An old scar—a freak-out scar. Froze up solid, refused to go on. The next pulse hit up against it and turned aside, then another and another, kept flowing but always less easily, always a bit sticking to that spot until it became a huge tangle, now jammed up.

What was the freak-out in the first place? Little girl squeaking, shrieking, squealing, screaming, silent scream, silent screams, there's nobody here to scream to, what's the use of screaming? Don't scream this time, don't scream, don't scream, find another way around it. Little unscreamed screams, building up, piling one on top of another, damming the flow. Damn the Flo. What do you want to scream? WHERE ARE YOU? WHERE'S MY MOTHER? Don't scream, she'll hear you, she'll hate you, she won't feed you. She'll feed you when you don't want to eat, she'll make you eat what you don't like. Here, don't scream. Eat this. Don't scream. No, you can't have that. Don't scream.

Be quiet.
Be still.
Be stuck.
Ice cream.

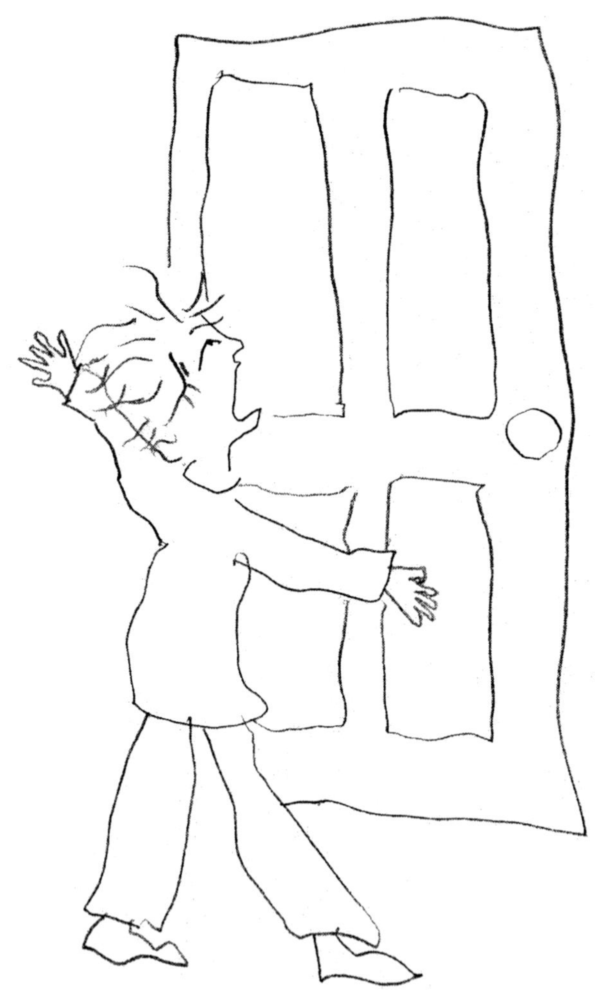

OPEN SESAME!
OPEN SESAME!
OPEN SESAME!
OPEN SESAME!
OPEN SESAME.
OPEN SESAME. OPEN SESAME
OPEN SESAME OPEN SESAME
OPEN SESAME OPEN SESAME
OPEN SESAME!

like a mountain stream, words come pouring and bubbling out from behind the music, cascading out into consciousness—funny, they're all in English, one wall built around me already before I even get to state my preferences for who I will be. Stuck with thinking in English, so different from French, so different from Hindi. I find myself using the Hindi words (Sanskrit, really)—*karma, bhav, lila,* how can you talk about them in English? You can take a pile of words and shove them around until they describe something, which is not the same as naming it—name it and you've got it, bang! The whole thing, alive, right there. Like the dolls—the one I bought, so beautiful, so carefully constructed out of simple materials, a Nature Spirit she called it—a doll picture of a Nature Spirit. And the one I threw together from driftwood, pieces of shell, sea urchin spines I picked up on the beach and stuck together—not a picture of anything—she simply IS. Is who she is. Ugly, twisted, gnarled, asymmetrical, alive, she stares back at me with total unconcern for who I am, who she is, what she looks like—she simply IS. You cannot do better than that, I say. Empty of all attributes, it comes as it comes, I am as I am.

The music rushes along, babbling over stones between its mud walls, past trees and deer and bugs, on its way to wherever it's going. When it arrives it will be on its way to wherever it's going.

Where am I going? Why am I going? I've used up this place, I guess—the solitude, the ordinary, plain beauty of it, the deer and skunks and porcupines and foxes and raccoons and groundhogs and squirrels and rabbits and crows and blue heron and ruffed grouse and bluebirds that fly down the chimney, the butterflies, the hummingbirds, the insect that looks so much like a hummingbird that when you show him to someone they don't believe you that it isn't a hummingbird till you show them it doesn't have bird legs. The mist on the hills. The smell of blueberry blossoms. The silence. The sky—my own piece of sky. The slow, empty vibration all around me. I've milked it for all it's worth, I guess—stayed here one year longer than I stayed in Paris, can you believe it? Time to move on.

The brook rushes on, carrying me with it. I abandon all illusion of being in a canoe with a paddle—I'm just a leaf, carried along by the current, sometimes slow, sometimes fast. I'll either go down down down to the sea or I'll get hung up on a branch, a log, a rock and stop, still, stuck, deposited—I'll find my new home.

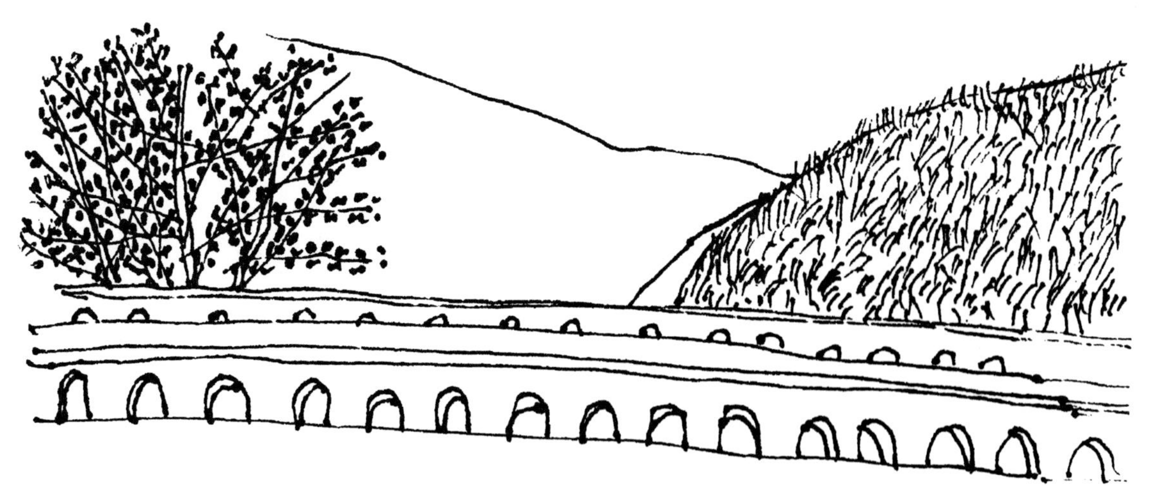

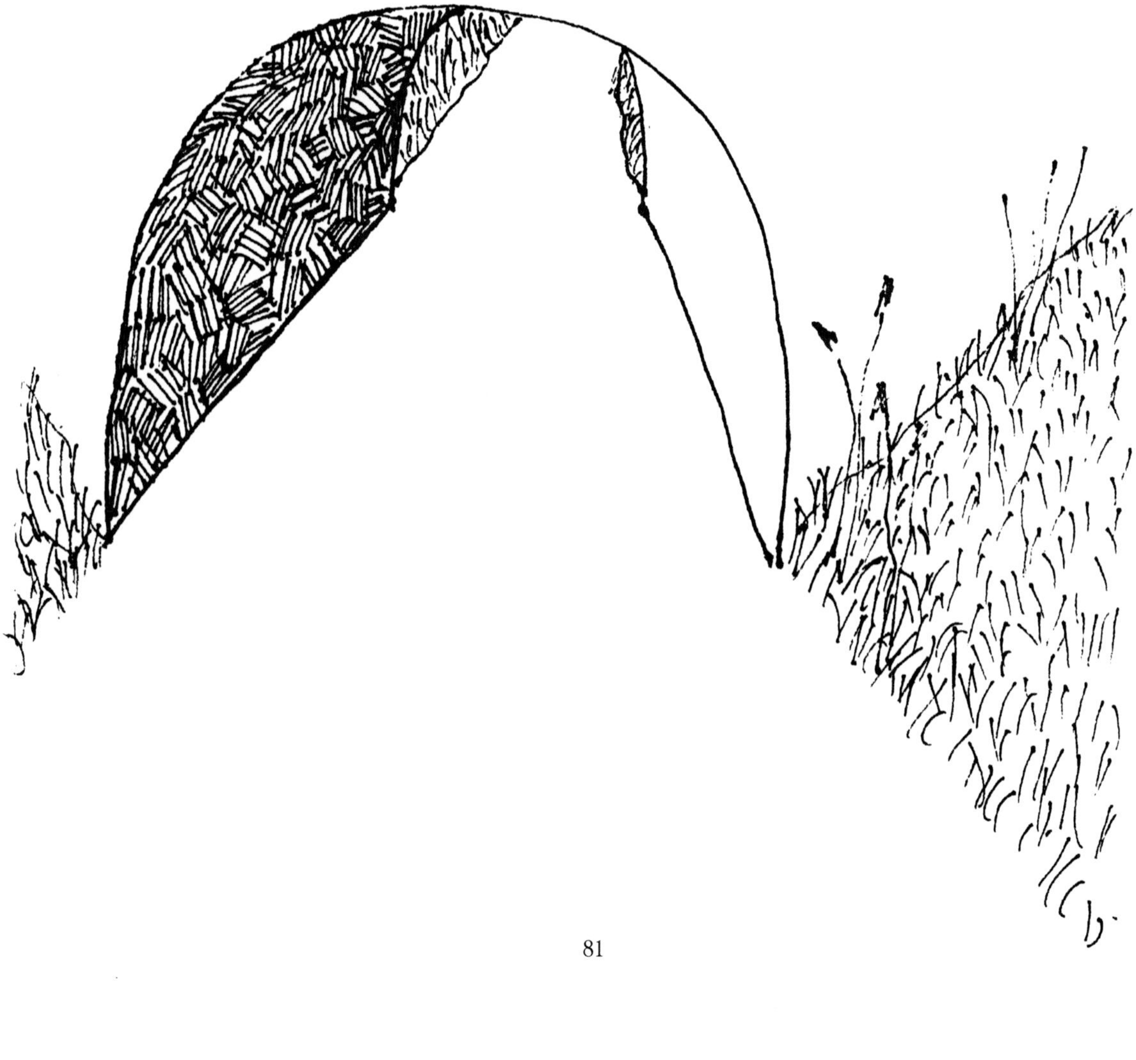

i have not written in so long my hand is rusty my pen is dry. To whom am I writing? To me to you to the page to the air I breathe to the stars to the universe and beyond. I am tired what a long journey there and back to carry my words in a small leather suitcase with worn out corners out to the farthest star.

DO YOU HEAR ME?

I hear you—turn inward, it's easier. I am in there too if you look deep enough.

HOW DEEP? ARE YOU THERE YET?

Here I am the farthest star twinkling in your belly button. Relax—you are dissolving. Your atoms are stars and your spaces are growing wider. It's a very long way from your shoulder to your knee. Look at Orion splashed all over the night sky. Even his sword is bigger than your house bigger than your town bigger than Mount Meru I mean BIG. That's me, spread out splat against the sky, too big to see from one end to the other, where are my hands? My face is gone, who am I now, who cares, I'm stretching out, MAKE ROOM!

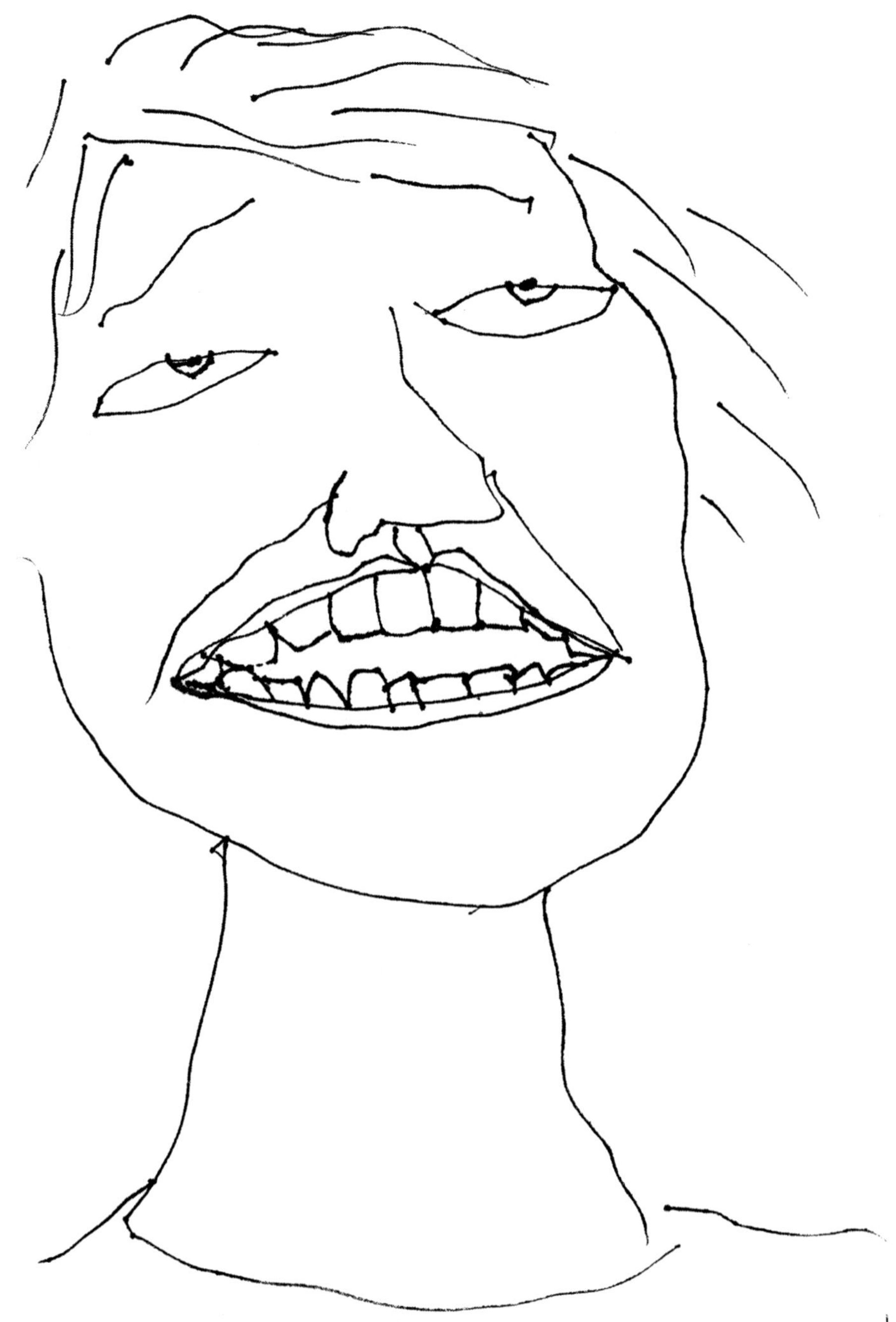

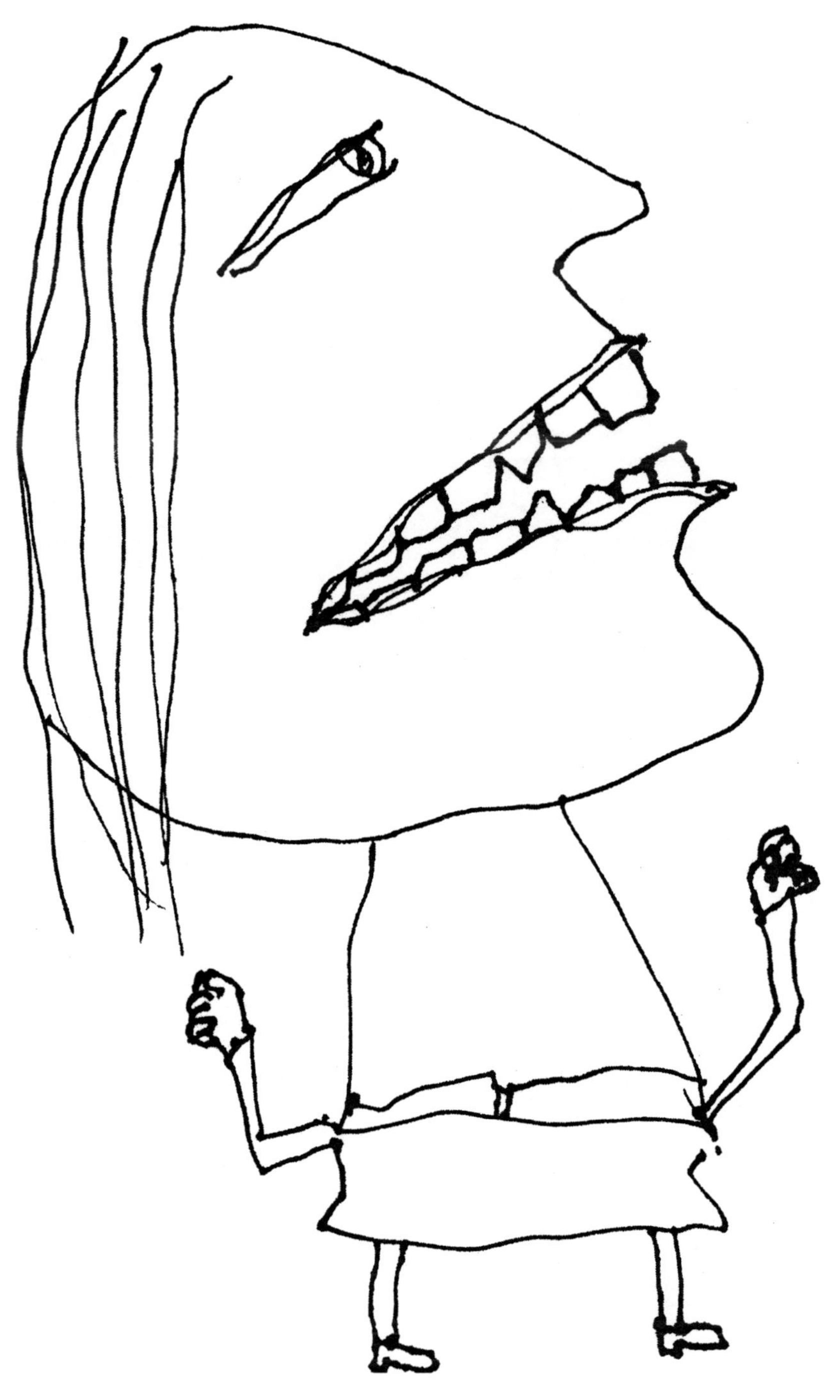

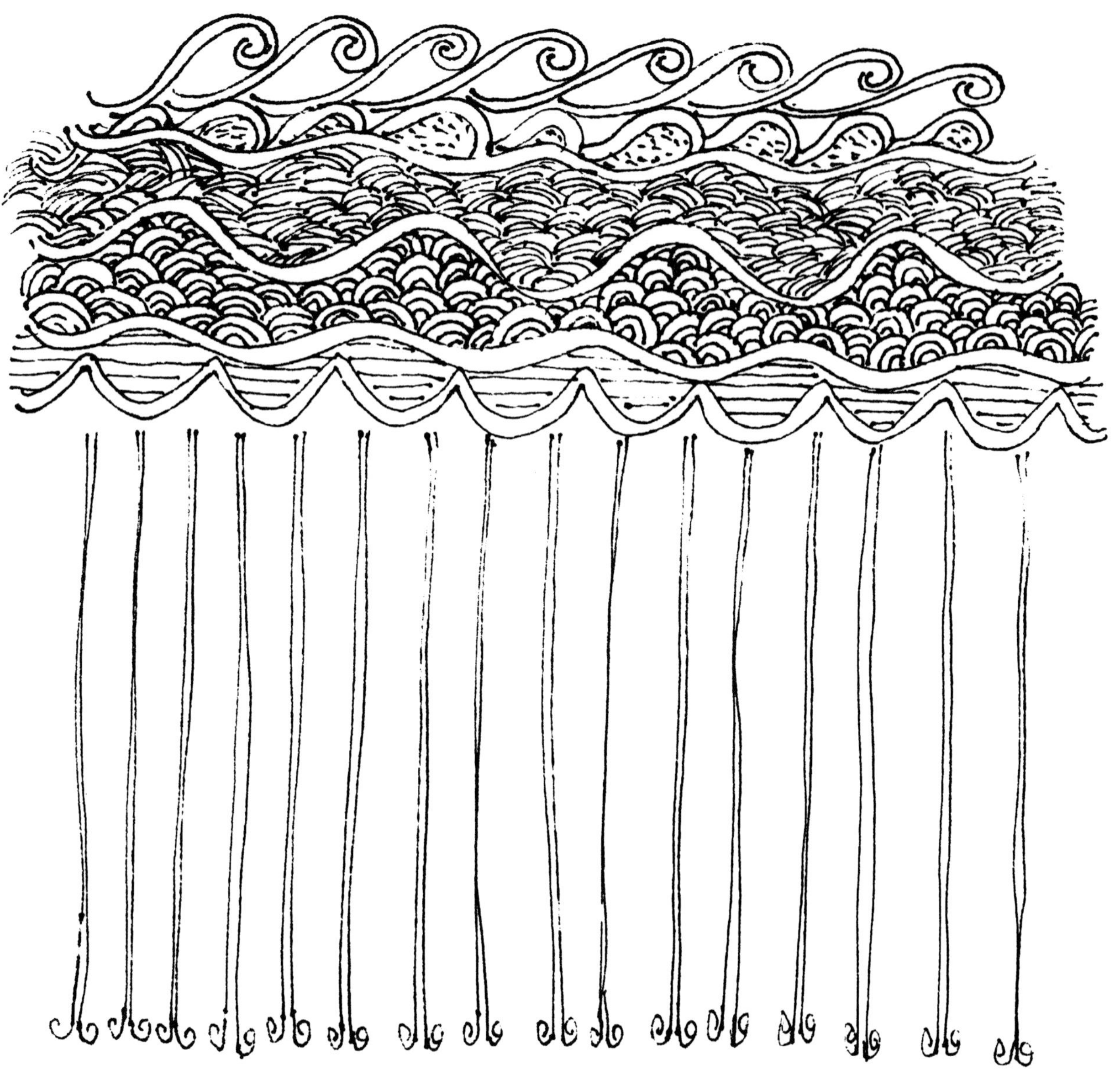

My mother has crawled inside my head the way a fetus curls up inside the womb, resting there like a dream-symbol brain tumor to remind me now that I'm within two years of the time, of the time when a brain tumor grew in her head and took away her life in a few short months. So this is how you felt, Mother. Why do you want me to feel it now?

The urgency to have me know what you felt is stronger by far than any need you feel to protect me or spare me this experience. So you curl up inside my head, like a memorial. Not in my heart, where you belong but were never comfortable. Maybe even beyond the wall of death you still don't know how to curl up in my heart. I felt you there once—remember?—but what a big deal you made of it! Announcing your coming in loud cries like trumpet calls—"Here she is! Here she is!"—as I lay half-sleeping with a crystal in my hand. My insubstantial dream-arm rose behind me slowly, while my physical arm lay on the bed at my side, and your voice called out the announcement of your coming, and then like a charge of electricity you entered the crystal in my dream-hand, which felt then more real to me than my "real" arm lying on the bed, and like a bolt of lightning you flowed down my arm and into my heart.

I saw you there—your face, in my heart. I felt you there too, with a tremendous peace that put to rest all the surge of fear and excitement that had gripped me when I heard the loud calling and felt that surge down my arm. Then I lay there, half asleep half awake, and felt you in my heart. For the first time. And the last, since you have not revisited me in that way. Now you prefer to inhabit my head, a constant dull ache that constantly asks the same nagging question: Am I brain cancer? Are you going to die the way your mother did, at the same age or even younger?

Or are you going to live to be an age where you'll be even older than your mother ever was, and forge your way into new territory, a woman older than her mother, self-created?

Anything is possible. I think I'll do that.

Get out of my head, Mother. Find your way to my heart. I'll join you there, and not in death. Not yet.

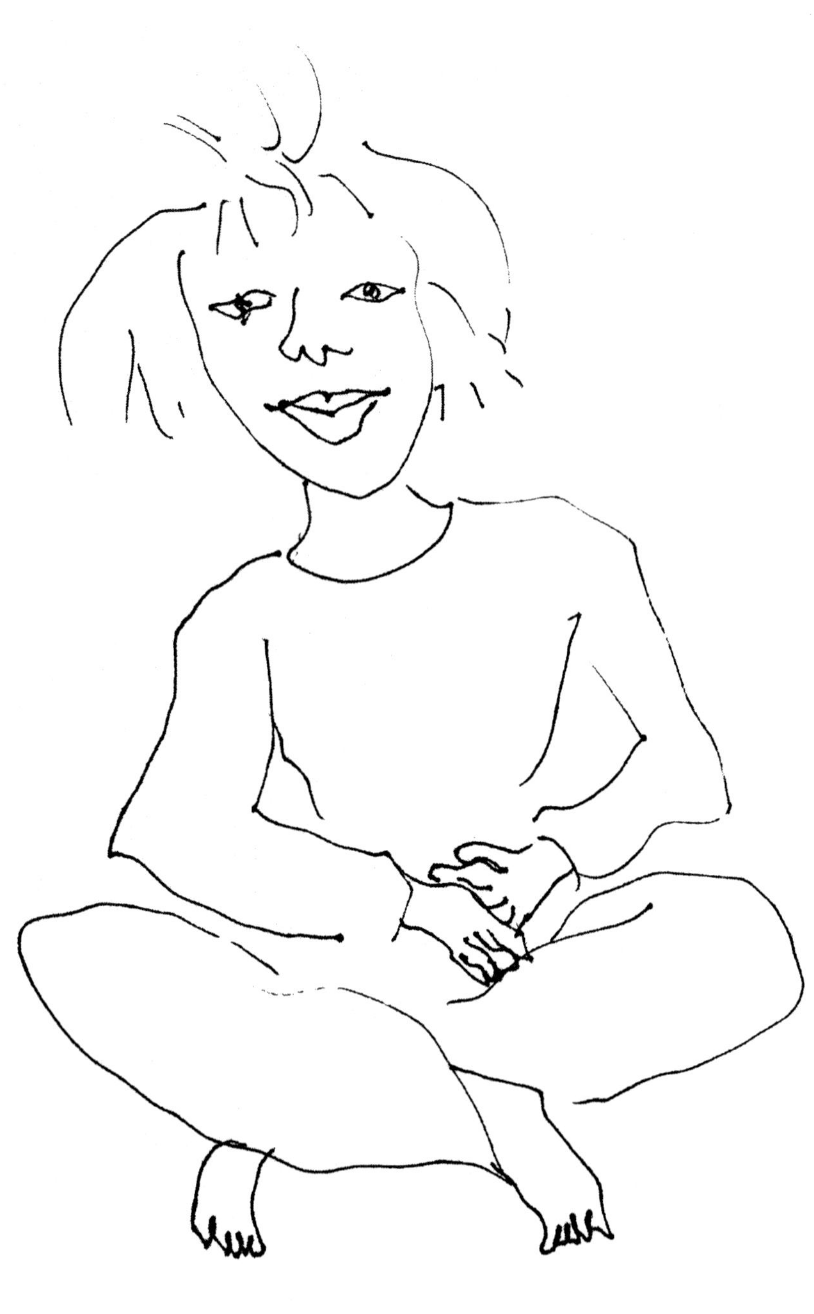

ALL ALONE

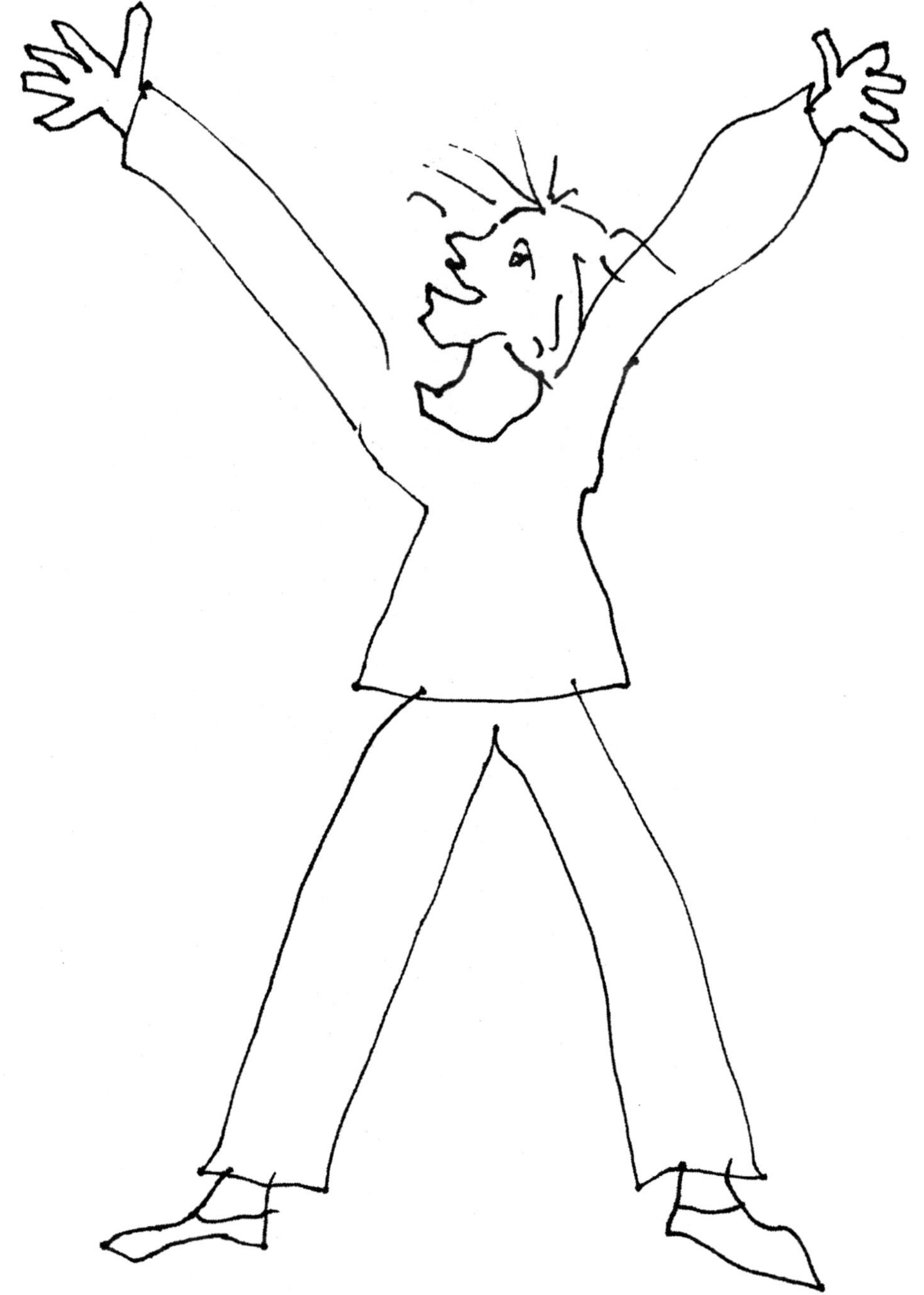

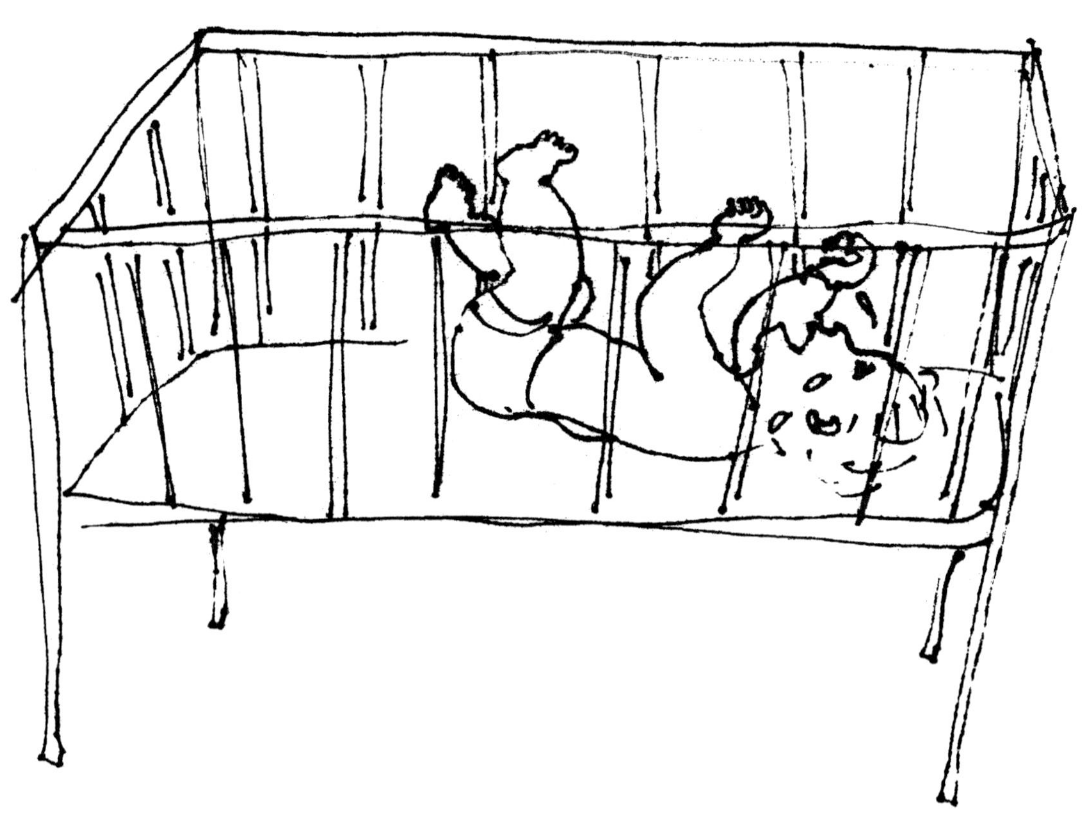

there's something about a piece of land that belongs
to you, land with your own house on it, the land you live on—it becomes like a piece of
your own body, alive and conscious, consciously breathing and happening day and night,
awake and asleep. Like your own life extended out beyond your skin, seeping through
your pores into the air and out, into the earth which breathes as you breathe. Green living things unfold and blossom, ripen and seed, wither and die with the passage of your
own time. Animals roam secretly in your extended living body, visible in the daylight,
unseen but there at night, wary and distant always and yet part of you. You know it and
they know it, but still they keep their wary distance, one eye on you as they go about their
animal business, tolerating you up to a point and then bolting if you get too near. Still,
they know and I know that we are parts of the same whole, belonging to this land that
foolishness decrees belongs to me. My life plays itself out in the same scenery as the deer
and foxes, but I pay taxes and they are free. Free not to think, but to keep a wary eye on
me and go ahead and graze or chase mice and rabbits or dig burrows.

I used to live in cities, and the rhythm of my life tied in to other human rhythms, invented like artificial daylight—powerful as a tide but neither acknowledging nor worshiping its sources, the great burning sun, the great Mother Earth. Diurnal rhythms ticking
in us all, but in the city we rise and fall again like automatons, unfolding to the ringing
of alarm clocks, blossoming in the subways, ripening in tall buildings, shedding our seeds
on the sidewalks, withering and dying alone in tiny rooms. Sitting on the grass in front
of my house my mind spills out and down the hill, rolling and green and warmed by the
sun. Animals play in my thoughts or lurk at the edges of my mind. Birds fly in its blue
spaces, and my body expands to cover the land from border to border. Stone walls surround me, a brook runs through me, trees put down their roots in me, flowers grow in
my hair. The earth breathes me, the sun gives me life, the moon illumines me, and the
stars roll overhead as I pull the black night sky around me and lie down to sleep.

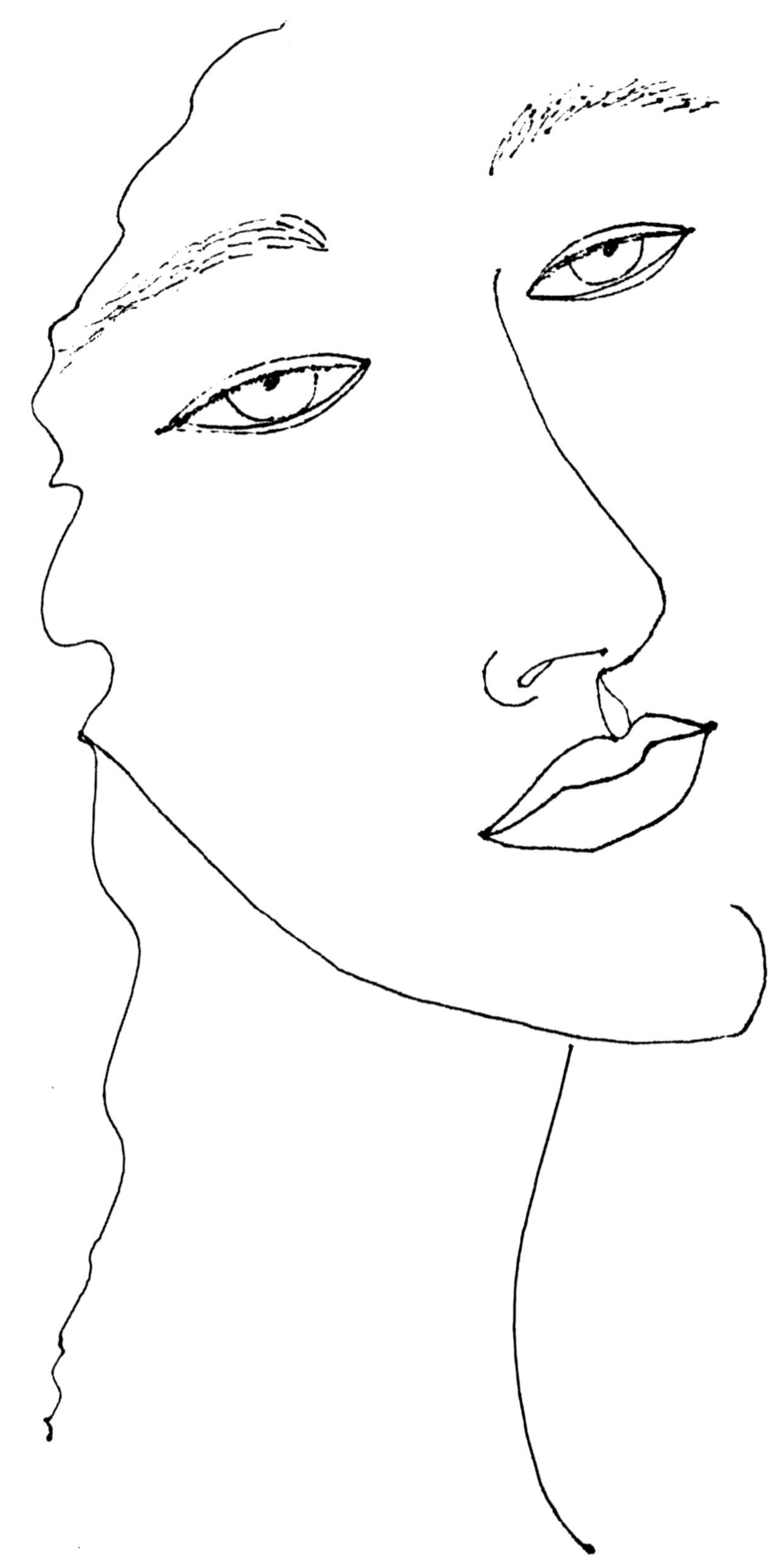

Square page, round thoughts

Square page, round thoughts spiraling round like starry tracks in a liquid mind, spirals of stars like the bubbles in a glass of champagne, coming up out of nowhere and spiraling to the top in an unending, hypnotizing stream. Where does it all come from, this play that comes from nowhere and crystallizes into solid form while we sleep and dream, unknowing? In the morning we wake and Lo! A world has crystallized around us—a floor to put our feet on, a bed to get out of, walls that make a room, a mirror in which to discover, with a shock, ourselves.

Who is that, and who is it just behind, unseen but definitely there? And who looks out of those eyes I stare into? It's definitely not me! Where did I come from anyway? Was I born from last night's dream? And that person in the mirror, where did she come from? The back of the mirror? I peer into the distance of the reflection in the glass, looking for the spot where the bubbles start. It's no good, though—there's always another bubble behind the bubble you are looking at—a new one is always popping into existence at every moment.

Of course, we know what black holes are—they are the rabbit holes of our existence into which we fall, like Alice, down and around and through the nothingness to pop out on the other side into some new universe, like the bubbles in a glass of champagne, ever newly created from nowhere. Nowhere is just another name for the doorway, the black hole that takes us to zero and starts us going again somewhere else, the mirror image of where we came from, in a backward universe where black is white and the spiral goes round the other way.

And so we grow young there, and are born again back into this world where another black hole waits to chew us up and spit us out whole again, inside out and upside down and racing at breakneck speed from something to nothing and then back to something again. Just a cluster of atoms being juggled in space by a playful universe too big to notice how scared we are as we bounce.

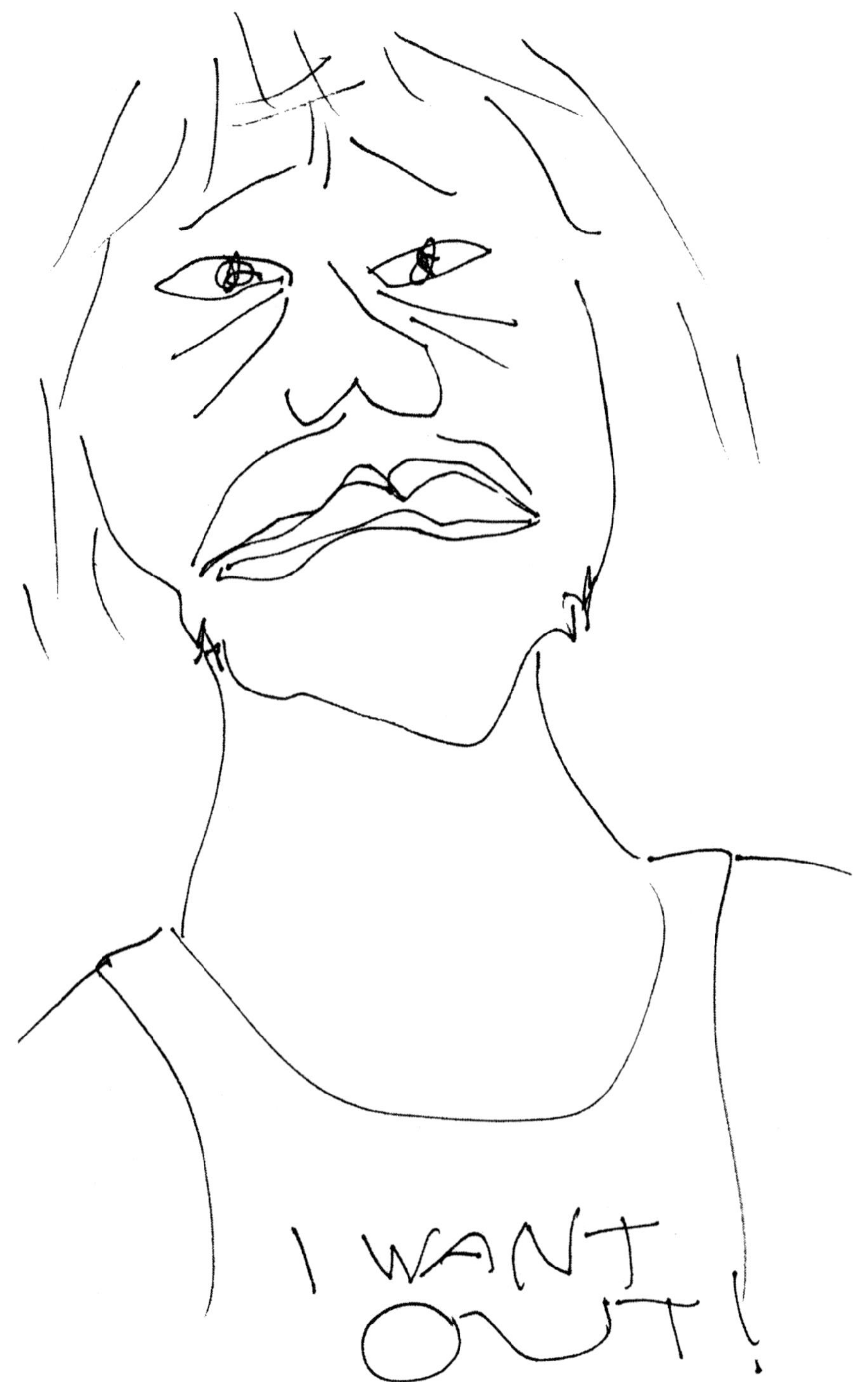

I WANT
OUT!

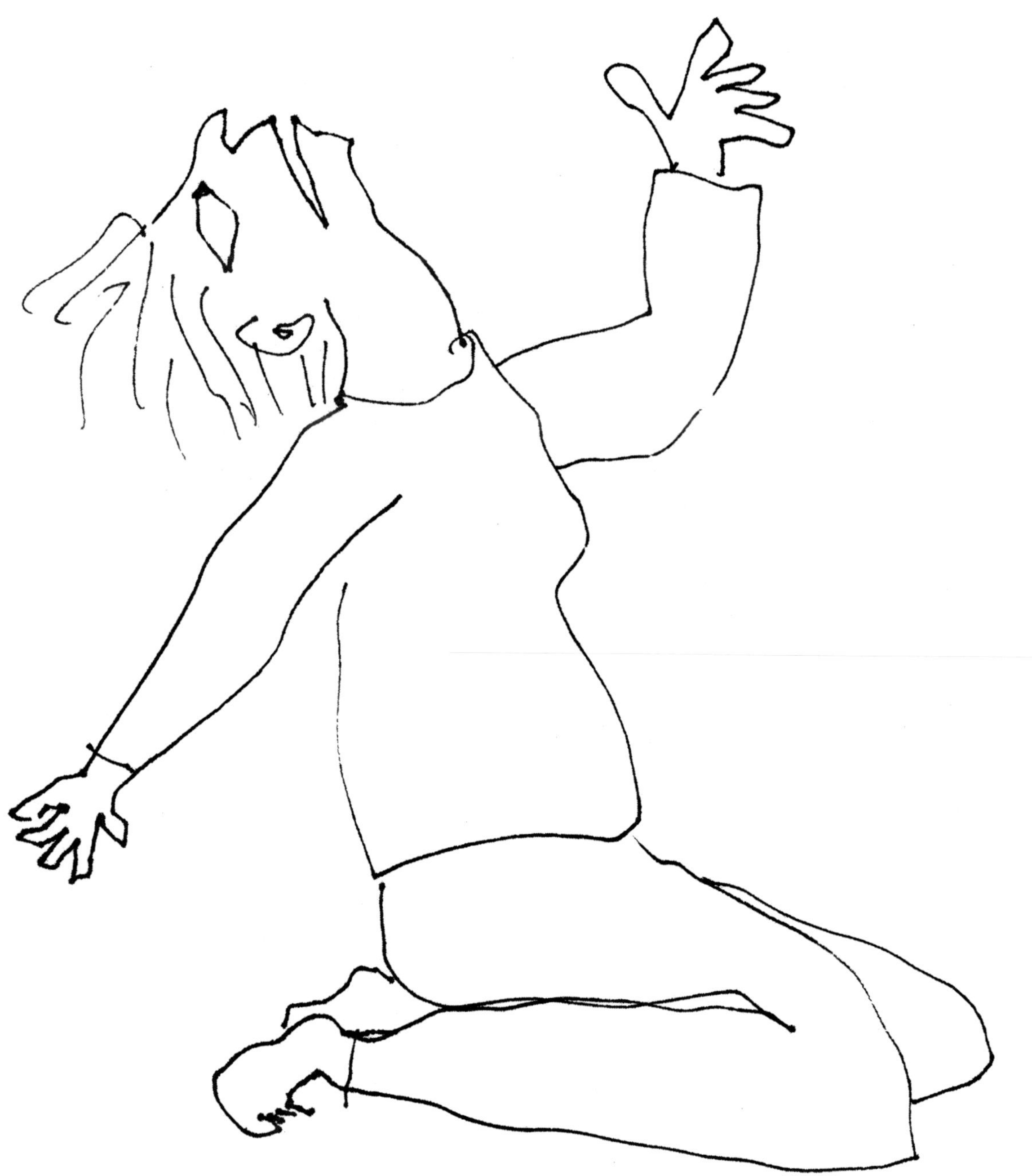

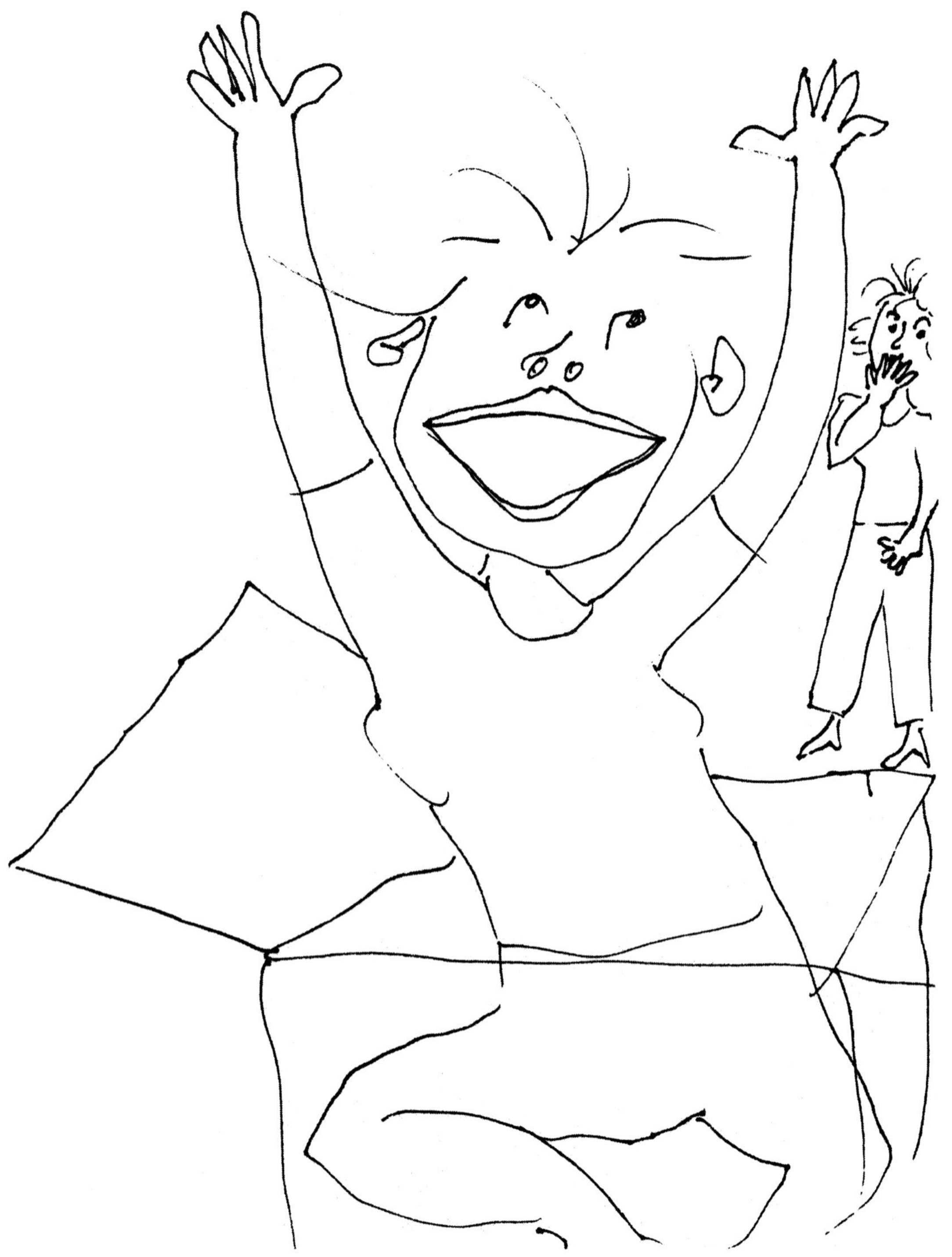

My mind is bored rattling around inside my head, thinking the same old thoughts and looking out of my brown eyes at the same old scenery. My mind would prefer the farthest reaches of outer space for a neighborhood, and it's always running off there when I'm not looking, slinging its small bundle of possessions tied up on a stick over its shoulder like an old comic-book character, and hitching a ride out to some distant star. And there it sits, gazing out at gigantic billiard balls floating and shimmering in the blue-black gleaming emptiness, resting and refreshing itself there where it knows I can't follow it with my lists of things to do, worries to worry about, and endless insurmountable obstacles to overcome. I sit here curling up the corners of my notepad while out there it contemplates the beginning and the end of time as it bathes itself in the cooling waters of eternity. Quarks and muons are its companions and galaxies its playground, while I sit here obediently playing the silly role life has cast me in, trying to remember what it was I told myself I must remember not to forget.

Universes explode into being around my mind, and in the twinkling of a thought snuff themselves out in the unimaginable depths of black holes while my mind witnesses the cosmic play, pretending it doesn't hear me calling it. Somewhere beyond space-time goes my mind, losing itself in the fountainhead of streaming matter arising in luminous rainbow sparks from nowhere and returning inward back to its source, out and in, out and in, infinite universes creating, colliding, and vanishing while I, complaining, look everywhere, in drawers, on shelves, under papers, behind books, for my lost reading glasses.

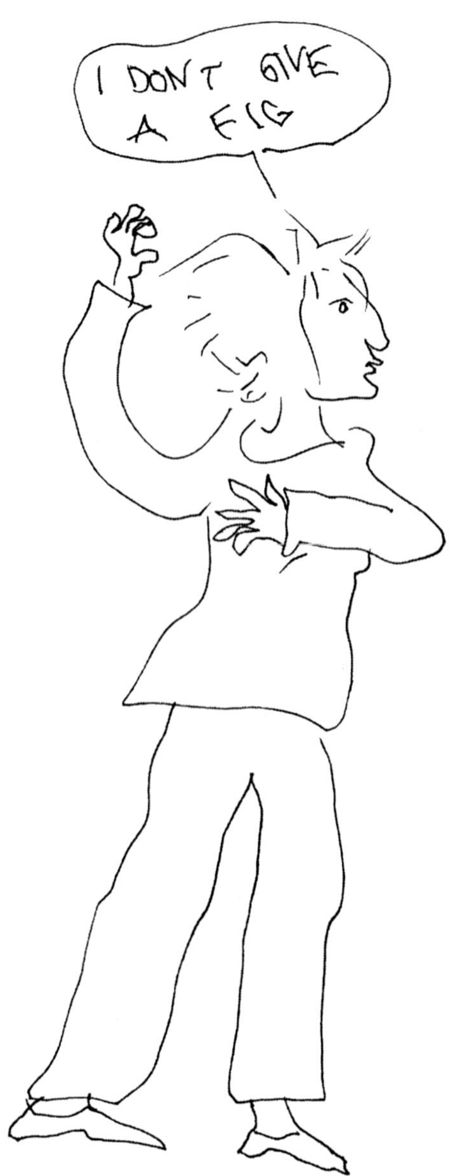

I DON'T GIVE A FIG

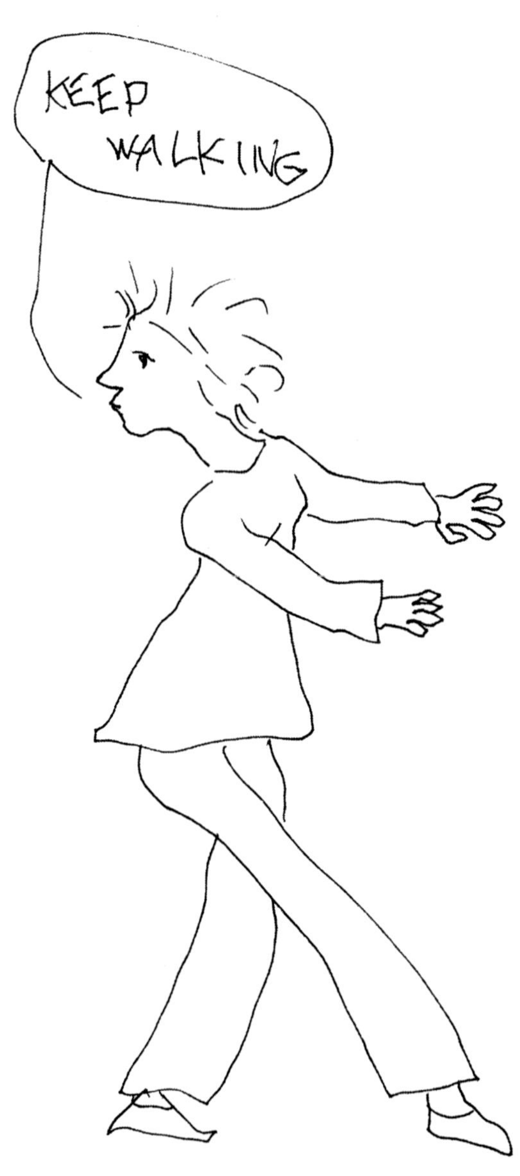

KEEP WALKING

Inbreath and outbreath over and over day and night week after
month after year after year all my life I breathe in and breathe out, keeping it going
through all the easy places and the hard ones, not choosing to, but being breathed by
something that wants me alive, wants me to partake of all else that is alive, and to give
back of my own essence to that pool, unimaginably immense and smaller than the small-
est dot my mind can imagine. Gross matter supported by the rarest, thinnest wisp of
is-ness, fed by nothingness and sent on its daily rounds willy-nilly, wound up with air
and set in motion by a will that lives ever outside the flecks and chunks of material that
cluster together to form the person I am.

Yet who am I? I was once the baby I was, and still am but am no longer, grown much
older, larger, fuller and emptier, dumber and wiser, and much more tired. Looking at
her and then at me, even I would fail to make the connection if my parents had not told
me, "This is you." Which is what they told me, from the beginning and all the time I was
making myself up, struggling against and bewildered by their pronouncements of who I
was.

And it took me forever to clear myself out of the you they said I was, or rather to rise
above it and observe it from a safer distance, doing its ritual dance of who I was supposed
to be, following the tracks it had been set upon and thinking the appropriate thoughts
that could explain it to itself.

And having risen to that safer distance, I empty myself as best I can, tossing overboard
like dumped baggage whatever I can lay my hands on of the you someone else told me
was me, waiting and hoping and working to see if there is anyone left after the cleanout.

And I begin to see through the emptiness that there is someone there, though she or
it is as unsubstantial as the air that breathes her and keeps her cells turning over in the
unceasing coming together and falling apart that her living consists of.

And in the center of the emptiness a few things shimmer and remain, refuse to
go—the upwelling love for her children, who are one of the names of God; the act of
creating something beautiful, which is the endless dance that defines her living; and the
marriage to a house and a piece of land that became her body before she even noticed it

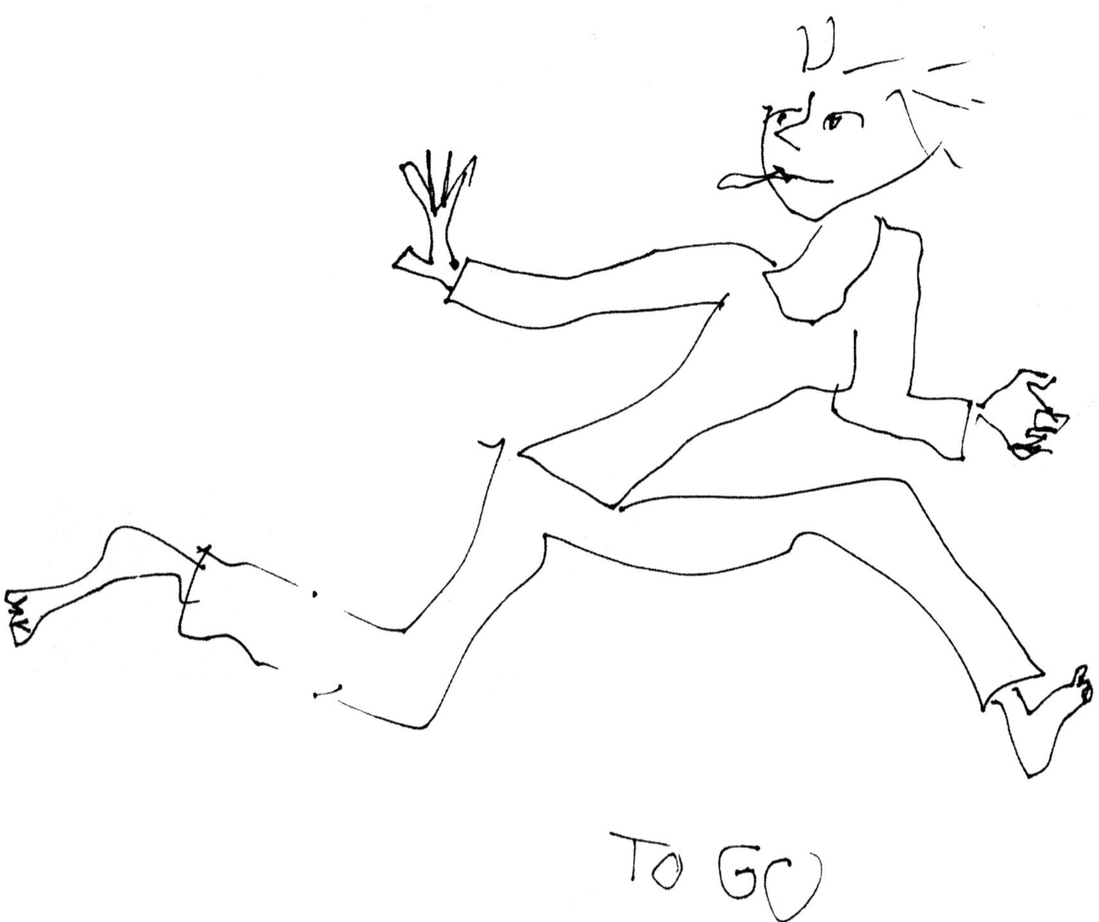

was happening, so that now when she is away from it she is unmanifest. Everything else can go—those things remain, fed by the inbreath and radiating forth to every corner of the universe as I breathe out.

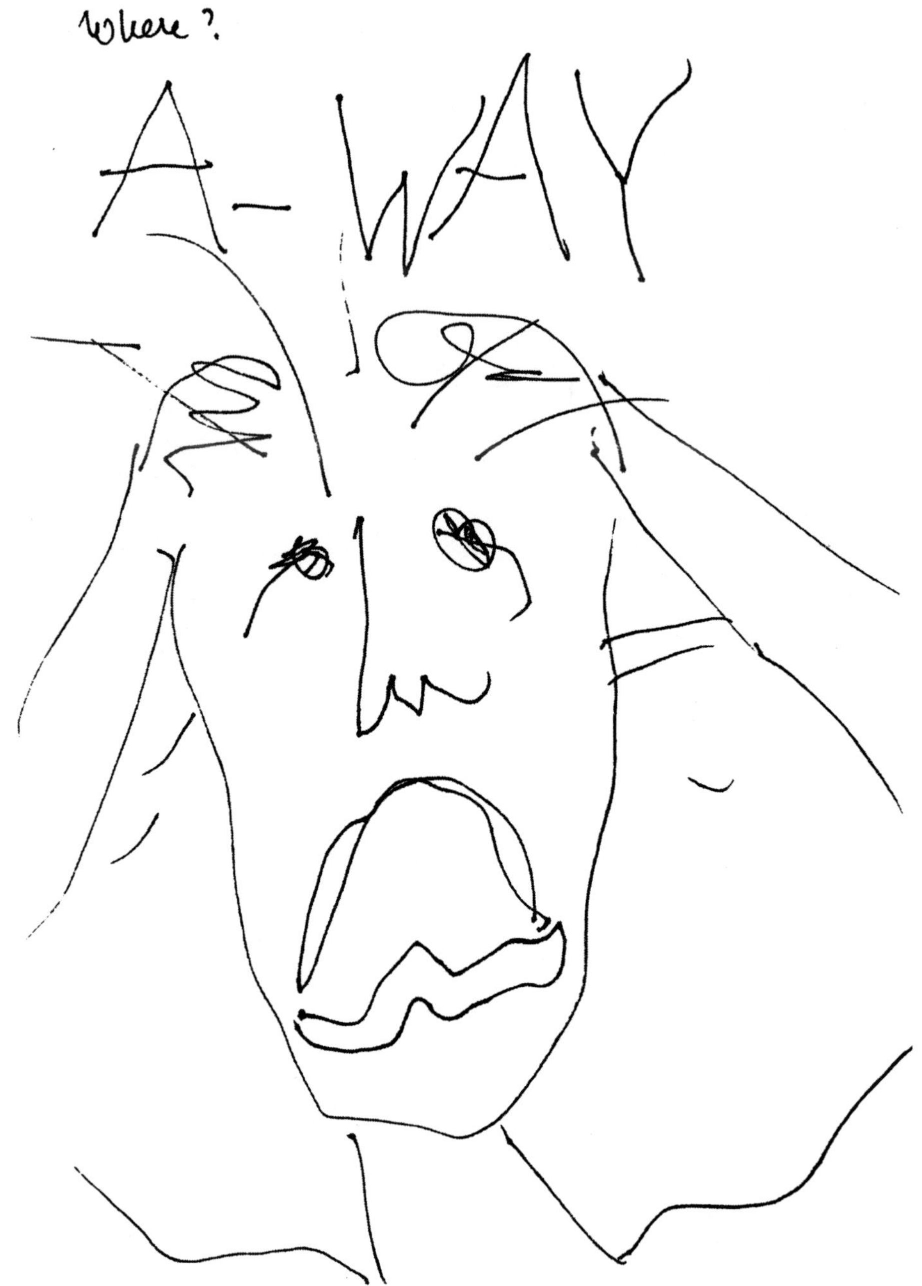
Where?
A-WAY

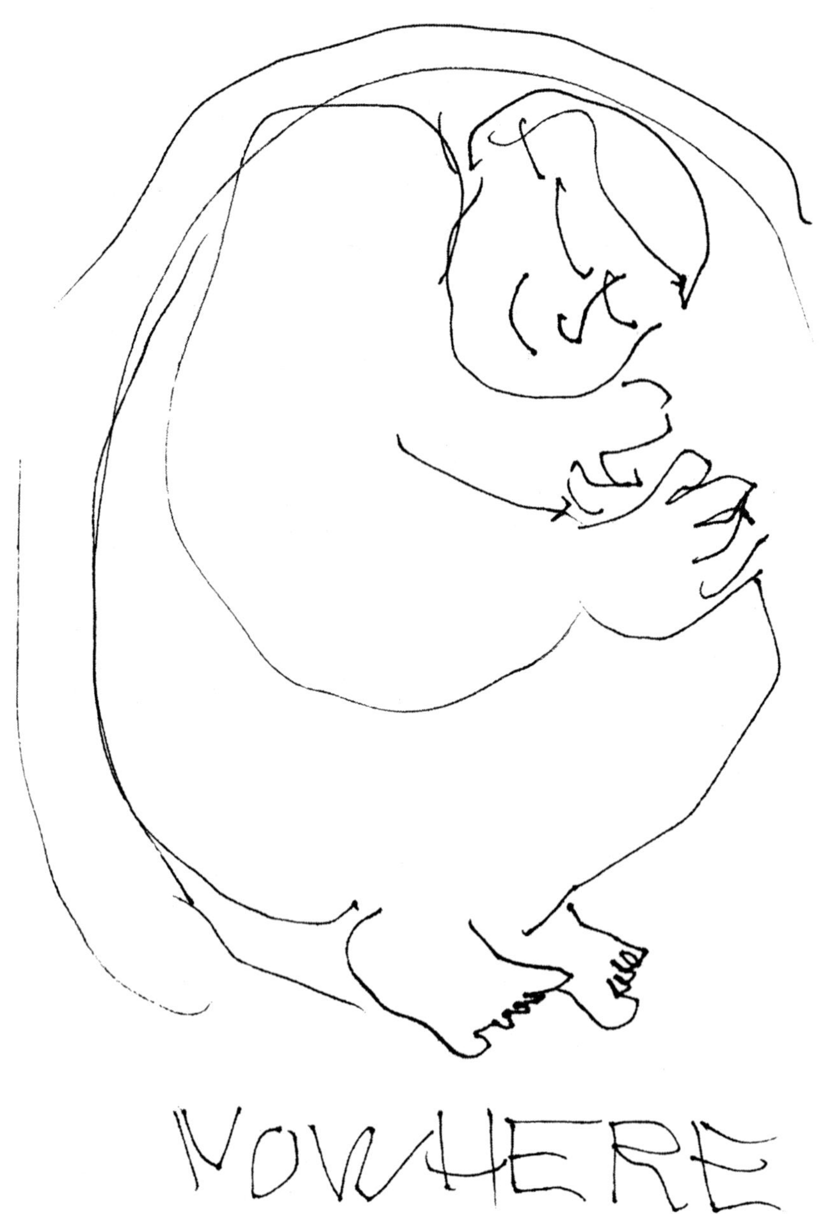

Then where will you be?
NOWHERE

Shapes float out of the candle flame the way words bubble up in my mind—not always sure they are my words—whose are they then, someone else inhabiting my mind, that most intimate territory that seems so incontrovertibly to be me. Just as the bacteria inhabiting my gut turn out to be an indispensable aspect of who I am, so are my thoughts maybe their thoughts? As they surely were, that time I took flagyl and had to stop because I could hear them all screaming STOP—YOU'RE KILLING ME!

And what size thoughts do my intestinal flora think—are their thoughts the same size as mine, or do they have to get together as a group to think a thought that is audible to me? Easy enough for them, they are already a colony, a group, a community. How many people do I have to join with to think a thought that's big enough to be heard in the cosmos, and is my small mind permeable? Do those thoughts come back to me, like a reflection bouncing off a mirror and pinging onto my retina? Are my thoughts small, large, collective, mine, cosmic, human, background noise, and why do I give them so much power to toss me this way and that and give direction to my life?

Though we know, don't we, that it's only that they seem to give direction. They sit up there on the bridge—togged out in captain's blues with a spiffy hat and stripes on their sleeve saying, Helm alee! Port! Starboard! Full rudder, north by northwest, shiver me timbers—drunk with power—look, I'm driving!

Yeah, right, think again. The future in its implacable wholeness curves up over the ship of my life and grabs hold of it, sucking it forward into what already is but appears from here not yet to be, and I sail toward that future aiming here and there, wavering and tacking, pitching and tossing, but headed inexorably, unstoppably toward the future that not only awaits me but is pulling me toward it, creating forms and events in my life that hint of its existence, and about which I say, Oh, if it hadn't been for that, I never would have ended up here. When in fact it was because I was going to end up here that that came into my life. The future creating the past—the opposite of what we imagine. And my small boat—my body, afloat in the sea of experience, an organized collective of animate and inanimate matter, and not one atom of it is identifiably ME,

so who am I?

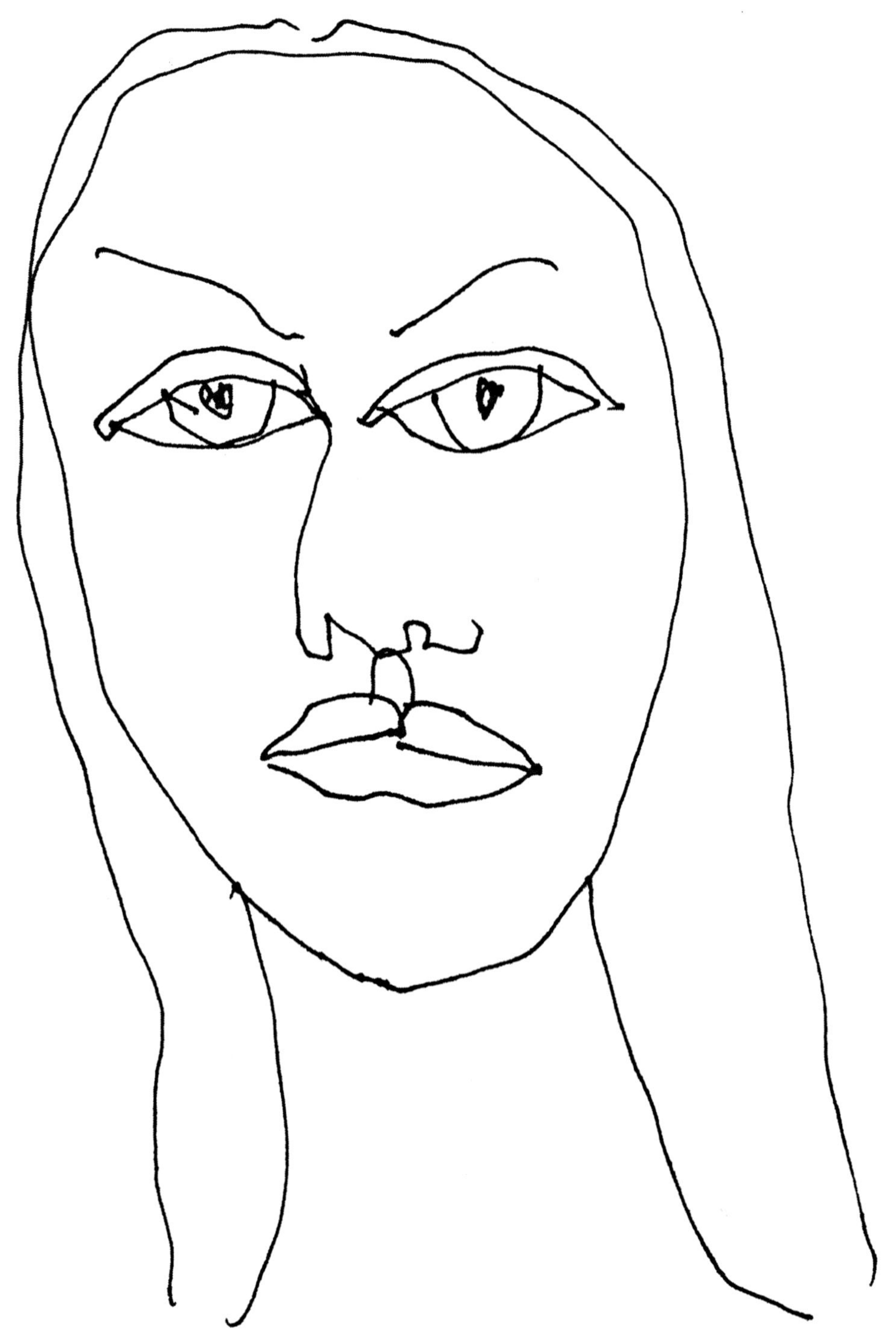

Climbing the ladder toward an unknown goal, one rung at a time, already in the clouds and too far up to go back down again, but no goal in sight. Have to keep going, something impels me ever upward. Been on this ladder since I was a child—will it ever end? Is there a top?

There have been mileposts along the way, dimly recognized as I passed through them, but clearer in memory—memorable, at last. The births of children. Painting—the flow of creative energy in my life. The discovery of myself and the awakening of the kundalini, fully experienced but recognized and given a name only ten years later.

The move to Paris—something happens in your brain when you become bilingual. You live on two levels, two different lives with different trains of thought, ways of conceptualizing, like being two different people in one body.

Cancer, a milestone and a first encounter with the god of Death. Meeting the Guru. The first miracle, when the structural concept of the world crumbles away and magic is born.

The death of the Guru, one way or another, and the accepting of the burden and responsibility into my own body and mind. Keep going, there's another rung, and another. Sometimes the clouds part briefly, permitting a glimpse of what might be ahead, but as they roll back I am left with only a memory of more rungs, going on and on and up and up into more cloud layers. Sometimes I hear faint echoes of angels singing, but when I focus on the sound it fades and the silence mocks me with its emptiness. I put one foot after another, climbing rung by rung endlessly, having abandoned long ago the idea of getting somewhere, but acutely aware nevertheless that there is no choice but to keep going **up.**

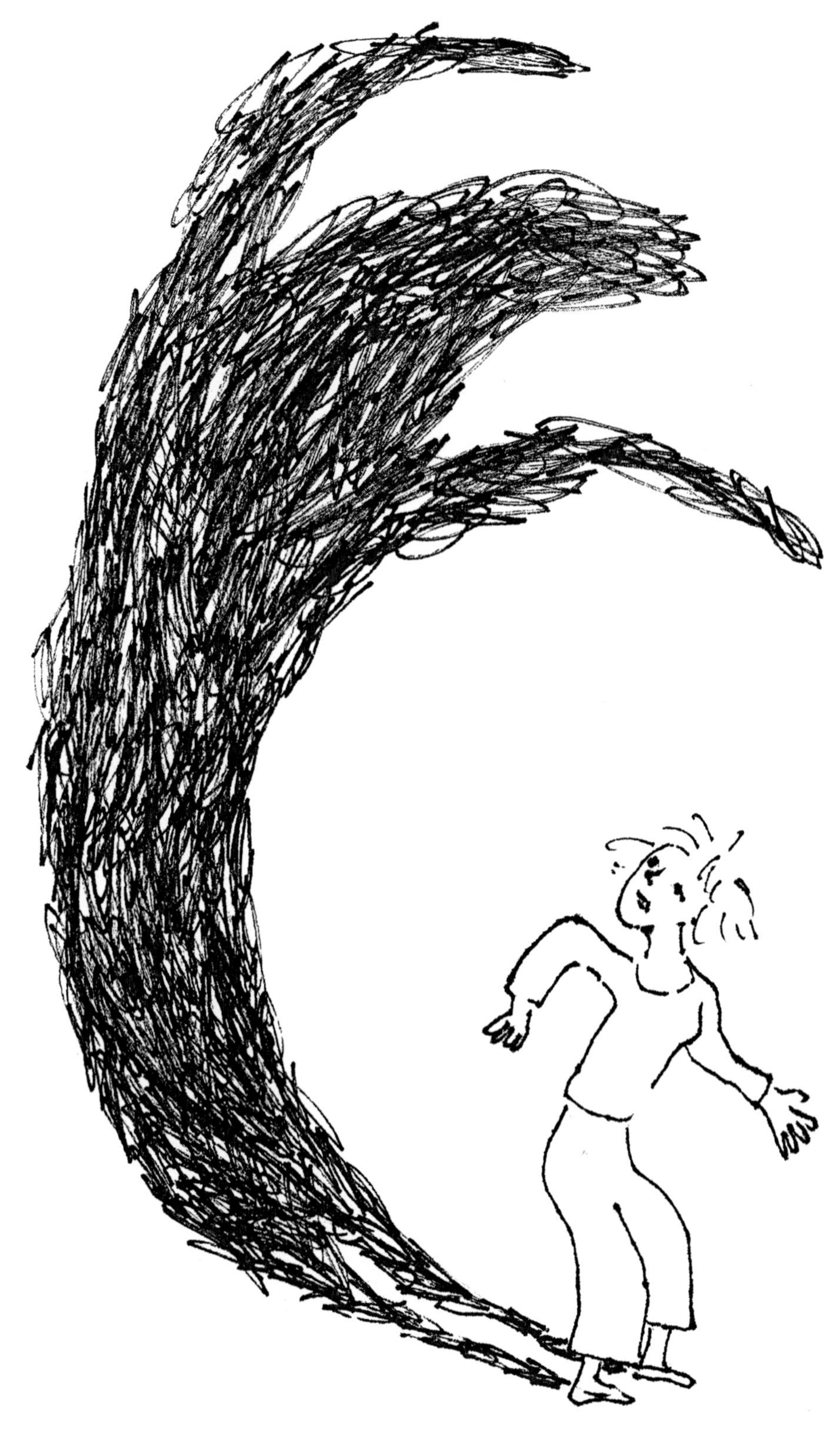

the cold weather descends like a blanket, snuffing out the warmth of summer. Leaves turn red, orange, gold, then fall from the trees, leaving a rustling red carpet on the green grass. The breeze picks up bite, and gray clouds roll across the wide blue sky. The deer come out in their new brown coats and eat their fill while there's still time. The outdoors no longer calls teasingly, invitingly to come and play.

I have to bundle up to go for a walk now. I say good-bye to the leaves as I walk, for I know that one day next week, or soon after, a hard rain will come carrying stiff winds with it, and when the sun next shines the trees will be almost bare.

I am not afraid of November, not afraid of the retreat indoors and the hours spent by the warmth of the woodstove. Late next month when the sun sets, the bare trees on the hill opposite will glow with a violet light. Sometimes I think it's even more beautiful than the green of summer. Then the house begins to come into its own. Spurned in the summer, when the call is to be outdoors, the house now shows itself off as a place of shelter.

The kitchen invites with smells of baking muffins, and warm soups dance in the kettle on the stove. The family draws together in a smaller space. The vegetables we carried so lavishly from the garden in August are cherished now as they dwindle. We are thankful in November for the gifts we've been given.

Could I live without the change of seasons? Paradise, all agree, is a constant 72 degrees, and we walk around in it scantily clothed, never putting by wood for the winter. But what happens to the human soul that never knows the reawakening of spring, the new hope, the tender green, the early flowers, the scent of blueberry and wild cherry blossoms on the air? That never knows the sudden luxury of summer—the unfolding of all that promise, the long, languid days? And the bittersweet blaze of autumn glory, a celebration of death at its most beautiful?

What happens to the human soul that never experiences the inwardness of winter, the chance to put down the hoe and retreat indoors by the fire, knitting sweaters and doing small repairs, the family coming together, singing songs in harmony by the fire to pass the long dark winter nights till spring's sweet mercy releases us from cold and dark, and the Earth wakes up before our adoring eyes?

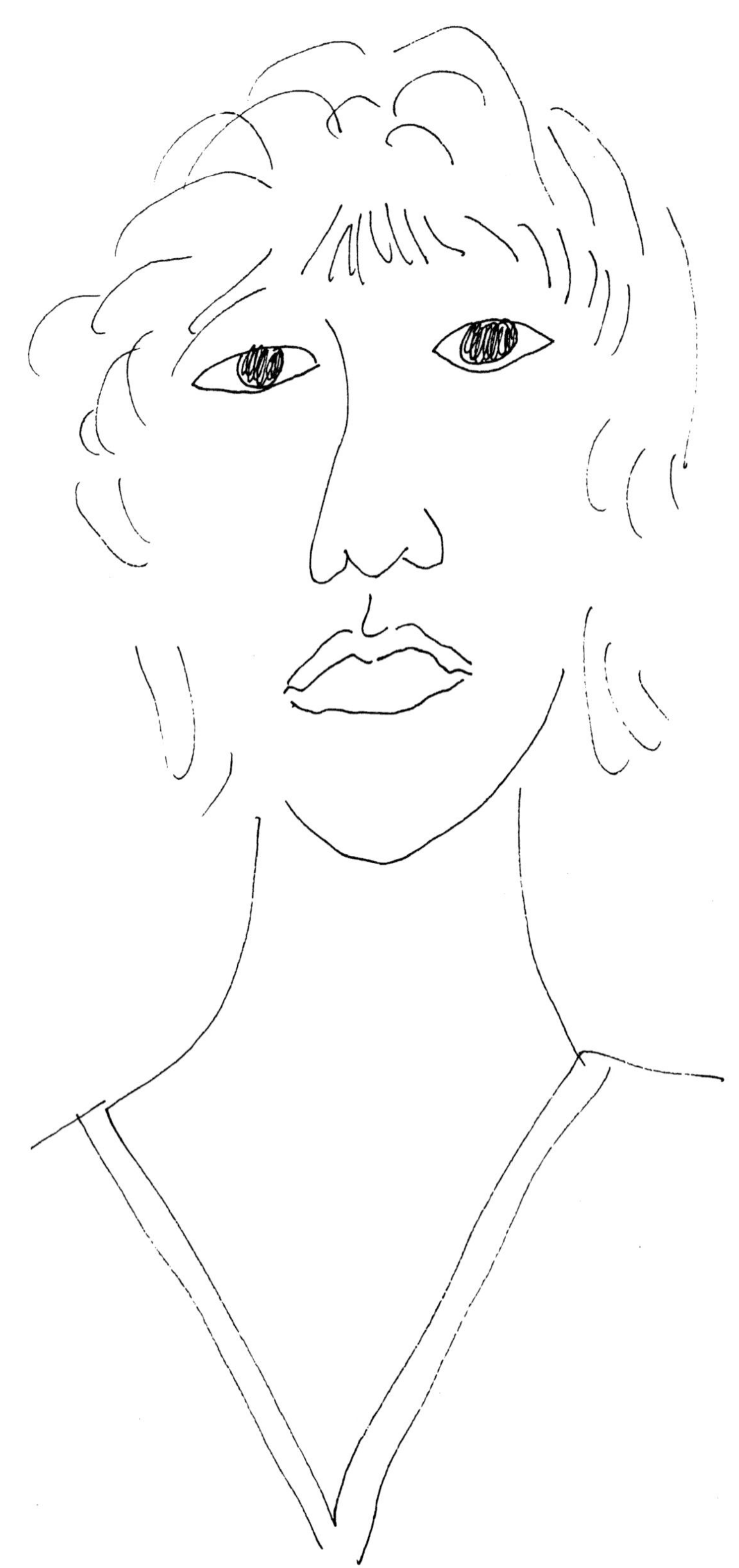

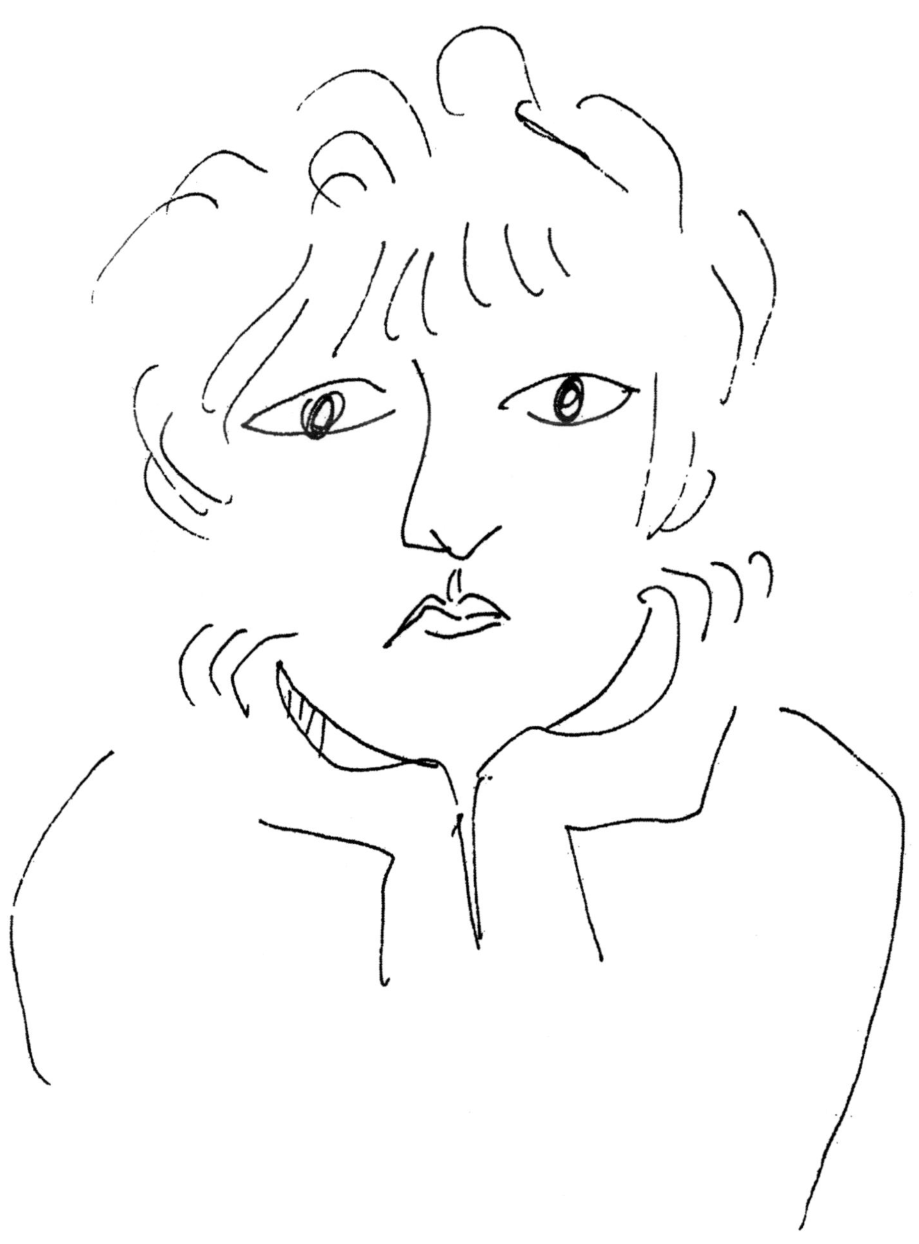

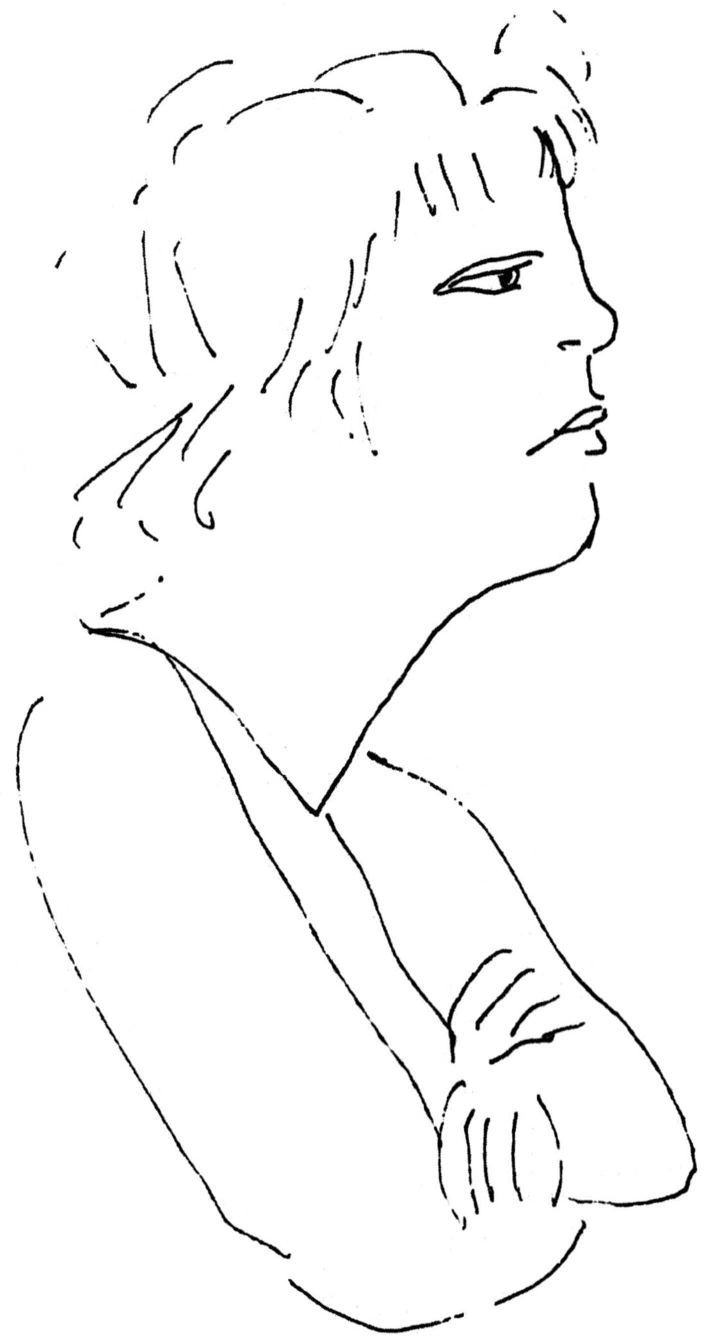

baba's eyes are the flame of the candle—representing the light, life, movement. Feeling close to Baba these days, even though I'm leaving his house. He hasn't been around for a long time now—several years—no dreams of him, no practices, no ashram, no satsang. Everyone so angry at him—why?—for dying and leaving them? For not being a good boy? For not explaining who he really was? Who was he really? I've no idea—I just know I can't get rid of him. He is the form or he is the events that happen or he is my house or he is the cause of everything—whatever happens, he's always there in some form or no form.

The truth is, I haven't been as happy since he died. I thought and feared it would be that way, and it is. Seems stupid—I should be happier, no? Free, enlightened, all the rest. Everything I didn't mind giving up to be near him now hangs heavily on me—I don't have them and he's nowhere—everywhere and nowhere. Does he have some intention for this house, or is everyone right—do things happen meaninglessly, and the only thing that matters is to make yourself more comfortable and avoid getting hurt? Can't avoid it though—hurt is around every corner. An Irish terrorist kills an English policeman and we think, "How terrible," and then that night God shakes up the Earth a little bit and 900 men, women, and children die in an earthquake in Tibet.

What did they ever do to you, God? Indeed, I am sick of it—disillusioned, discouraged, tired, tired of trying to make it better, tired of trying to think it's okay. The Buddhists say that is the beginning of wisdom, but I say it's spinach and I say the hell with it.

I am always requiring proofs of God—do this and I'll know it's okay, I'll know you're taking care of me, I'll know you exist. It's because I believe it's not okay, no one is taking care of me, and like the Buddhists, I have no conviction that God exists. If there's a God, I can't imagine what it is. If there's a Cause, why isn't there a Point to the unfolding of it?

We are in the soup here, slices of carrot bubbling around in a hot pot trying to make sense of the turmoil and agitation around us.

I need some rest.

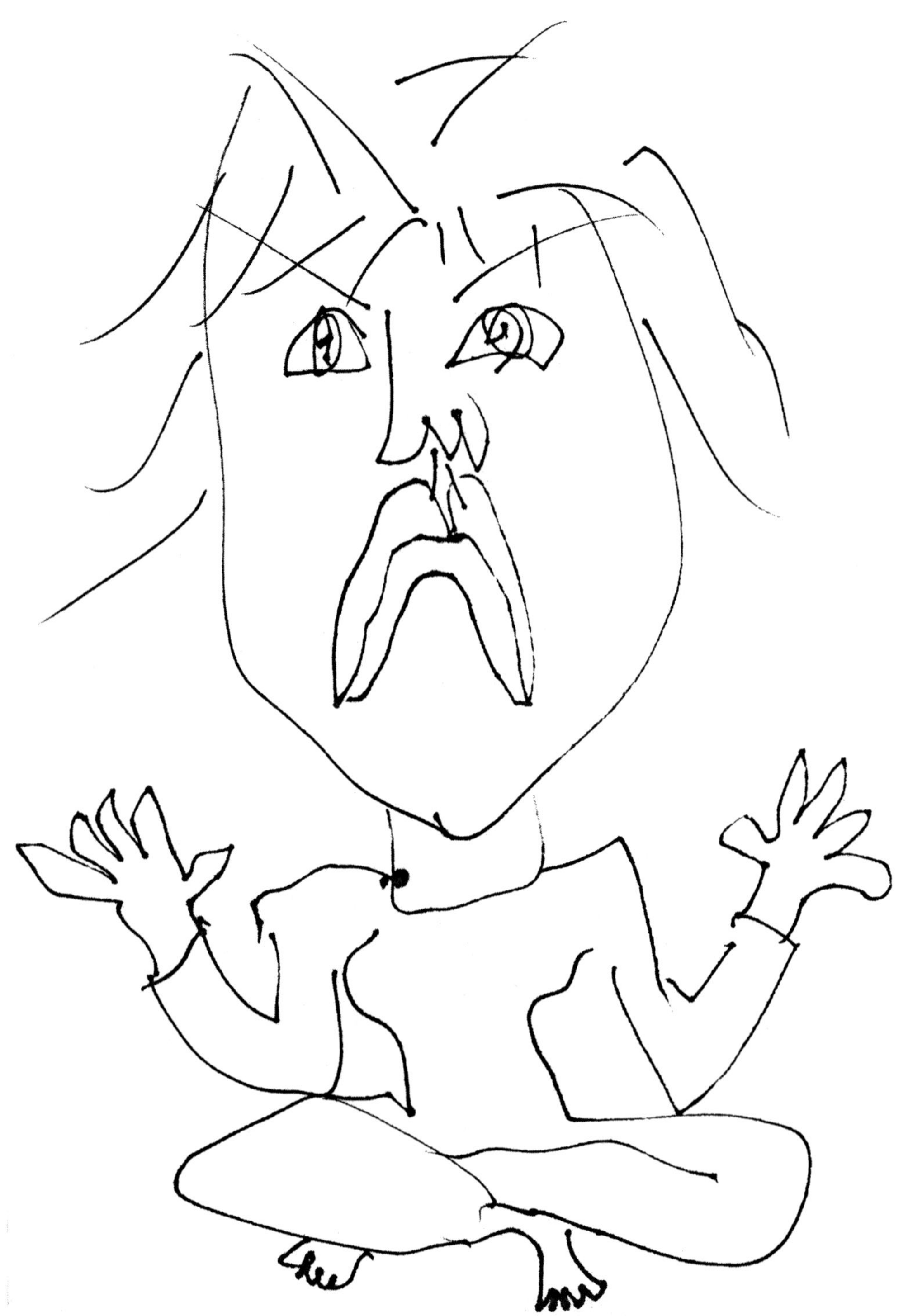

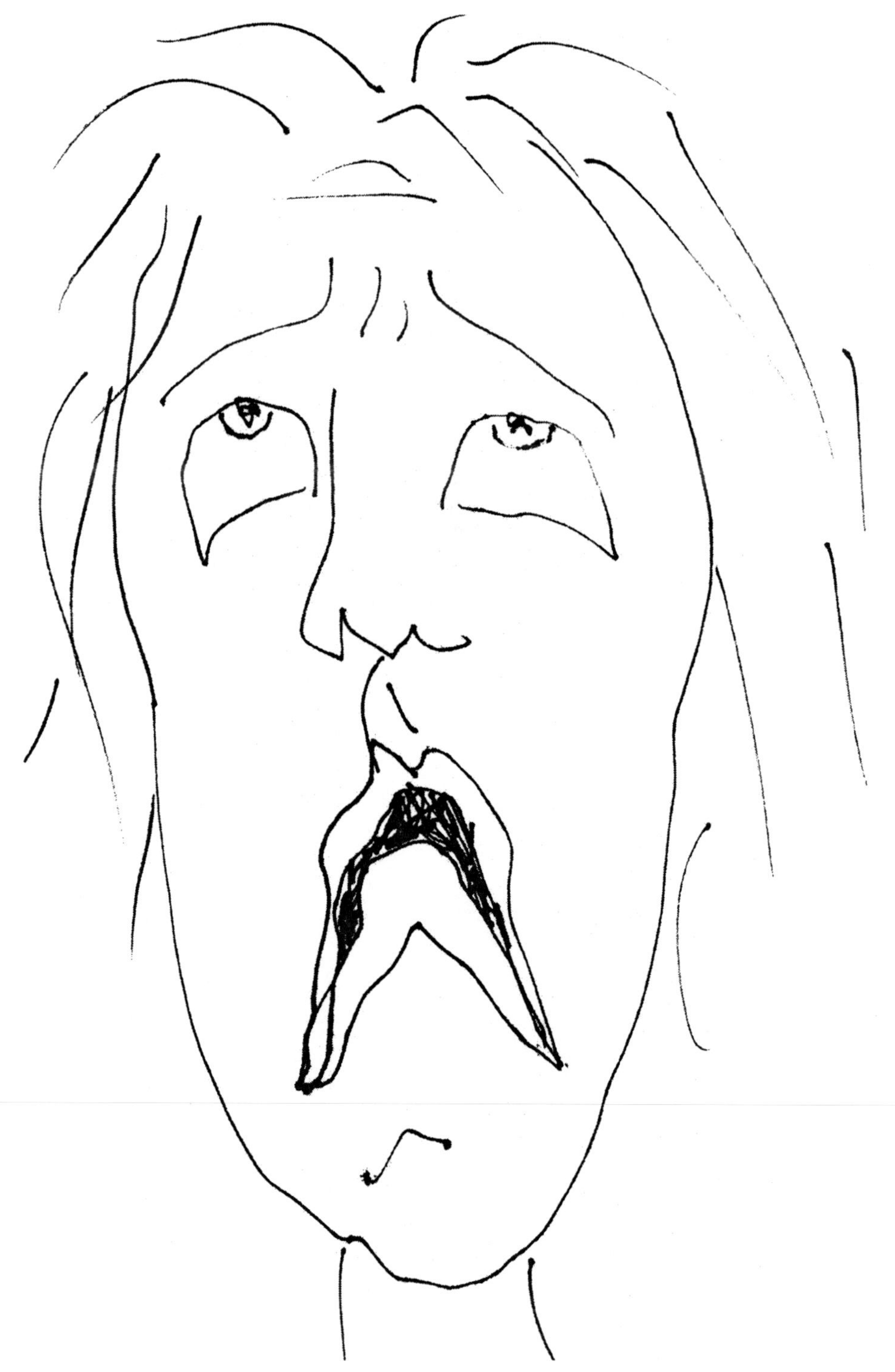

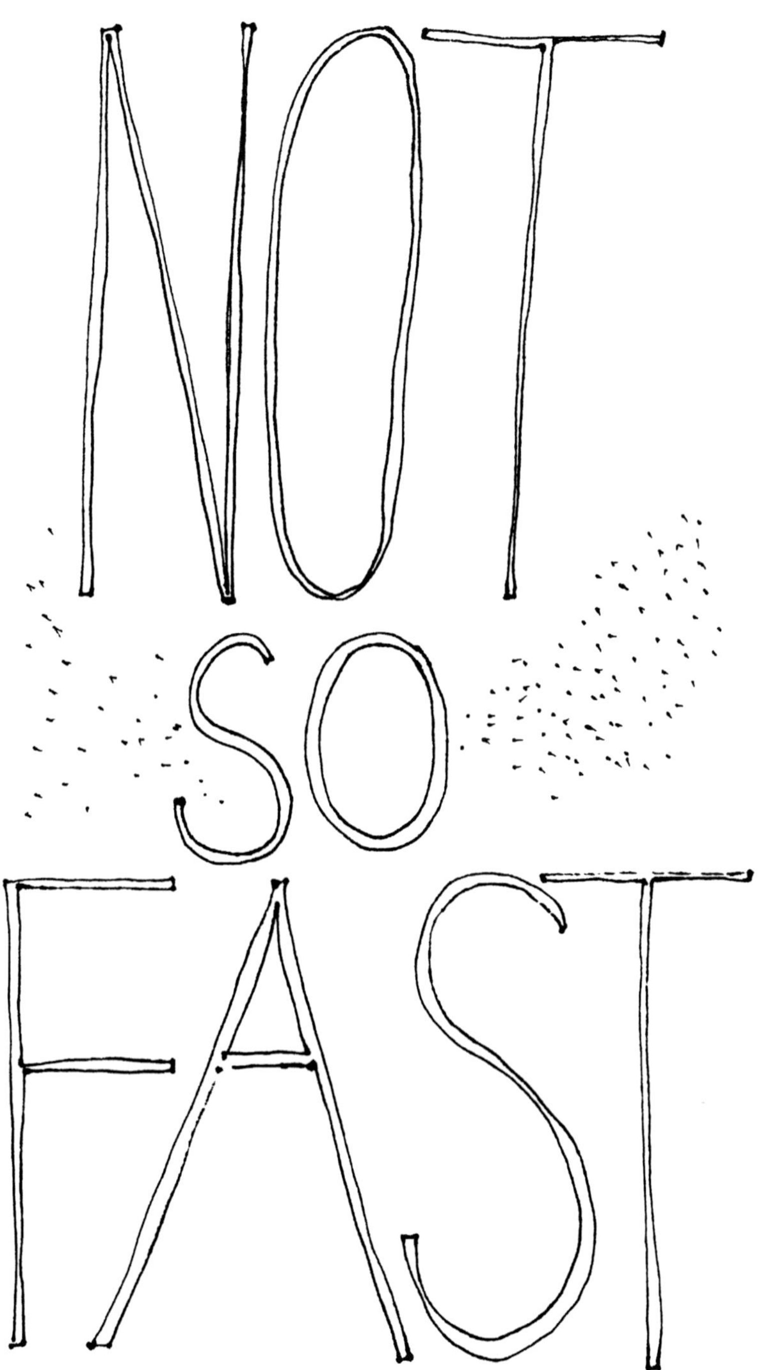

NOT
SO
FAST

Write right. Right-hand write. White write. White while I write. Wait while I write. Write that down. Listen for it, then write it down. Somewhere behind the words, bells playing. Deep gong bells and their vibrations, filling in the spaces behind the words. The words are the flowers in the tapestry, the bells are the canvas. The warp and woof of the world. Is it all made of sound then? So they say.

A little brown-robed, white-haired person appeared behind my eyelids, and he wouldn't go away. I'd never seen him before, but he made himself at home, turning and taking different postures in my inner vision as though he were out there in outer three-dimensional space and I was looking at him with open eyes. He had a funny hat with wide flaps like a brown wool version of a little Dutch girl's cap. His brown wool robe came down to his ankles. Did he have a long mustache and a little gray beard? Maybe.

I thought he was just a somebody, a nobody, but after he stayed for a while I realized he's a wise teacher. Come to teach me something? I bowed to his lotus feet. Okay, I'm ready—teach me. Where am I going? Why am I going? Am I going? Or is there something else you've come to tell me?

Once upon a time—

Oh, please—no stories! Get to the point!

Your whole life rises on a stem like a drop of water shooting into the air after a pebble is dropped in the bowl. How will it fall? For a while it pauses in midair, all of it packed into a droplet of water, shimmering, transparent. If you look fast enough you can see your life in there—your house, your furniture, little things you like—feathers, stones off a beach, telephone insulators from France, gold-embroidered cloths from India. A painting in three-dimensional objects, a pleasing patchwork.

Something has sucked it all up into the air the way the funnel of a tornado sucks up trees, cars, cows—everything it touches. There hangs your life, standing stock still, done with its up momentum, not yet started on its down.

All the things, the things I've put together in bits and pieces from here and there, spread around the three dimensions of my outer space to make a place in which I can find my way around, so familiar, so *me*. A velvet couch, a grandfather clock, a Persian rug, a brass kerosene lamp, two glass angels, a feather duster, a basket of knitting yarns, an inlaid table, a Chinese wind chime, a beeswax candle. If I empty them all out of my space, will I find my way around? Is the whole point of this exercise to get rid of my beloved objects?

This *kriya*, this *spanda*, this *lila*—there are no words in English for this process—the thought of leaving this home we created and going somewhere else, we know not where. Or why. Or when. Or how. Or even if we'll really do it, because when it comes right down to it we can always back out. Or so we tell each other, squirming together in our restless, impatient anxiety.

Old man, if you think I've learned anything from you, you're wrong. Please teach me louder—but no violence, it hasn't come to that yet.

The old man is still there. At least I've made him smile.

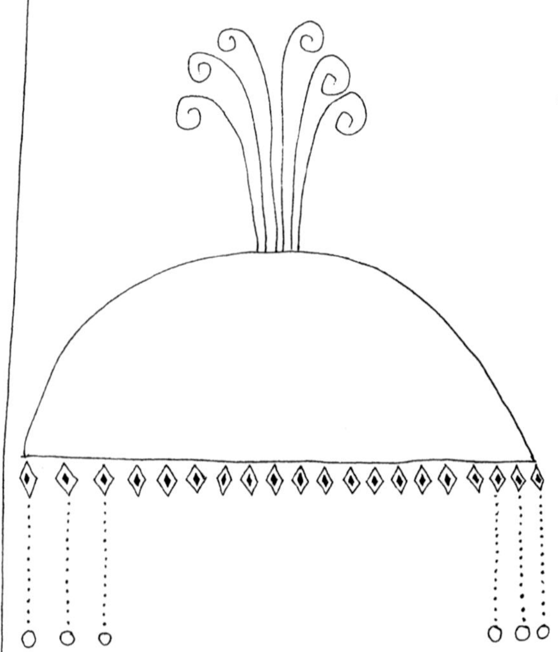

When I bought the land it was just a little hill, partially cleared, mostly woods and scrubby hardhack, as the locals call it. I have no idea why I bought it. I've only discovered over the years what makes it so idyllic. On a crest of the south-facing hills, near the top where it levels off, we carved out a space for a house and dug a hole, into which we poured the house that had taken shape between the architect and me as we worked over his blue-lined drawings.

The well was dowsed and dug and came in cool and pure and abundant. The house, solar, sat on its hill and gazed at the sun, while I fretted over the downhill slope it occupied, feeling always as though the house were sliding down its hill. Then one day it hit me that we could build a wall in front and terrace it to make a flat apron in front of the house. That was our first summer's project, and it made all the difference.

Next we put in a tiny, timid garden, now grown to good size and teeming with worms and the wildflowers I can't bear to pull out of the soft, loamy earth. Apple trees came next, and a plum, a peach, and two magnolias. Then we cleared away the hardhack to make a vast sweeping expanse rolling down the hill in front of the house.

Meanwhile a second solar house had sprung up, and later a red barn. Now the trees that had always been there began to take shape in the space left when the scrubby bushes went.

Perfection called for a pond, so we put one in, and though it gave us three years of grief, it ended up a sparkling jewel in the hollow at the base of the rolling green hill below the two houses. As soon as the pond filled the whole place burst into bloom like a symphony, one flowering bulb, bush, or tree after another. All the little hopeful twiggy plants we'd put in over ten years suddenly burst forth into manifestation. And the birds came as though we'd put ads in all the latest bird magazines—a family of bluebirds, Baltimore orioles, swallows by the dozens, hummingbirds, goldfinches, flickers, chickadees, a blue heron down by the stream—an incredible display of bird life every day.

All this is coming to fruition at the moment of our departure. Somehow we are done here. We feel it without understanding it any better than I understand why I bought this land in the first place. The apples, the first real crop we've had—the plum tree laden with plums for the first time—the tiny peaches taking form on the baby peach tree—all will be eaten by someone else, who will perhaps think of me.

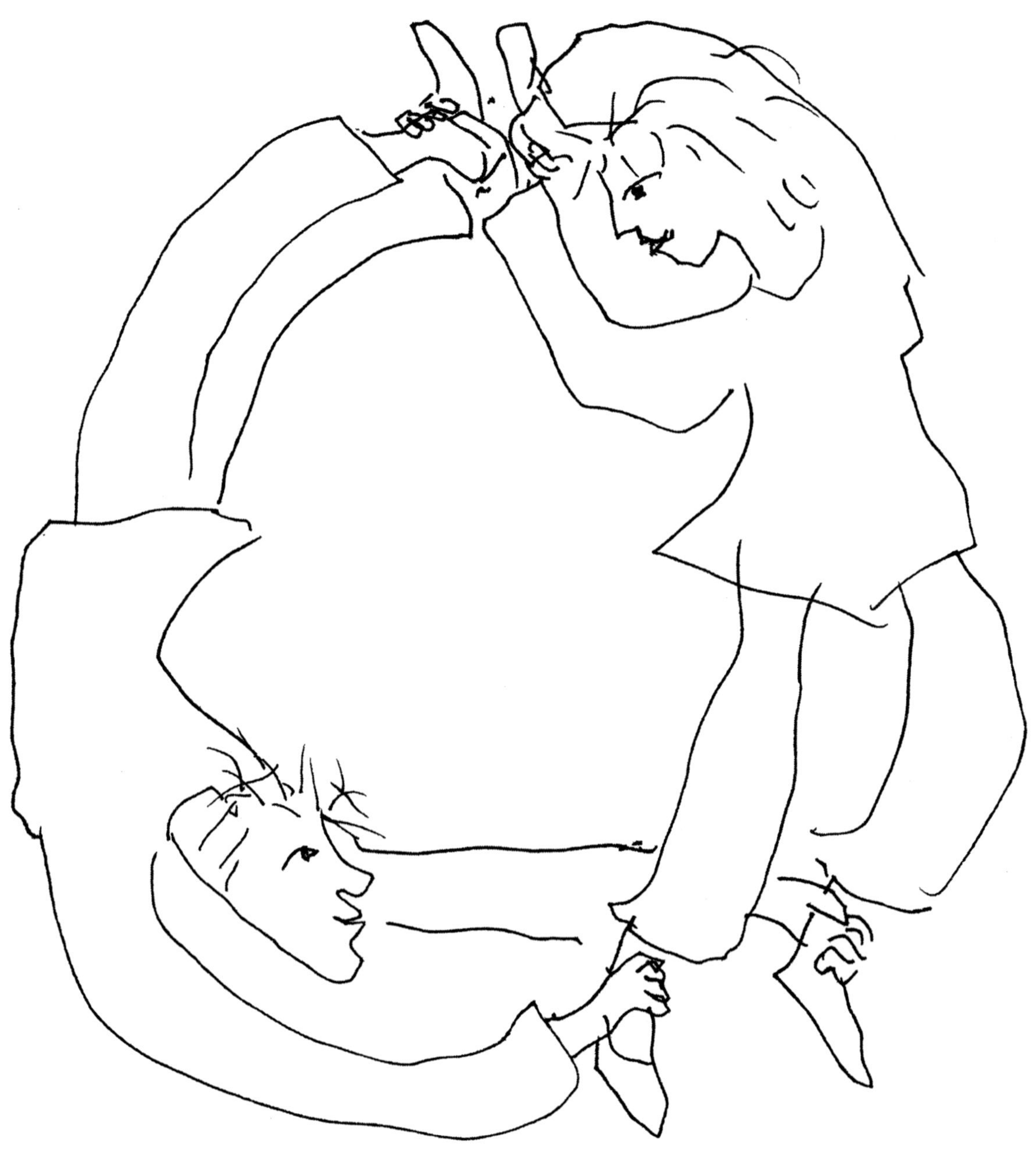

April is almost over and I am going, but I don't know where, don't know when. Who will buy my house, made like a second skin, the wall around my subtle body with one enormous glass eye that gazes out and down the hill like some prehistoric monolith, watching the world build up and crumble, build up and crumble while it sits, impassive witness to the pain and joy of it.

Who else could fit here, with no one but the sky and the deer for neighbors? Will the animals choose? Will the trees call to someone, "Come, it's time, we're waiting for you." Will someone walk through the wide front door and recognize this place out of some dark corner of an unremembered dream that never rose to the light of consciousness? Will someone know this place as his, hers, theirs?

The worms in the garden, the family of bluebirds, the fox that cries in the night like a banshee, raising old memories of terror along the spine? The blue heron at the pond, the porcupine who sleeps in the tree outside my window, the flock of wild turkeys, the deer deer deer—are they all moving on, out of my mind and into the possession of someone else?

And what about my memories, do they stay with the house? Is someone else about to walk into my skin, to occupy the last ten years of my life like a suit that belonged to someone else, but fits? Just so does a queen pass her power on to her successor, handing the scepter and the crown to waiting hands and sighing as the burden slips away, along with everything she once thought of as herself. Just so does the queen slip through a small door and out of the palace, pulling a dark cloak around her and merging into the shadows beneath the lighted windows.

Where is she going? She knows not where, only knows she is being called by some voice she cannot hear, that pulls her as a magnet pulls the iron filings. As she glides forward in the shadows the palace falls away behind her like the skin of a snake. Inside the palace someone slips easily into the crown and thinks no more of the absent queen.

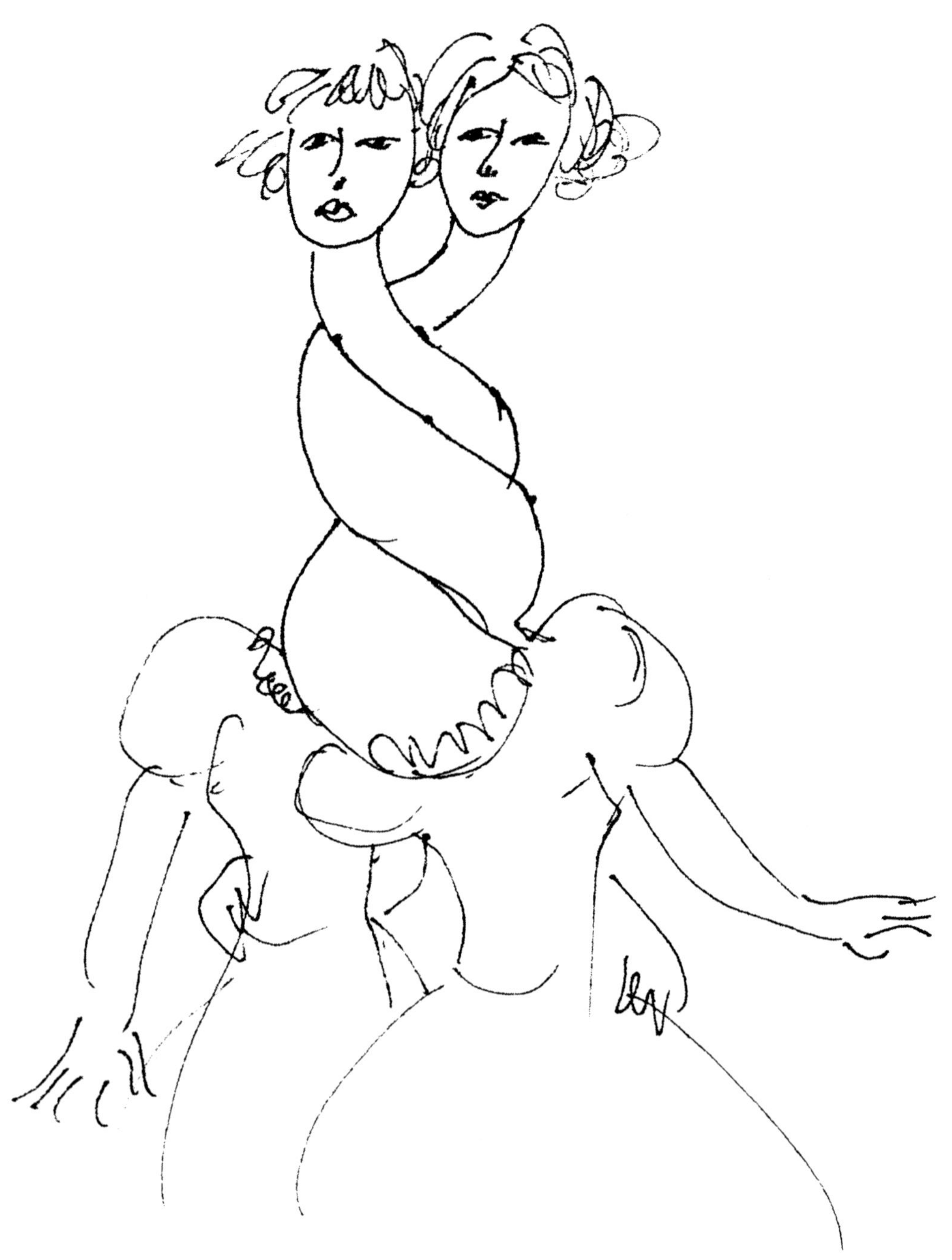

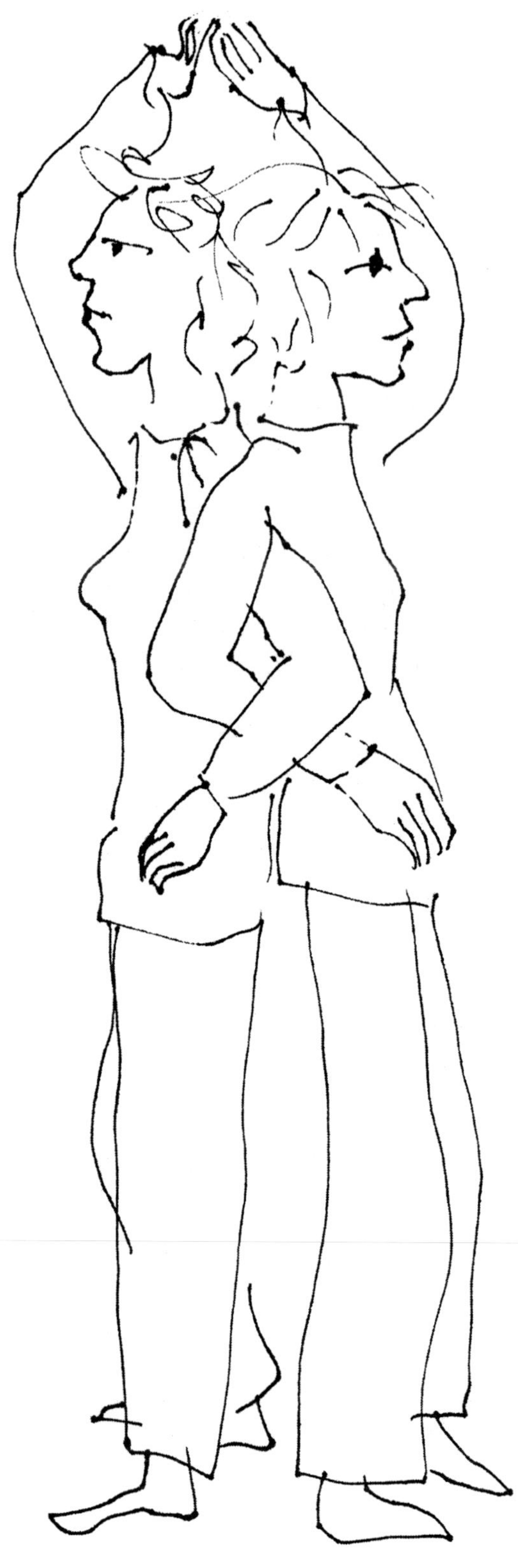

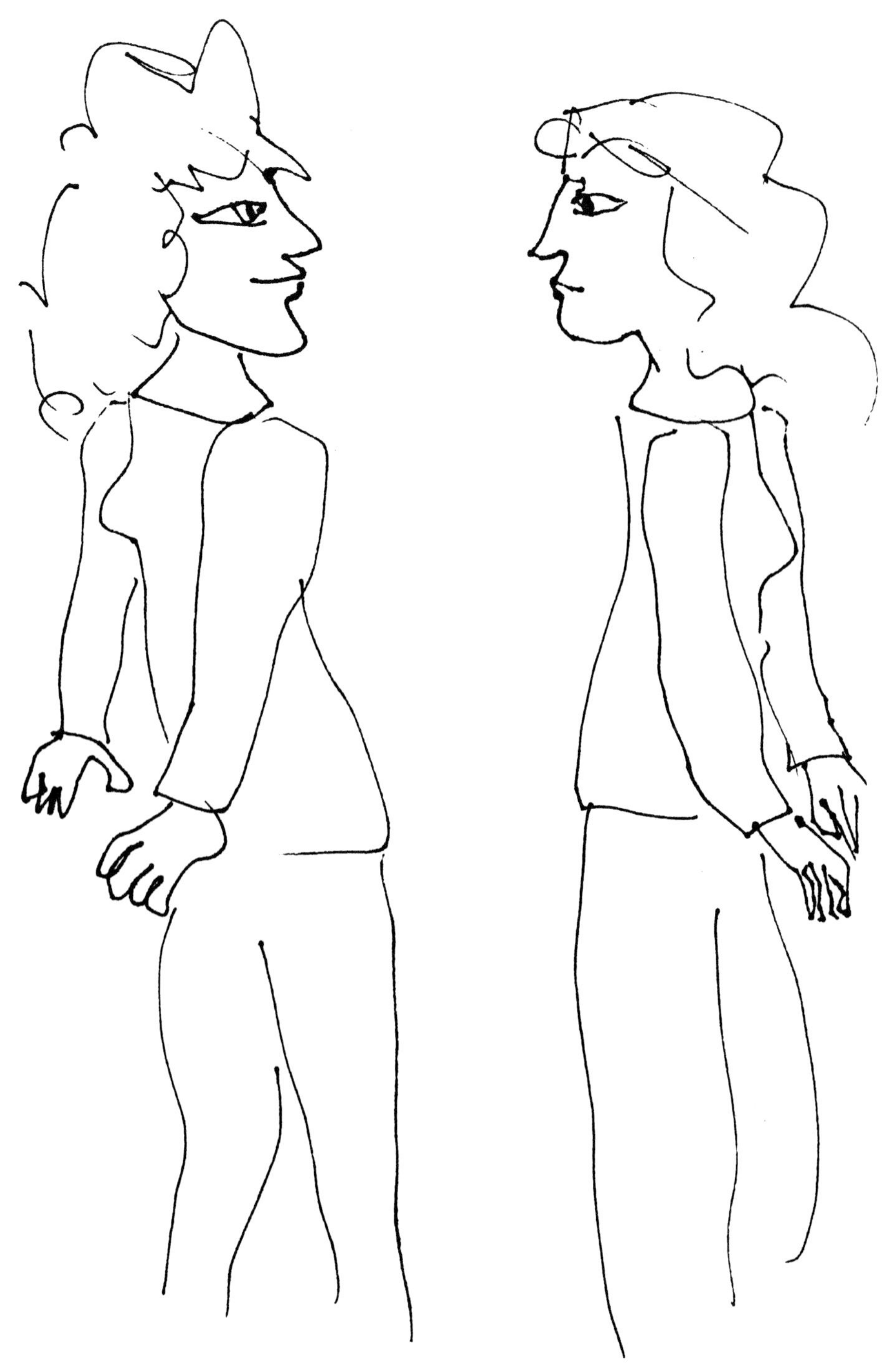

Unhooking my life link by link, like a string of barges
untethered one by one, floating free and away. Going, going as I myself am going. First
the house, the garden, the land, the future of the trees. Then the furniture, the clothes,
the habits, then the thoughts of the future. We have no future here. Then the past—I let
go to create a new now. Now the now I know gets unhooked and floats away. What will
be left of me? Off I go into the misty void, holding my breath, shutting my eyes, clenching
my fists in terror and awe. Let it all go, the building and the planning and the hopes and
dreams, trade it in for a large handful of nothing.

Now the air rushes past my ears and I am falling, floating, like Alice down the
rabbit hole maybe. For with my eyes tight closed I have no idea where I am or where
I am going. Do I miss the past? You bet I do. I miss the past I wish the past had been.
Do I fear the future? I stare into its ferocious jaws, which open right in front of me, its
pointed teeth gleaming, its long red tongue hanging down as it growls a low growl and
prepares to devour me. Black-faced Kali, wearing a necklace of human skulls, is about
to have me for breakfast. She crunches my life between her teeth like a crust of bread
and licks her lips like a lioness. Fainting with fear, I offer myself—food for the Goddess.

Going willingly.

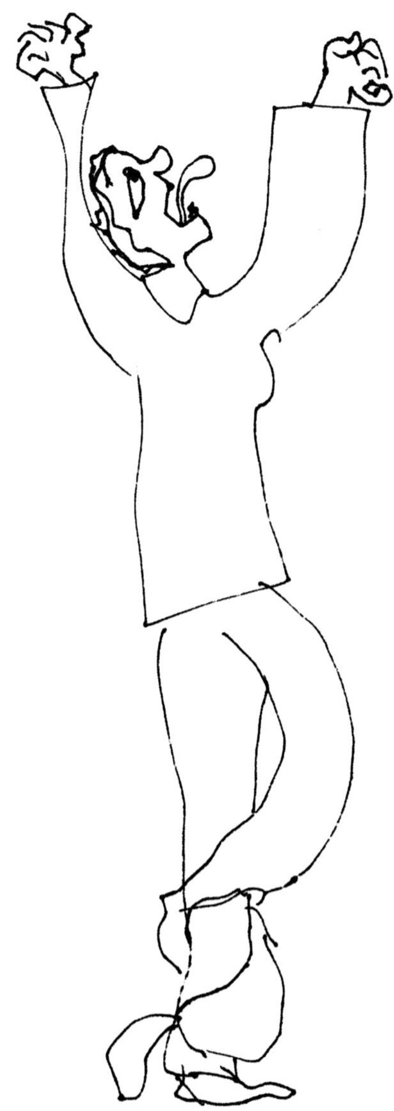

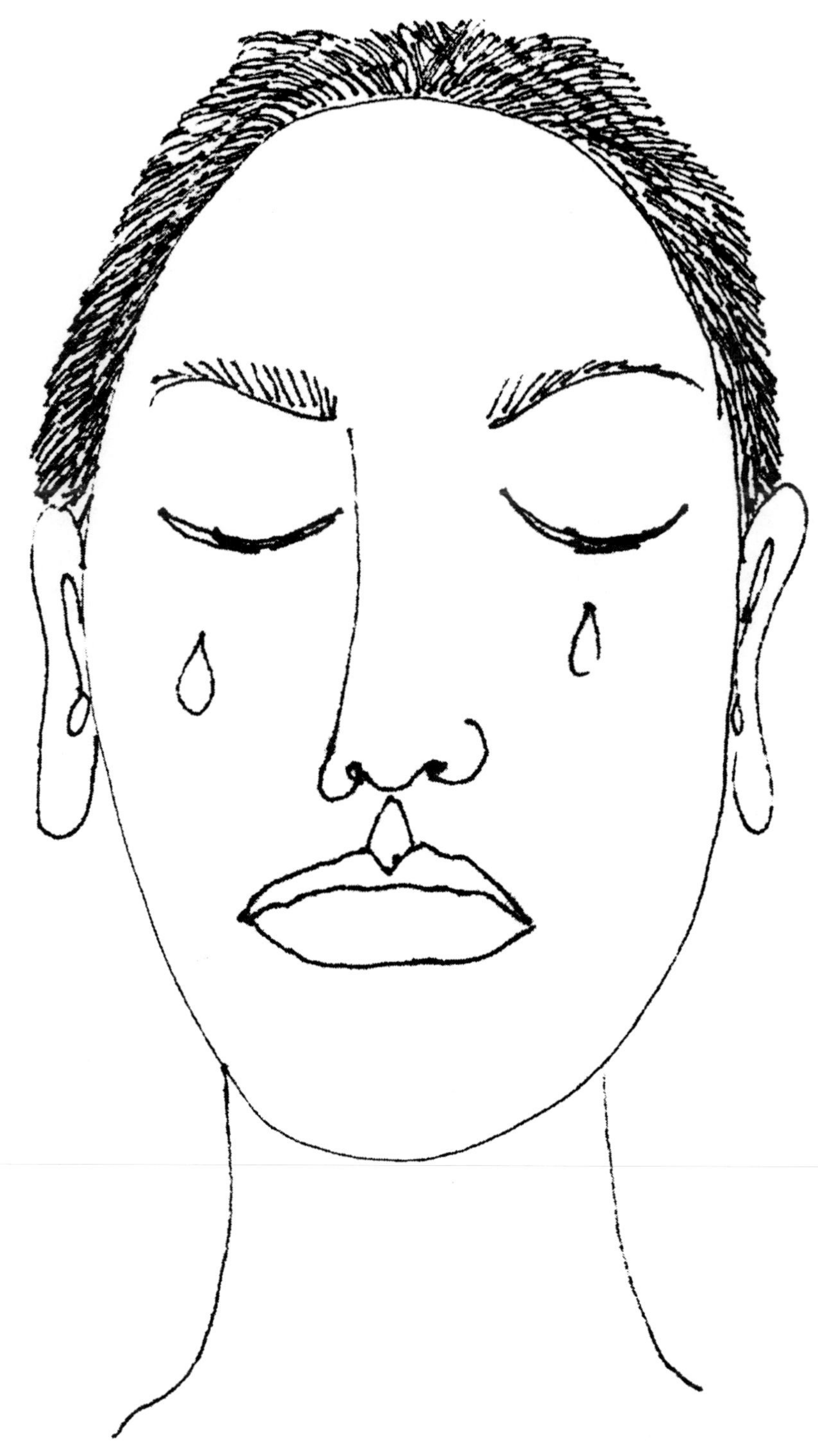

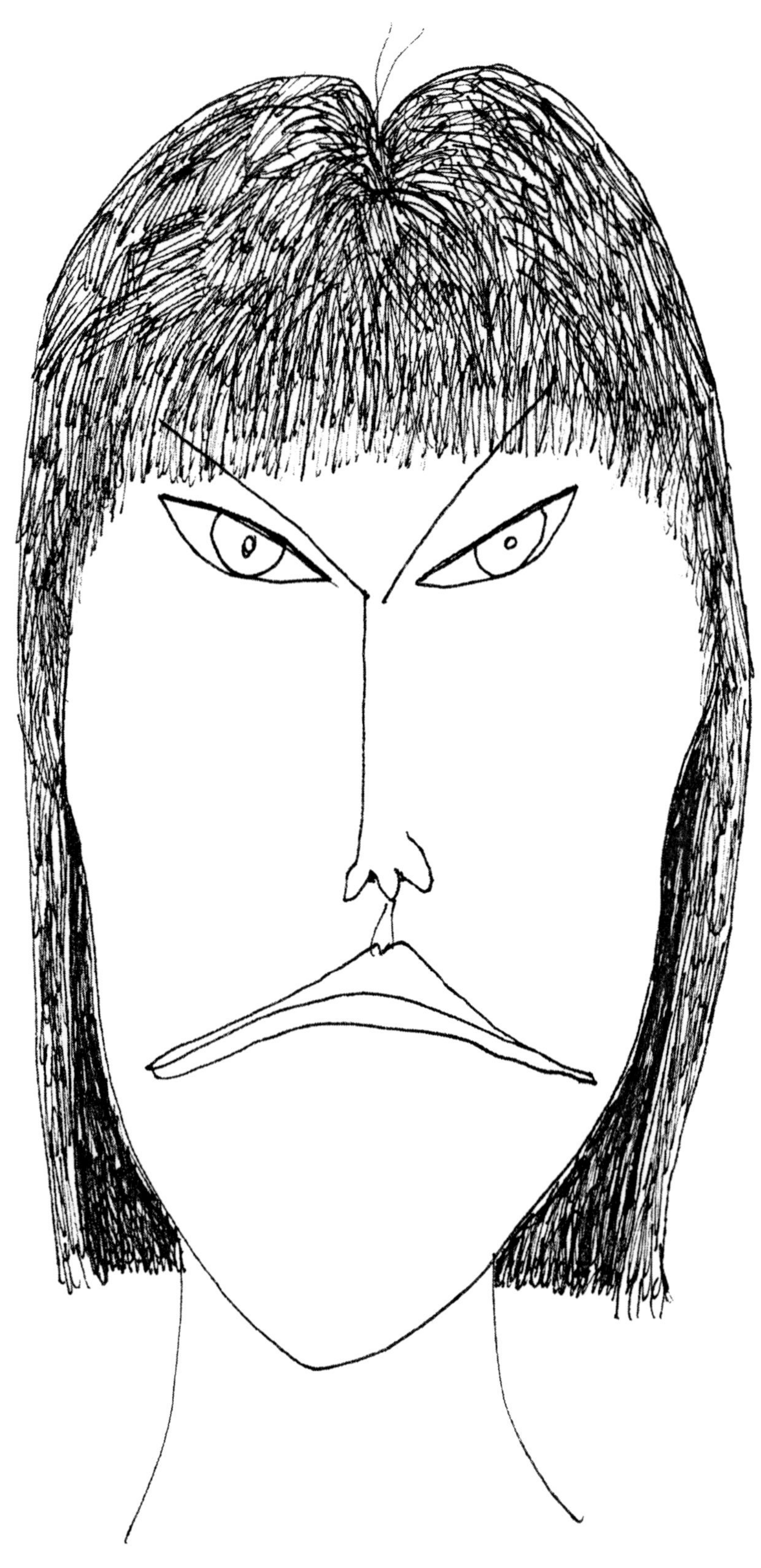

Who would have thought it could be so painful, trying to leave here? I once said Baba had nailed me here with the meditation room, and now it feels like it's true. Every time I tug away it tugs me back. As soon as I let go of it for good, the daffodils burst into bloom, then the tulips, the plum trees, the apple trees—every last one of them, for the first time ever!—and the peach tree, and now the lilacs, filling the air with their perfume while the peonies wait in the wings, and the quince, the beautybush fading now but the weigela budding up, getting its trumpets ready to start calling hummingbirds. Where will I find a place like this?

I don't want a place like this! I want a place with more people, more room in the house, less land, flatter, places to walk, things to do, people like us around to play with.

Time rolls round on an endless wheel here, and nothing ever happens. That's what I like about it, too—but it's time to move out of that, though I don't know why, don't know where. Don't know how to find it, since I don't know what I'm looking for. Don't know what I'm looking for that I don't have here. Every place has its dissatisfactions. How do you know till you live there if it's better or worse than where you came from?

Always before, I've gone to be with someone—Dan, Jim, Jacques, Baba. No one to be with now. A giant koan that calls into question all meaning, including the meaning of koans—a black hole, pulling my life into it piece by piece till it disappears, swallowed up, crushed into oblivion by the weight of the mass of nothingness spinning at the center. Nowhere to go, but I can't stay here anymore.

The Guru fails to speak, I fail to listen, God goes off into the black hole and time spins around the edge of the whirlpool, slipping toward the center as I watch, appalled and frightened.

Silence. Heaven speaks not.

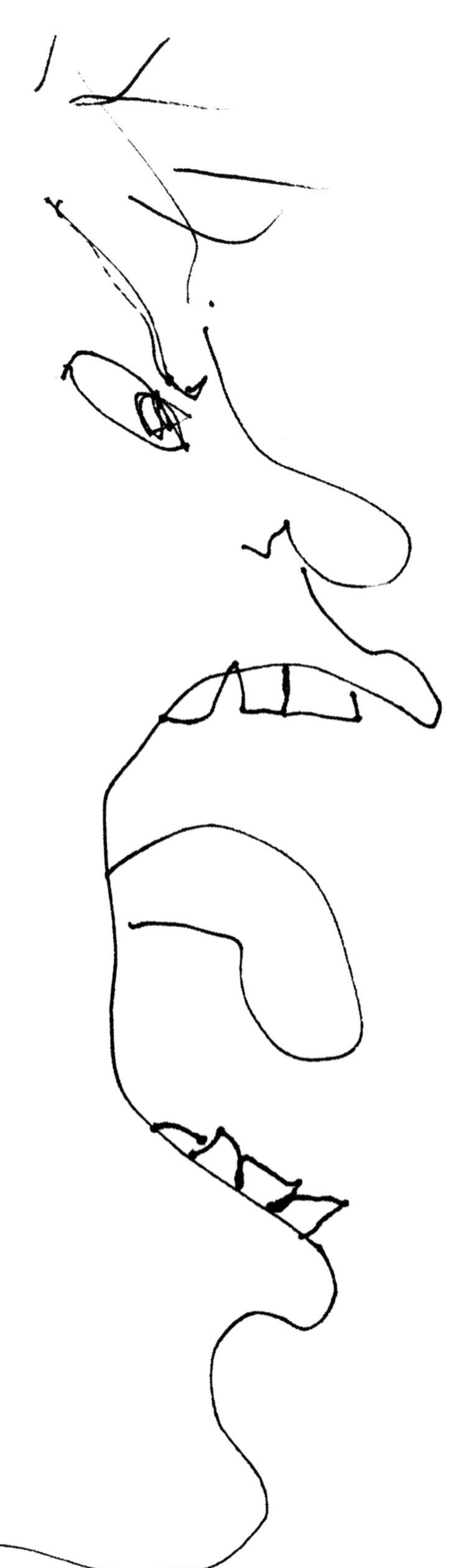

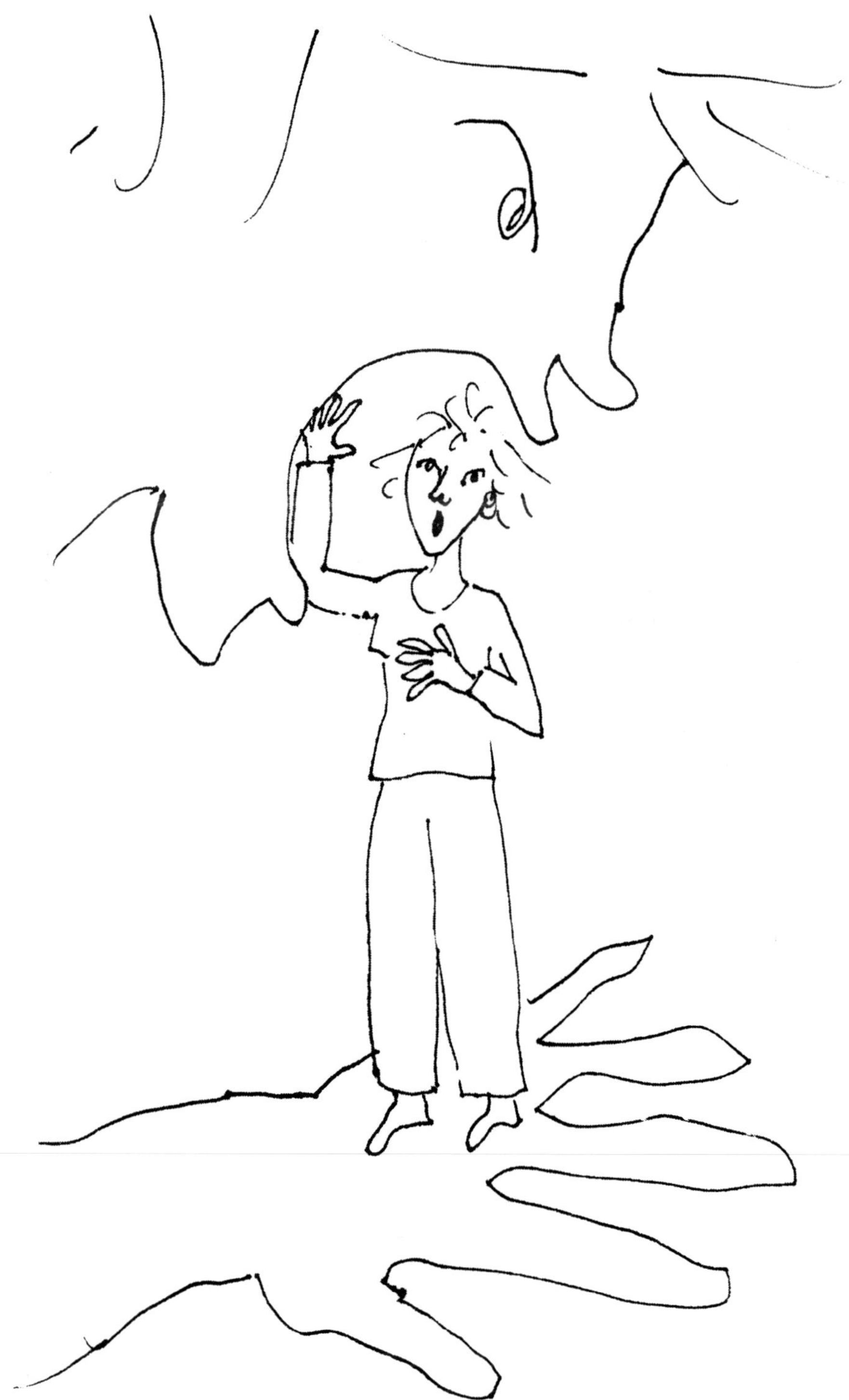

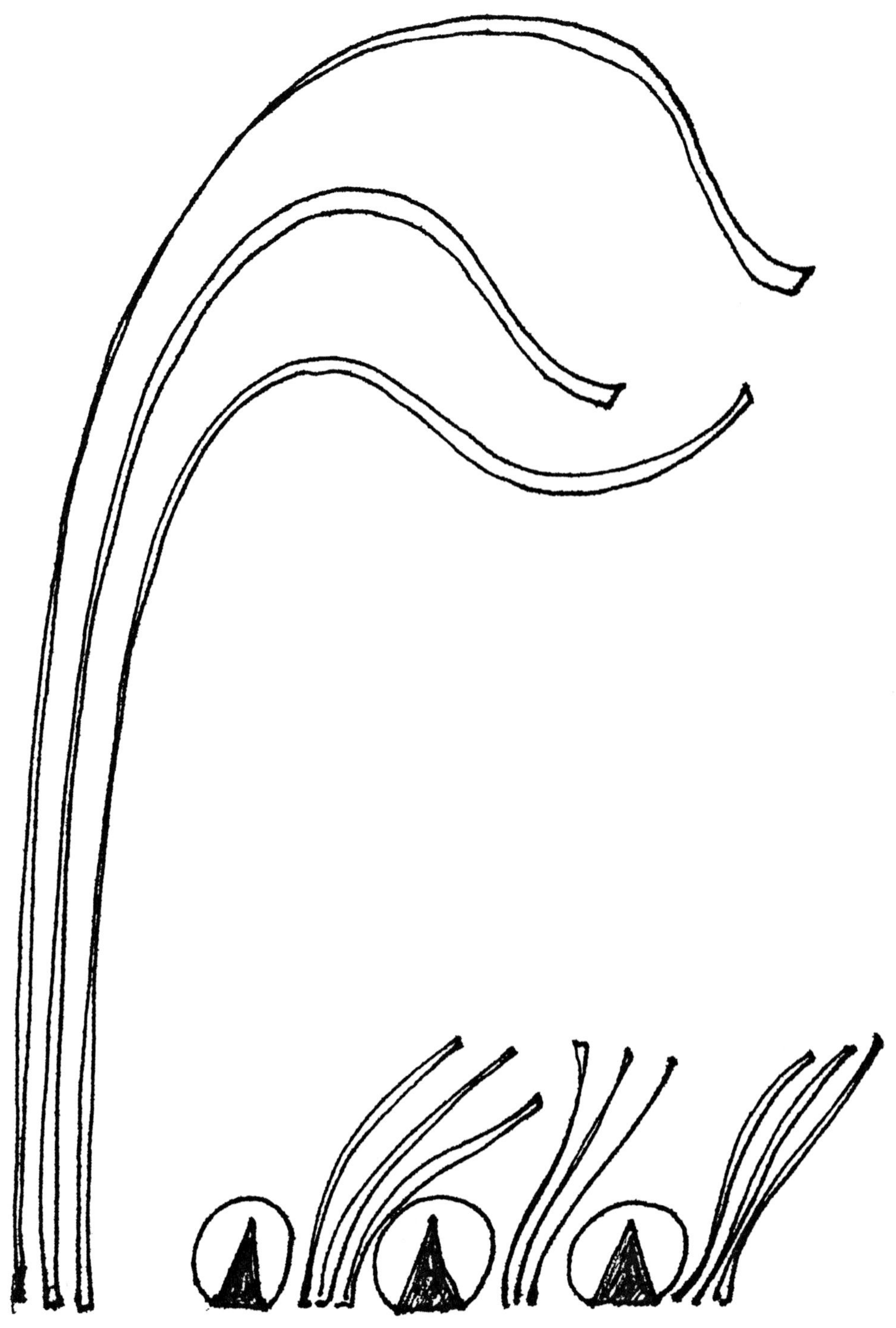

Order disorder the crystalline emerging into space of a thought form grown solid, six-sided clarity of thought and matter, columns tumbling over each other as they grow helter-skelter in preordained patterns, the patterns of the universe writ small in our lives, who decided this? Who decided this move, who is sending me off the edge of my flat earth into unknown, midnight-blue tomorrow?

My toes cling to the edge, I'm not going, though I know I'm ready, know it beyond any doubt, but still, I'm not going unless you give me a REASON! And who are you, out there, to whom I can address my request? Who pushing me from behind, whispering, "Jump! Jump!" I'm not jumping, not yet, anyway. I want to look around first, in case I want to remember this place, in case I ever want to come back from my free-falling, bottomless plunge into infinite inky void. In case I change my mind.

Want to tug off me the ropes clinging to my arms, my ankles, the strings that tie my heart to this place I never wanted but loved anyway. Can't even remember the love, now—so caught up in the jumping. Ready—set—no, I'm not jumping yet—first tell me WHY! I built and built here, planted, planned, dug, prepared, envisioned—I thought I had forever to work on it—or at least, *time*. No more time now, the doing is over, nothing left but the going. And the giving. Someone else will do it now—what will they do? Will someone else love it, want it? Is it my own folly now, ownerless and unwanted?

I'm not leaving you till there's someone else to love you! And then where will I go? Somewhere else to work the same folly, planting and planning? No resting place, just way stations on the way to nowhere, which is where I'm about to go anyway.

Leap into nowhere, end up somewhere. Happier? Healthier? Better off? Disappointed? Regretful? My mind is having a field day, useless appendage, worse than an appendix. The doctor took mine out without so much as a by-your-leave. Not my mind. Nobody took that out, it still rattles around inside my head like a dried-up walnut meat.

THE RESISTANCE

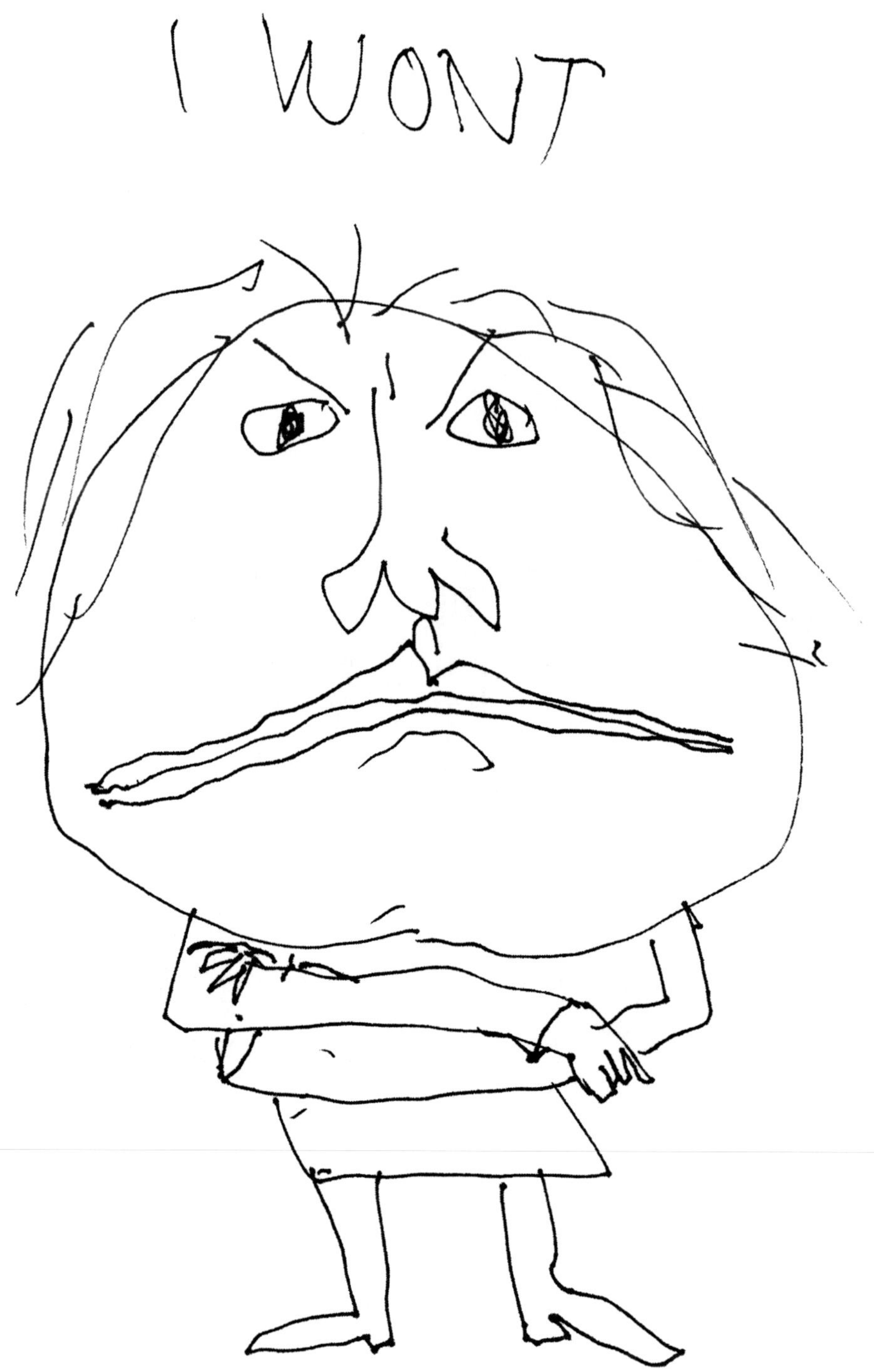

I WONT

AND YOU CAN'T EITHER

My mind doesn't seem at all interested in looking at itself now—usually it likes nothing better! So quiet, calm, and empty, no emotions, no focus. The wind has died down and the trees stand still outside the windows, barely a leaf moving. I miss the wind that ruffles their feathers and bows them this way and that in a gigantic minuet. Even the birds are quiet—everything is waiting.

The sun is ready to set, shouldering itself along the horizon, preparing to take a dive. I am satisfied to be still, incurious, unmoved, unmoving. Each day is different, each day is the same. There is only now in this place—for what do I need the past or the future? The past is gone, the future will come—the now stretches out and down the hill and up, as far as the eye can see.

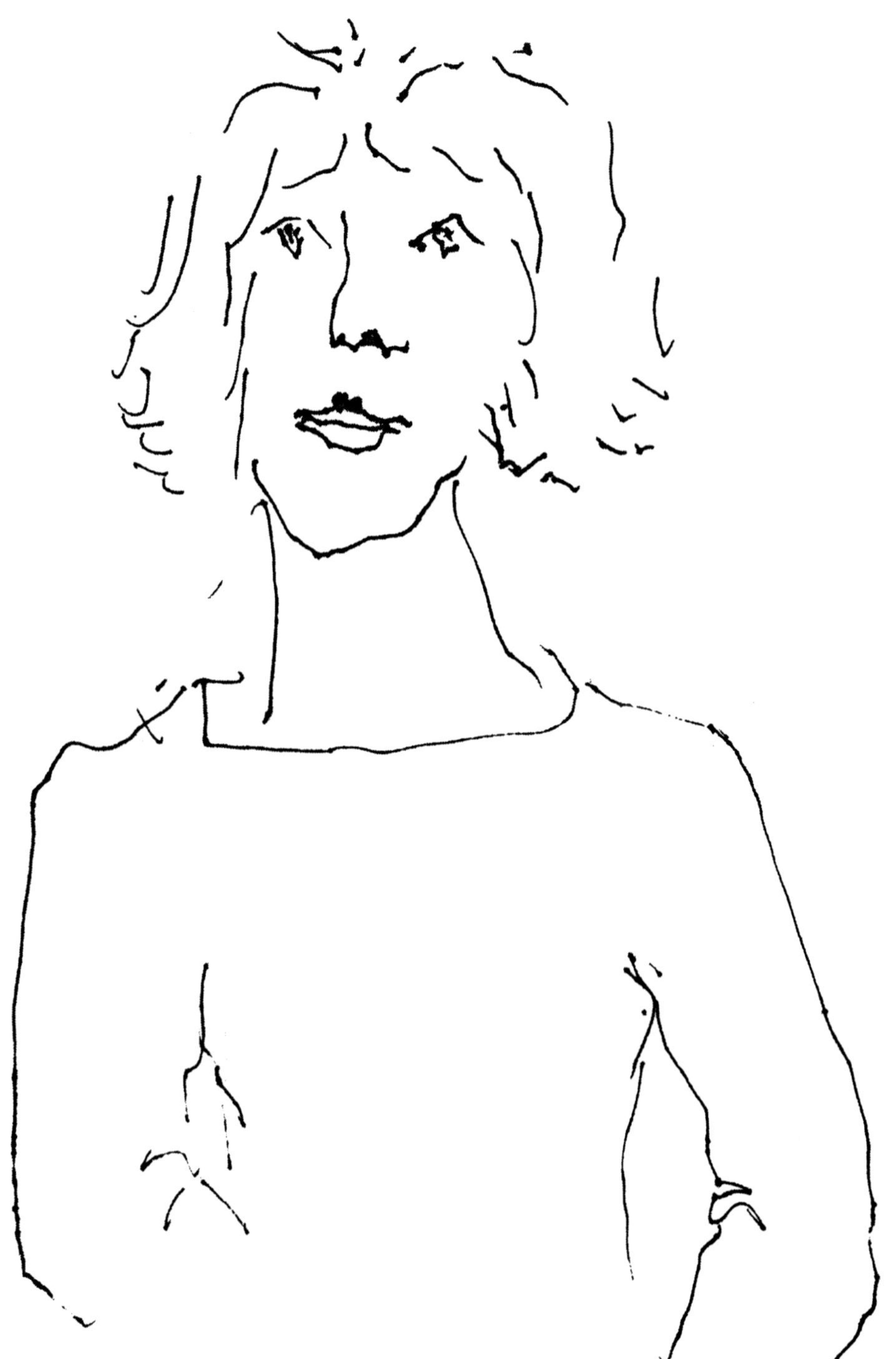

Sitting in my power-packed meditation room trying to figure out the source of this flow of despair washing through my words and over my head, drowning out the joy and bliss that used to bubble around me like the bubbles rising from the bottom of the champagne glass, tracing delicate spirals through the golden liquid in a never-ending stream. Gone, all gone—where did it go? As the bubbles in the champagne disappear when the champagne is drunk—an empty glass and a sigh are all that's left.

They left when Baba left, and all my efforts to recapture the joy are in vain—vain efforts, going nowhere. Everything turns to dust in my fingers, dries up, and blows away on the cool evening breeze. Is this the Grace? Is this where the Path takes me? The fruits of sadhana? The dried-up, shriveled fruits of spiritual seeking? My family blows away on the breeze, my house crumbles and follows, trails of dust spiraling out to the horizon. I watch as faith follows, and joy and bliss and friendship and even company. Everyone leaves, leaving me here in this dried-up desert wondering what happened, where did it all go?

No one comes, no one cares, the blueberries hang on the bushes and even the birds the bugs the bees the foxes the deer and I can't eat them all.

Nectar drips from the trees and turns to dust and blows away. The source must be tainted, like a poisoned spring, gushing forth bright, clear water whose taste brings death. The years slide away as I watch, and the nothingness sweeps forward like dunes in a desert, covering everything with the sands of meaninglessness, mounds of despair in the ruined, empty landscape.

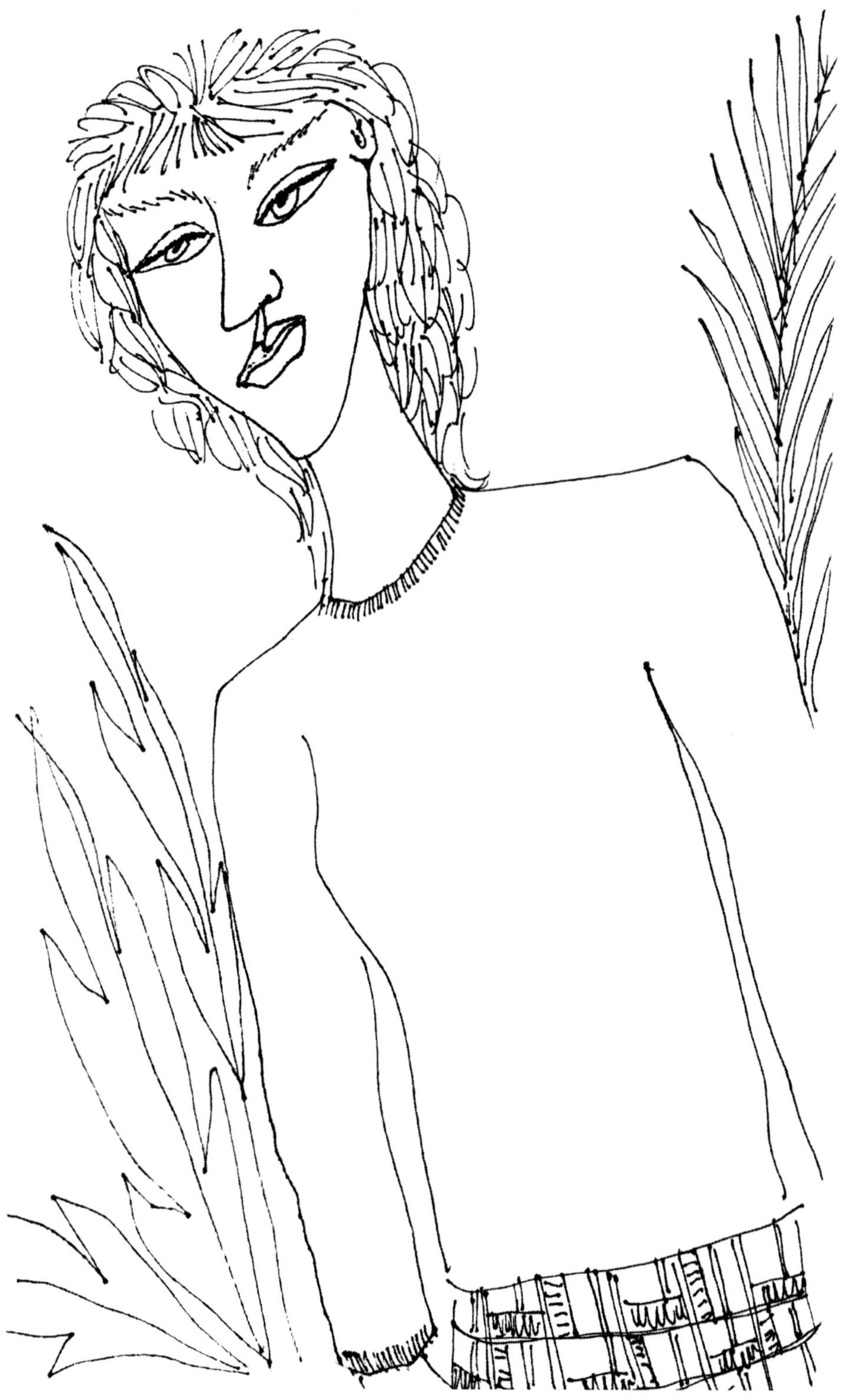

leaving this place I found and built myself, the places I invented, the place that became me, a second skin, a turtle's shell, my home. Starting from scratch, we dug a deep hole and poured in a house, taking shape magically from ideas first talked about, then written down, then bursting into three-dimensional form. Satisfying form, never boring. Warmed by the sun and lit by the sky, neighbored by wild animals, the house nestles into its hill and pulls a mantle of weather around it.

I thought it would never come to an end, yet suddenly, abruptly, it has. I am leaving this house for nothing, for I know not what. Terrified I won't find someone else to love it as it deserves to be loved. Terrified I'll go and then wish I'd stayed.

Life is a minefield of regrets, of wrong guesses and wrong decisions, of disappointments waiting to happen. Yet I cling to what I know, fearful of moving into the unknown, preferring the regrets and disappointments I'm already familiar with.

What could be worse than now? Only the past and the future. There is no salvation, only attachment. Attached to lethargy and inertia, to the now I know. Even the going is a now, but I don't see it that way. How I hate the pulling up roots, pulling apart closets, shoving things in boxes, folding up all the little habits that go with place, putting them on hold. I hate it, even as I know it is my salvation—shaking up the structure, shaking loose the encrusted patterns, discarding, discarding, discarding.

Life's moments crystallized in trivia—an ashtray from a French hotel, a matchbook from an ocean liner, a shell picked up from the beach, thousands of photographs stuffed in a box I never open. Memories, what are they good for? The older I get, the more I have. And things to match the memories, and memories floating around the things. Is all of life a rehearsal for dying? And what's so great about dying—it can't be any better than the life that produces it, can it? What is the profound mystery of dying? I'd like to know before I go there.

Now this house is dying, letting go of the life we filled it with, preparing itself for its reincarnation with some other occupant, new furniture, new things, new habits, new goings and comings.

The shortest day of the year. Things always look harder in winter.

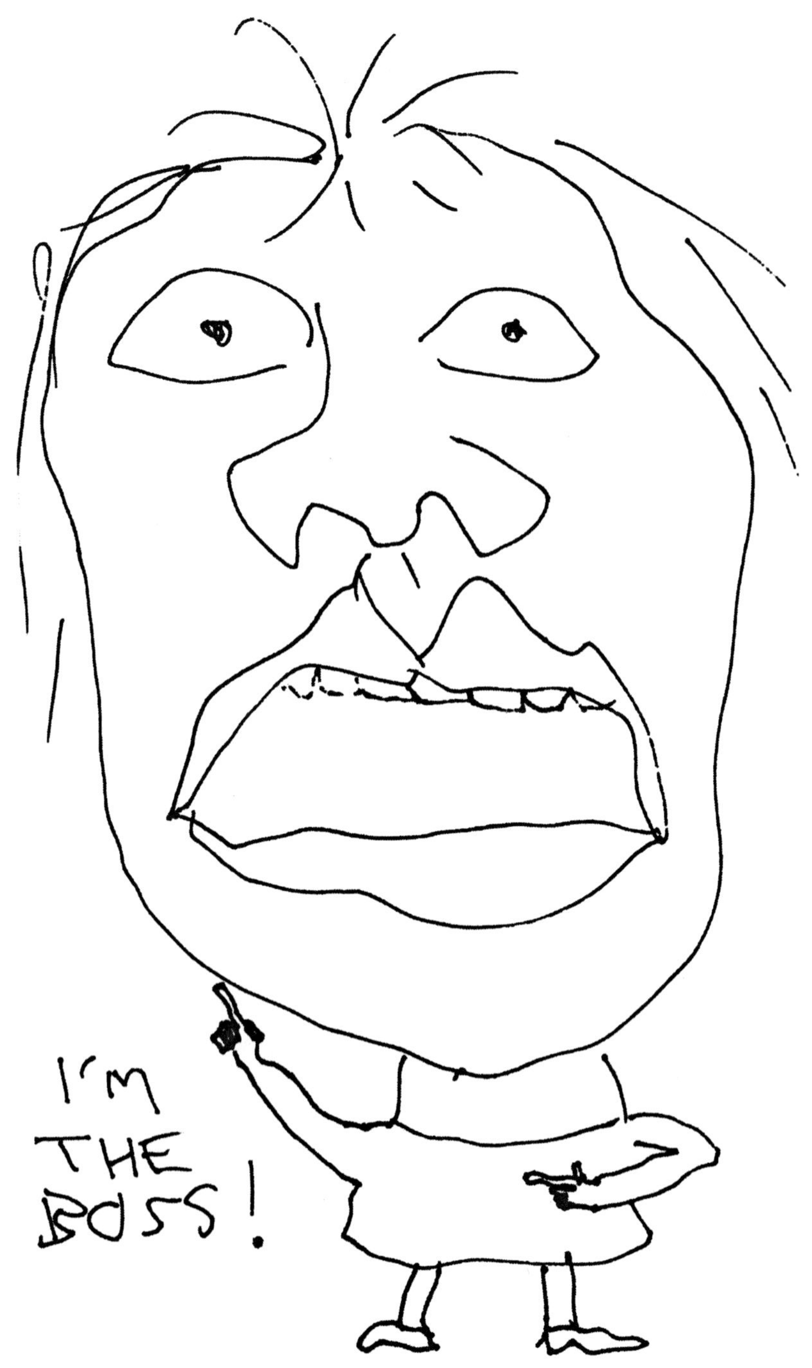

I'M
THE
BOSS!

End-of-the-year vibrations.

The 360-degree circle closes, and the five tag-end days roll around with their unworldly vibrations. Business quiets down. Minds are on other things. The year is drawing to its close. Last chance to do anything with it. It's slipping away now, and the new year hasn't announced itself yet. Five days of the void, neither the past nor the future. Too much now to suit me. It suits me, though, if I think about it. Doing nothing—my favorite pastime. Doing nothing is sanctioned, sanctified for these five days. Let the vibrations simmer down, catch a glimpse of what the New Year is bringing. A change of place, for sure—for lots of us. A different kind of life, maybe.

Rusty doors opening, their old hinges groaning. Always an effort. A breath of fresh air, of spring, comes through the crack. I must get rid of all the accumulation, things that arrive and settle like dust on shelves, in drawers, in closets, and stay there like encrustations of coral, like barnacles on a ship, like rust on the rusty doors of my mind.

How painful it is, pulling them out and getting rid of them. Memories go with them. Abandoning the past, unfaithful lover of old moments, moving on into the now. The future slips into the now and catches us in its current. Floating like a leaf in a shallow clear stream, streaming around rocks and over pebbles, going where the current takes me as it rushes down the mountain past grassy banks and sandy bottom, stream-washed stones and tree roots exposed on the banks.

Whirling motion, no time to look around and see where I am, I am nowhere, I am going, I am the process in process. Not even a goal in mind—just the rush of the water, which I allowed to catch me, to take me where it will. The water has no mind either—can therefore be trusted to take me where I must go. On these five days I relax and experience now the momentum of going—just go with it as it flows unceasingly downstream, downstream. The new year will bring a sudden opening into the future, and I'll have to start to steer. Not bad, for the present, to just let go and be carried.

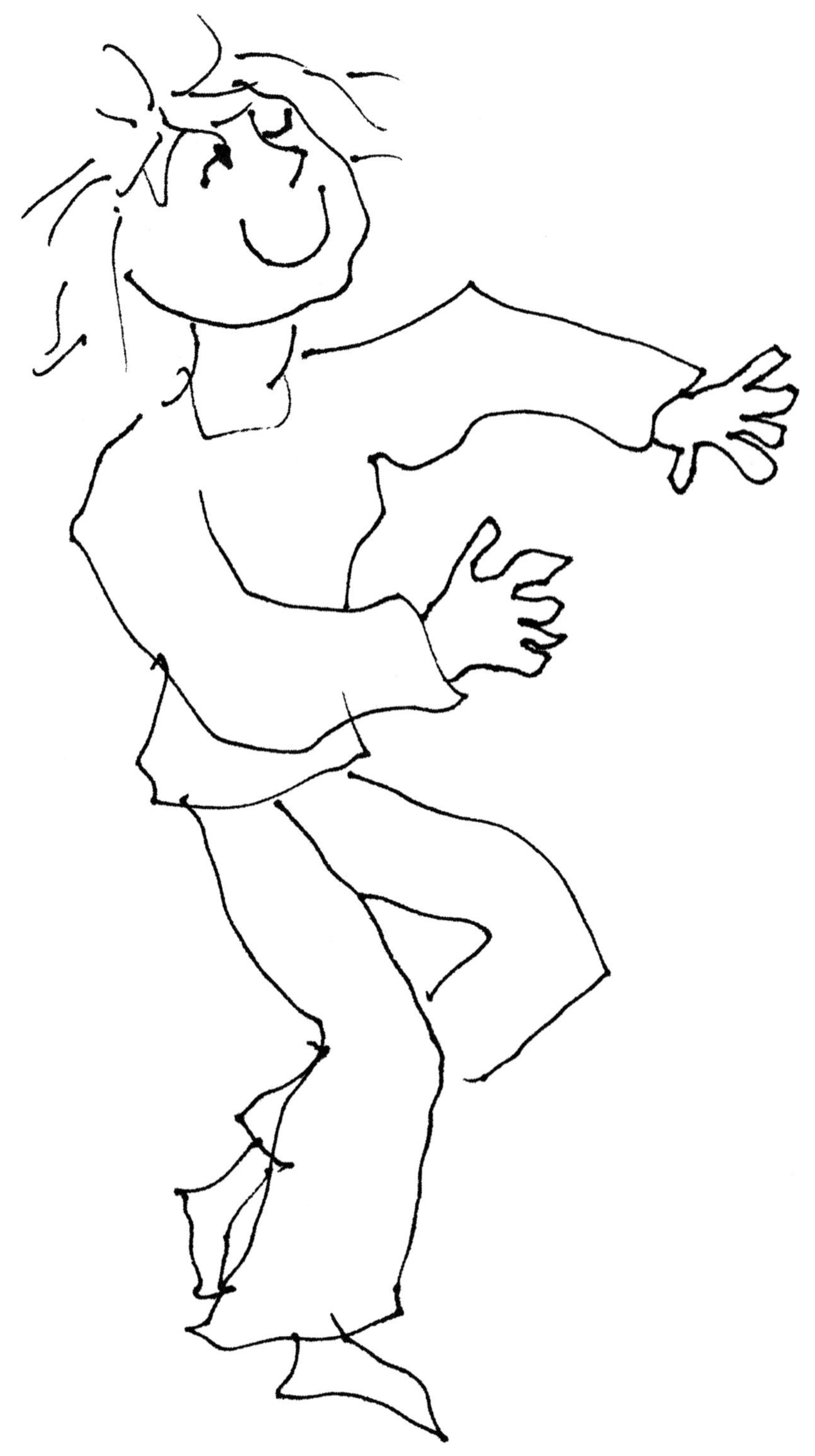

leaves twirling in the circling wind, making dry noises as

they tumble. The top of the tall maple moans as the wind pours through it on its way to Mars. Empty landscape, silver trees showing their true form, pink hills in the fading light that goes early.

The sun slips behind the hills on its way to Mars. I stand, small, straining to see over the horizon. The hills lie tired on this ancient land. Time passes, dragging its feet on its way to Mars. Space pours around my shoulders and around the maple tree, whose branches rub together and call out in the wind. The sunlight scatters, broken up by the naked silver branches.

This spot has used itself up; drained of trying, it lies down to sleep. Soon the snow will cover it as it sleeps. I will be gone by then, on my way to Mars. The tree calls good-bye and waves, the wind cries out a mournful farewell, the hills whisper they will still be here, and the sun sets knowingly on its endless round to tomorrows. Shadows creep toward me through the grass. Animals burrow in the cold earth. I turn my collar up and follow the shadows, going home.

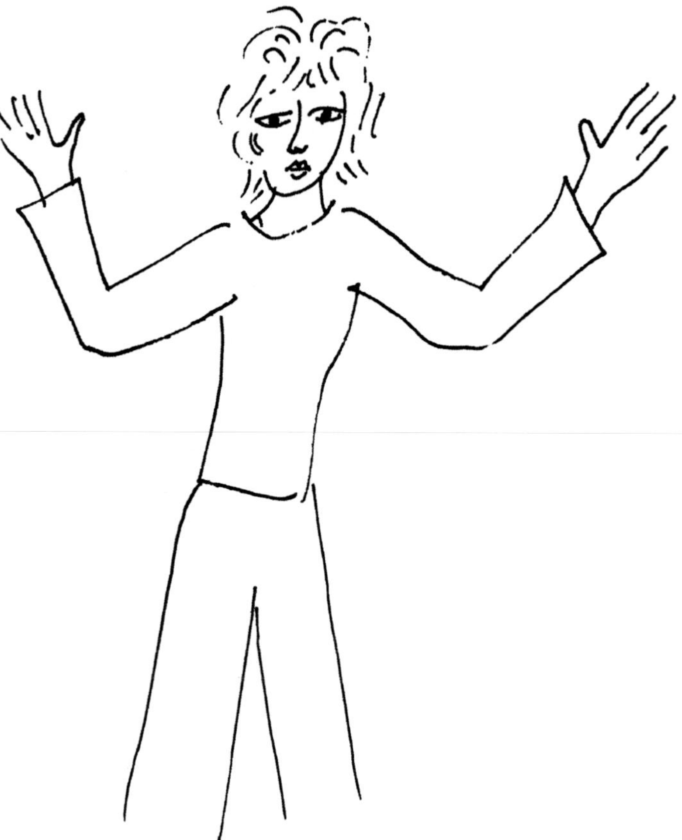

Creepy creepy this is a creepy state I'm in. Nothing satisfies me, nothing is real as I stand around saying, I'm confused. Why don't I just get on with it? I must be crossing a border, one I never crossed before, one that was taboo before, one that brings up my stuff, even old old stuff, and leaves me in a state of unknowing, floundering, daring to let myself be unfamiliar. Stay open to the previously unthinkable, all the while hating it, clanging alarms going off in my head saying, Danger! Stay back! No entry! Shivering, I stay anyway, creeping forward in terror, trying not to believe the alarms that have always warned me away from here before. Back to being alone, I want to go back to being one, and if I'm two then we two are one, and if we're three we are one, it's us against the world. It's Them out there. Stay in here where it's safe.

I'm so boring.

It is all falling away from me as I sit here with my legs crossed and the floor crumbles beneath me and the walls shimmer and fade and through them I see the blue-black expanse of nothing that surrounds me now as I float precariously in the nowhere having lost all reference points except my own body, which persists impossibly, holding on with fear to existence, attached to fear, leaning on fear, pulling the fear around itself to shield itself from the nothingness. Then it too begins to dislodge, atom by atom, as my mind watches, freaked out with nowhere to go. What's to become of me now? It cries, as though there were something to cry to, or a guarantee from somewhere that something would always become of it. Emptiness, nothingness, the famous void; spread out across the face of the void is a singularity that is supposed to be the next me, if I only existed and could only make the leap to inhabit it. But I have been used to a solid body with borders and edges, and the idea of becoming something that spreads out over the surface of the universe is repugnant to me, somehow beneath my status.

I'm not going.

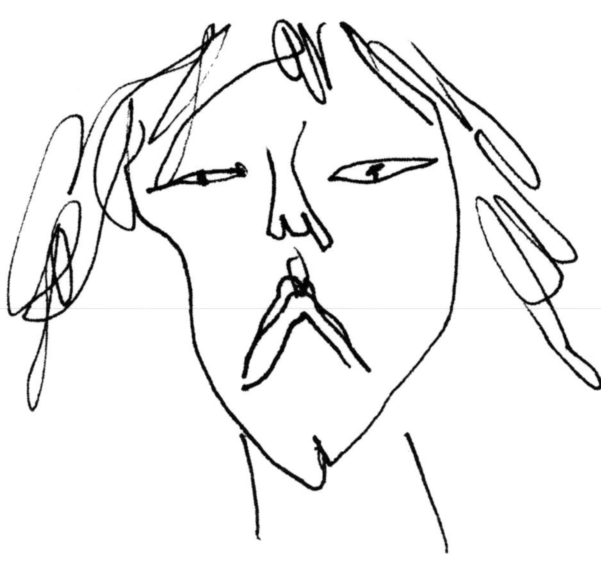

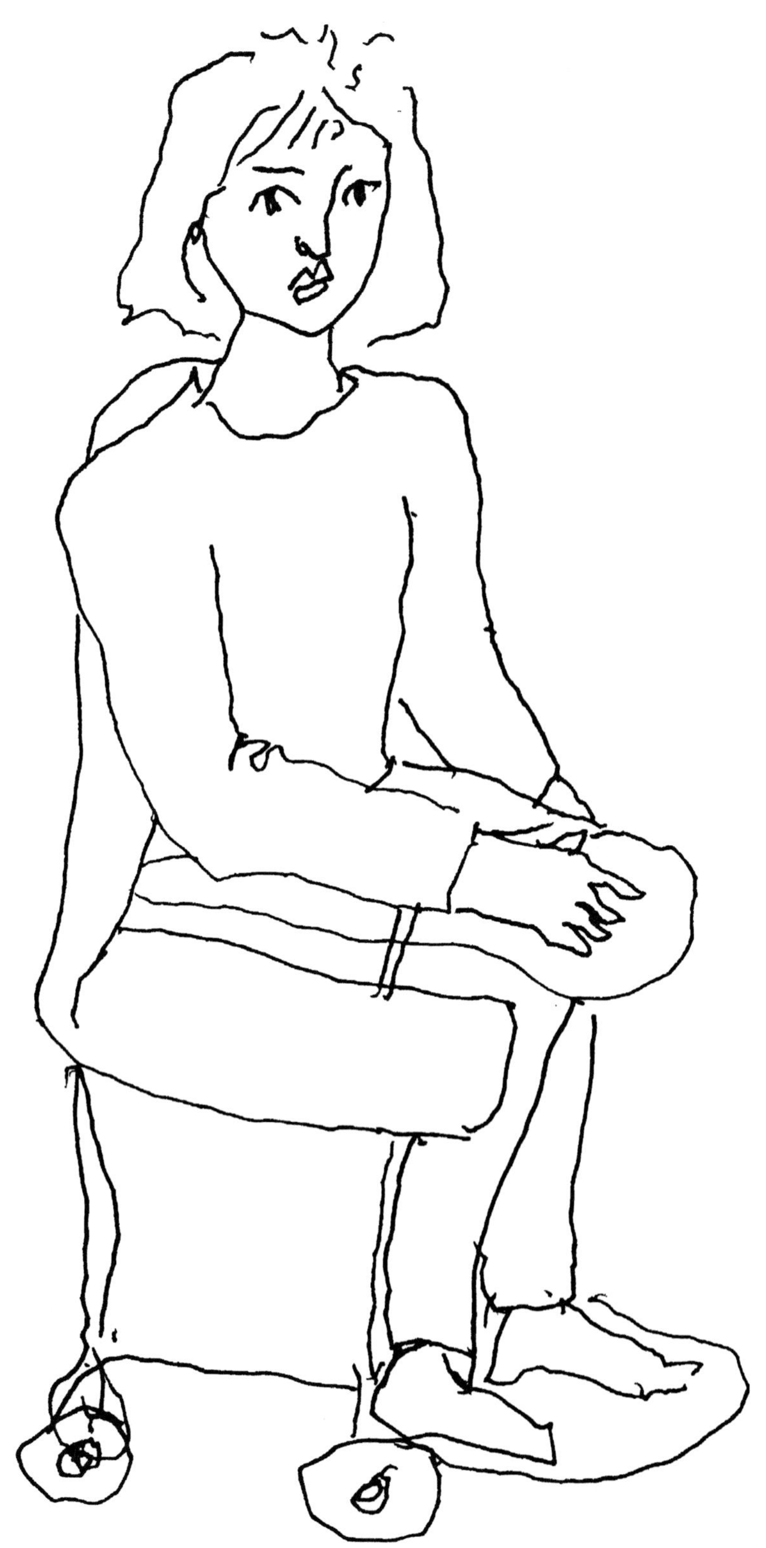

She has left her home, the house that became her character and personality, and the land that is her body, feeding her living as the earth feeds the roots of the tree so it can stretch its branches to the sky and sigh and bend in the wind. She has left because there were no people there, and because her daughter, the jewel in her heart lotus, had to leave.

In search of people, she went out into the world and immediately found some, an abundance of people she could love and who loved her. She even forgot her house for a time, forgot the land and the trees who watch her watch them, and even the one that speaks to her as she passes, creaking its branches in greeting.

She plunged into the new world of people and found new heart connections among them. They were a group, working together and rejoicing in their work, building a community, first of souls, and eventually hoping to materialize it into houses, clustered together as they had clustered so often to design and create it.

They are younger than she is, and have more to hope for. Their lives are as busy as hers is still. They have babies, jobs, husbands or wives, lovers, ambitions, and opinions. They are large of mind and heart, and they move her almost to tears of joy when she is with them. And yet, as the time rolls on, the house and the land it stands on reach out to reclaim her, demanding, insistent, persistent. So she goes back, like a visitor now, stealing time from her new life to find again that stillness, the emptiness that surrounds and pervades her there.

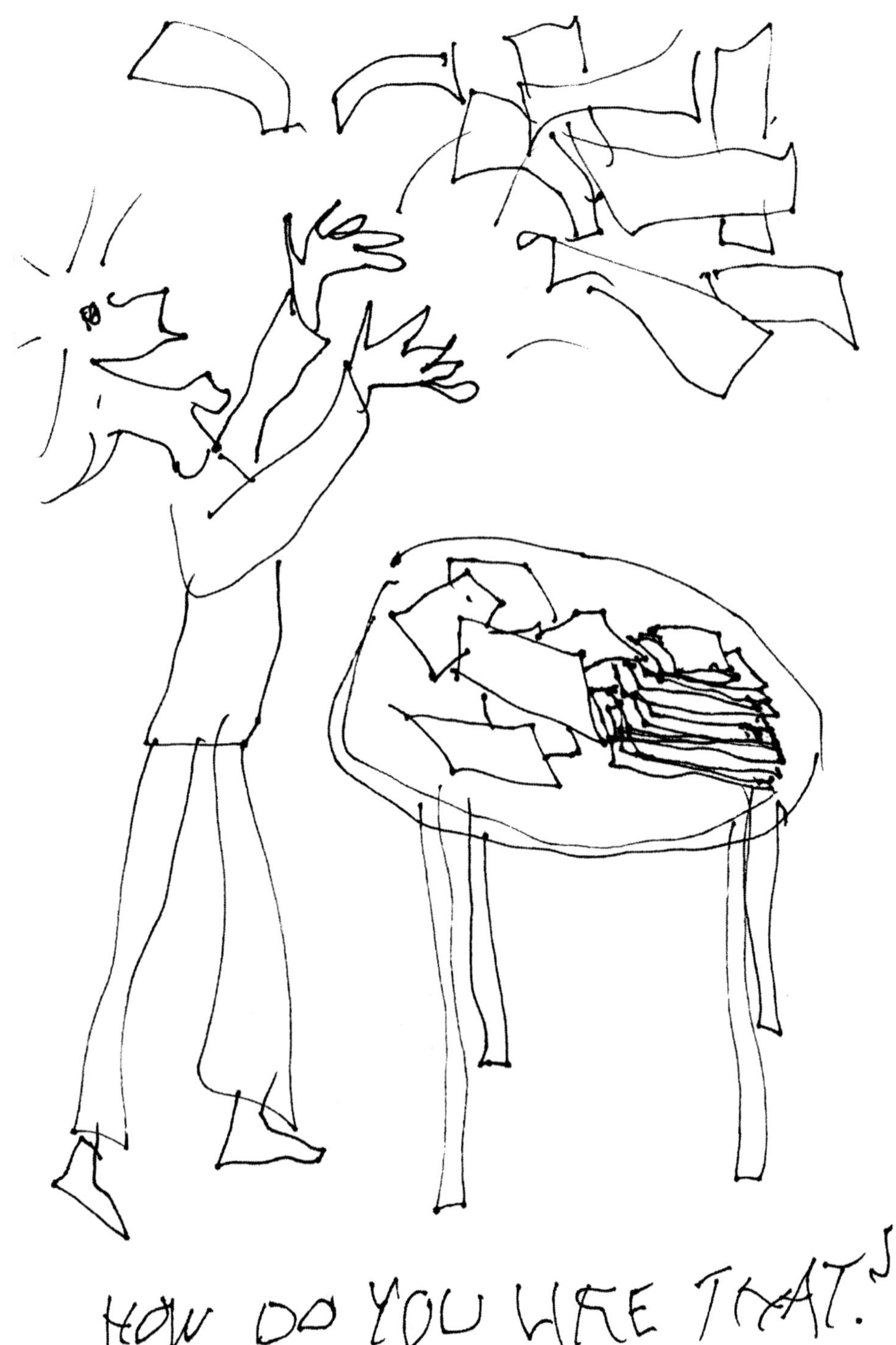

HOW DO YOU LIKE THAT.

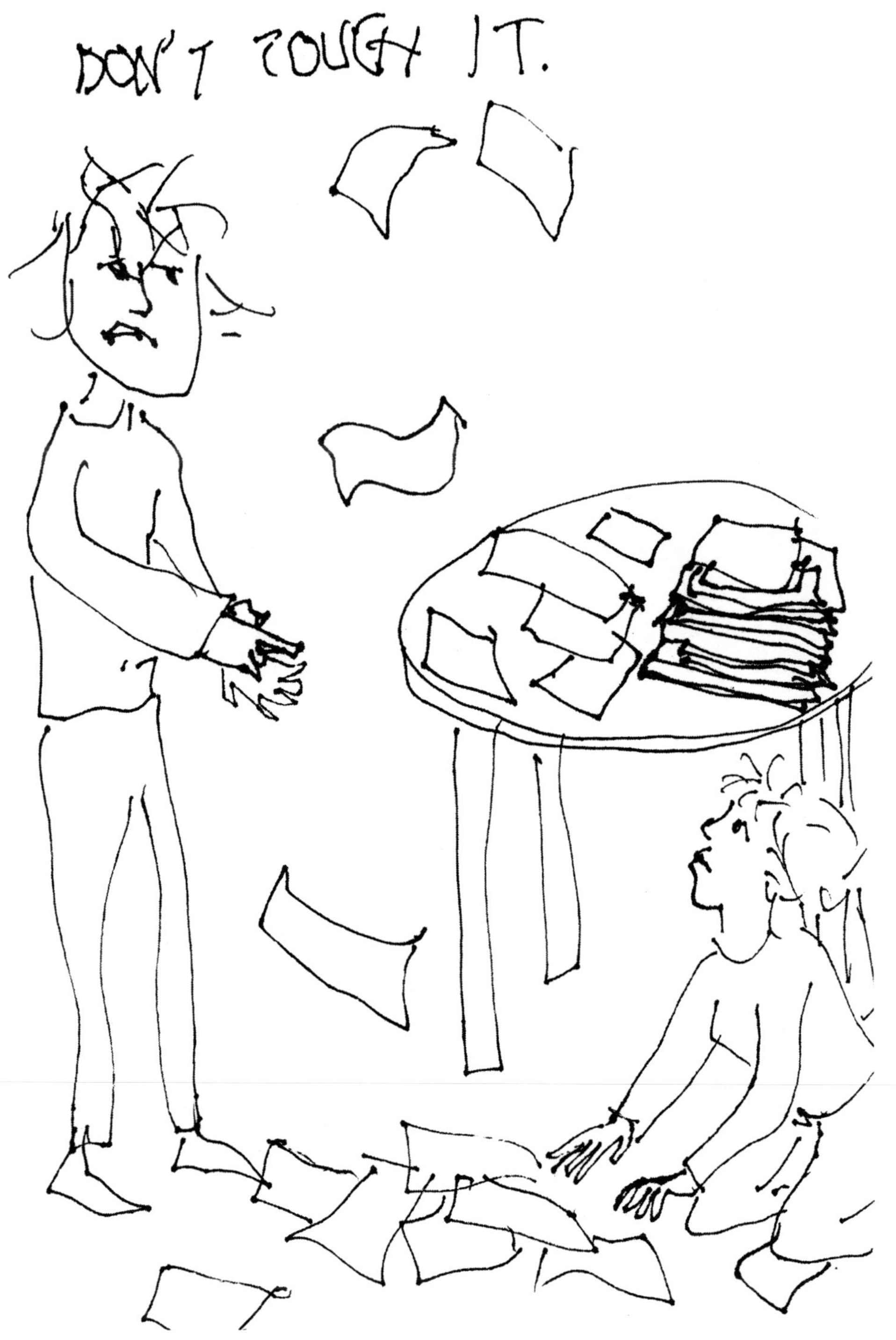

DON'T TOUCH IT.

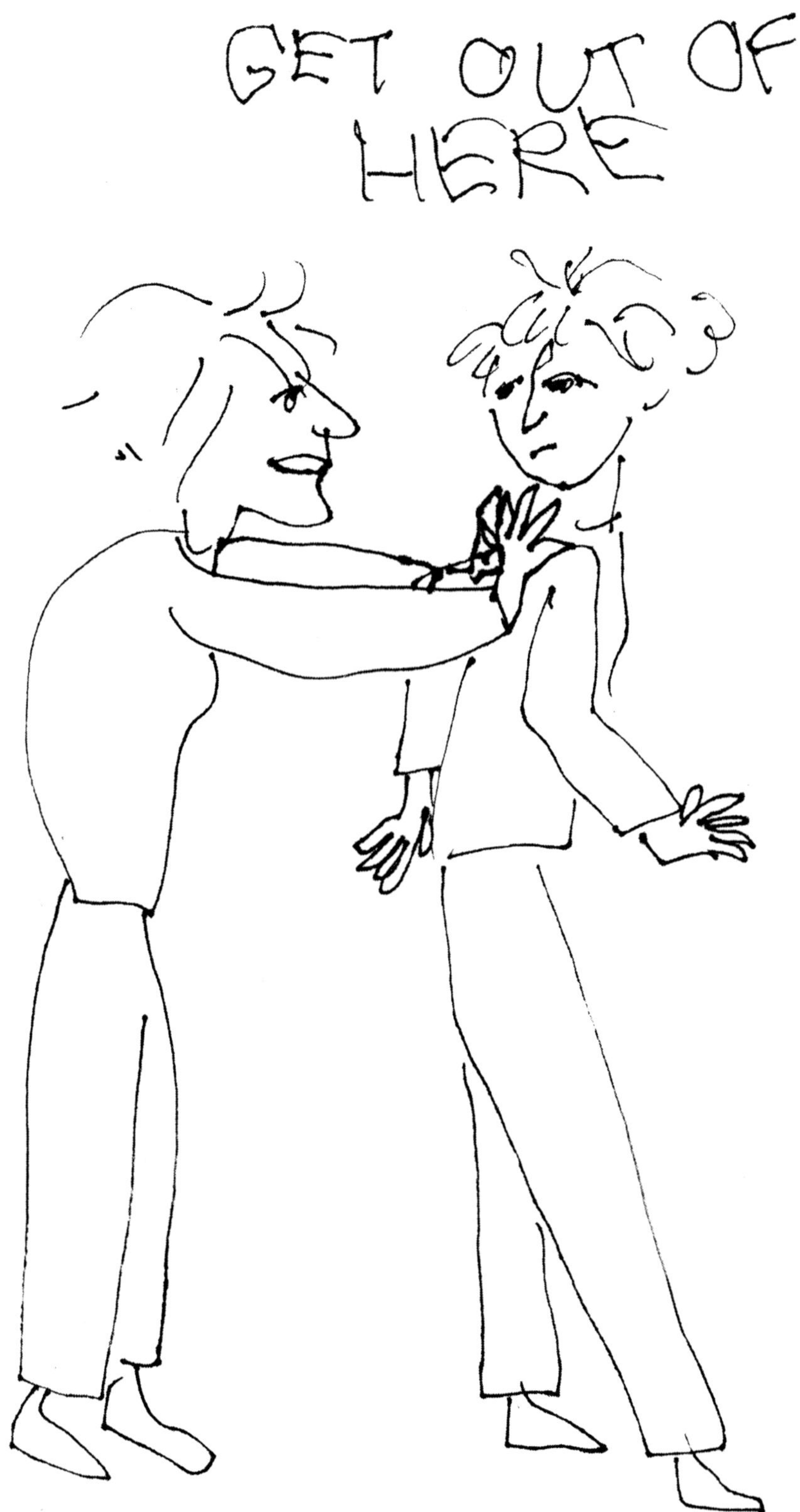
GET OUT OF
HERE

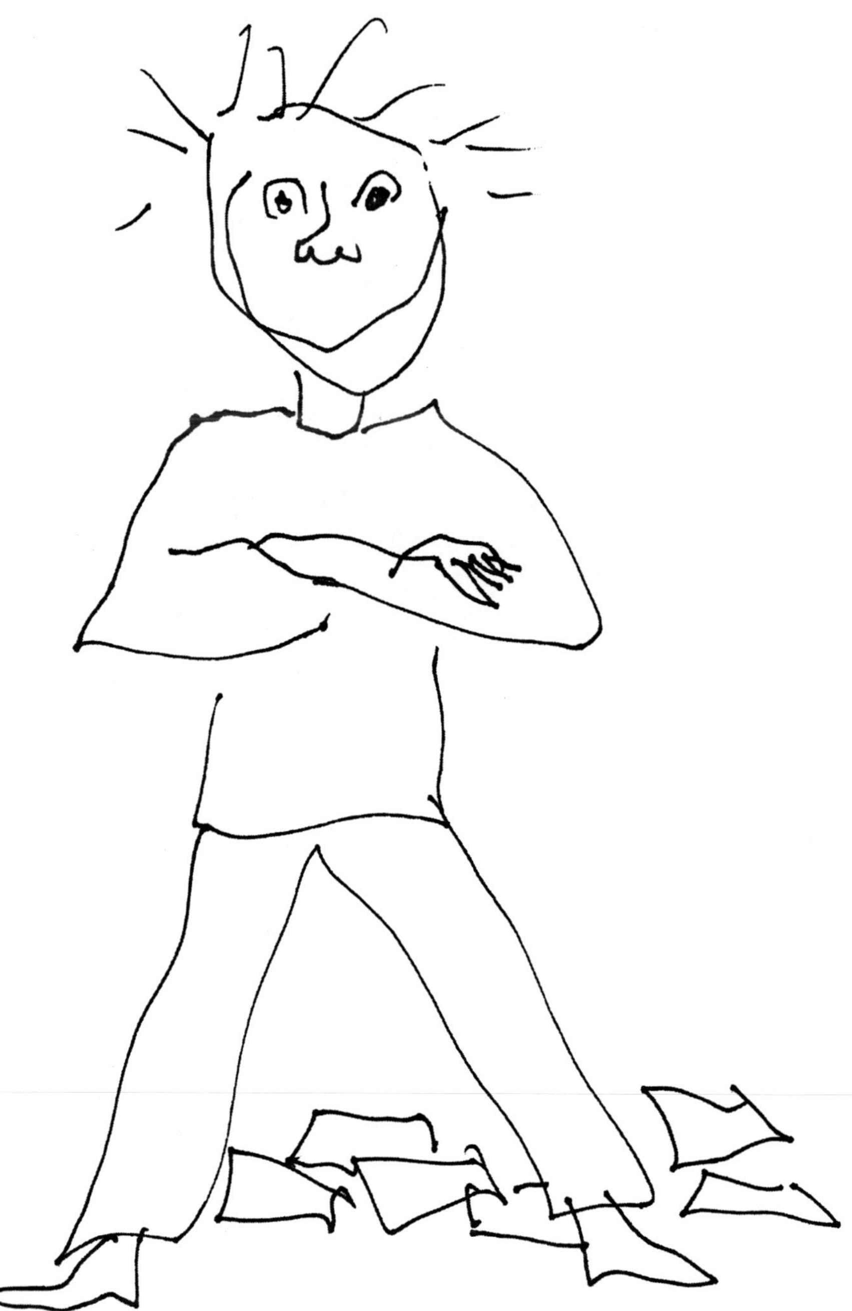

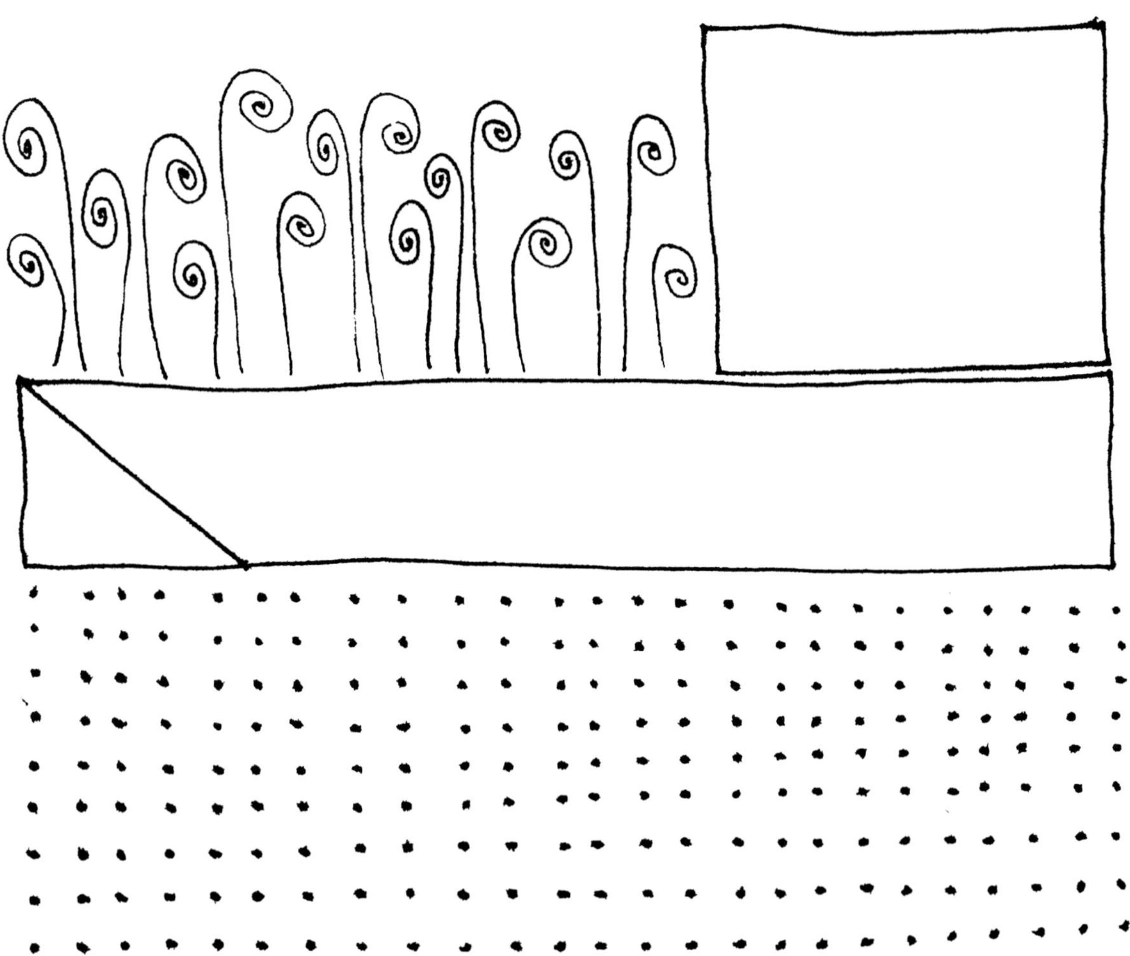

Winter is here again

Winter is here again and my body is pulling back into itself, tight and curled, looking for a warm space near the hearth. The wind whistles through my hair— I've always been a little scared of the wind, coming from where and tossing about wildly, untamed and uncomfortable and too cold, especially now that winter is here again again, too soon, always too soon for me. I'm never ready to face the hostile cold and deal with all the contractions in my body and in my life. And now living without a fire in the house, not only no spot to find warmth but no fire god at the center of the house. No more sun in my solar system, a terrible lack I just have to learn to live with. My Mediterranean soul rejects all this snowy blue-eyed winter of short days and long nights and polar bears cruising in the shadows. Cold nose, cold toes, cold fingertips, cold hands warm heart. The heart is the hearth, the warmth arises from it like heat waves hovering over the desert floor, rippling and baking. An inner sun I don't acknowledge and am not satisfied with. I want to experience that warmth outside of me, sit staring at the flames dancing gold and blue and cheering me, mesmerizing me, drawing me into the welcome warmth I need in winter.

Do I miss the flames in summer? No, because the sun is a heavy presence, close enough to bow my head with its weight, close enough to singe my eyelashes and make me look for shade. My Mediterranean soul understands shade, understands the weight of the sun, the yellow-green shadow of grape leaves, the buzzing of insects and the ease with which my body stretches out its length, finding comfort in the cool grass.

When I was little I stared at the sun, watching it until it became a golden disc surrounded by an intense blue halo, shooting forward out of a hole in the sky and then shooting back in, coming toward me and going away, a little private dance the sun did for me that held me fascinated so that I watched it over and over. Later I learned about the Indian fakirs who spent their adult lives doing that, a kind of penance or renunciation, a showy spirituality that destroyed their retinas and left them blind—but who knows what they saw then? Do blind eyes see something we don't?
Surely they had a reason to seek the sun in such an extreme way—and in India, where the sun is not lacking and there is no winter, not in the parts of India I experienced, anyway.

And is my longing for the sun Mediterranean or Indian or both, or is it just my body lamenting the cold and knowing the ultimate source of warmth and not wanting anything less? Wish I could enjoy the snow. The best I could ever do was enjoy watching it come down as I sit by the fire and warm myself protectively.

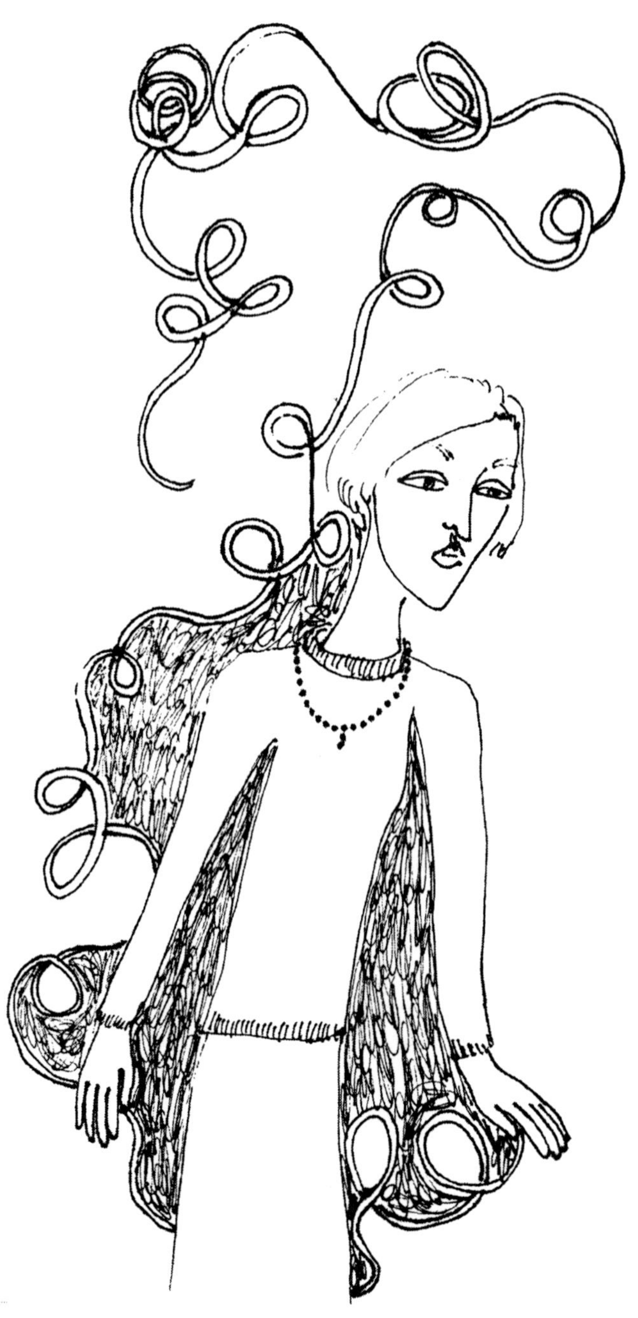

Swelling buds on the branches of the trees, early spring is pressing its way outward into form, the swelling takes shape—tiny leaves curl and un-furl, traveling the long path from yellow to bright green, suddenly mature with all the authority of the ripened adult—I am a leaf! Maple, they sing. Oak! Sumac!

Coming from the void, realizing the possibilities of the form they have chosen. Show-ing us, for a brief summer, what it is to be oak. Not just the one, that is not enough. Millions of oak leaves sing together on the branches, a finely tuned and wordless chant that, finally, says everything.

I pick up a brown and fallen leaf, holding it tenderly in my hand. What lavish gifts the Mother gives us, her perfection is everywhere. God is in the details. The edges of the leaf curl up. Soon it will be dry pieces, feeding the earth, going back into the ground from which it came.

Where will I go when my edges curl, when I turn brown and fall away from the earth, buried within her but gone? That part of me that will not go into the ground—that all of me, if you prefer. Does the one oak leaf in my hand release a soul, or is that "more" that the oak tree contains the sum of *all* its parts, and more—the trunk, branches, leaves, the leaves after leaves after leaves of succeeding summers, the time that unfolds around the tree as it pushes out of another tree's acorn and starts along the process of becoming itself. Already, just a baby, it throws out two perfect, full-sized oak leaves, just to let us know where it's going.

Does it know where it's going? At least it knows where it's going and never asks itself, Would I have been better off being born a maple? The leaves accept, no—rejoice in—their sameness. The trees, each so different from the other, celebrate their sameness. It is we, their human siblings, who look at each other and say, "I'm not like *that*. God forbid I should be like that. Thank God I'm not like that. There, but for the grace of God, go I." Why not "There go I?" What makes us think, so persistently, down to our toes, by God, that God thought so much of us that SHe took the time to make us, by the grace of God, different from all the others.

Nobody spends their life trying with all their heart to be like everyone else. Or do they? What about the cities? What about the suburbs? What about teenagers?

What about wanting, trying to be something other than what we are? I am the bag woman dressed in layers of discarded clothing, pushing a stolen shopping cart full of *objets trouvés*, my own art collection, muttering to myself insane wisdom as I cross the street, avoiding the eyes of those who walk by me turning their eyes away. The oak tree at the curb looks down at me thinking, What a beautiful one—so like the others, and so different! The woman passes the tree without a glance. The tree does not bow. Their hearts intertwine.

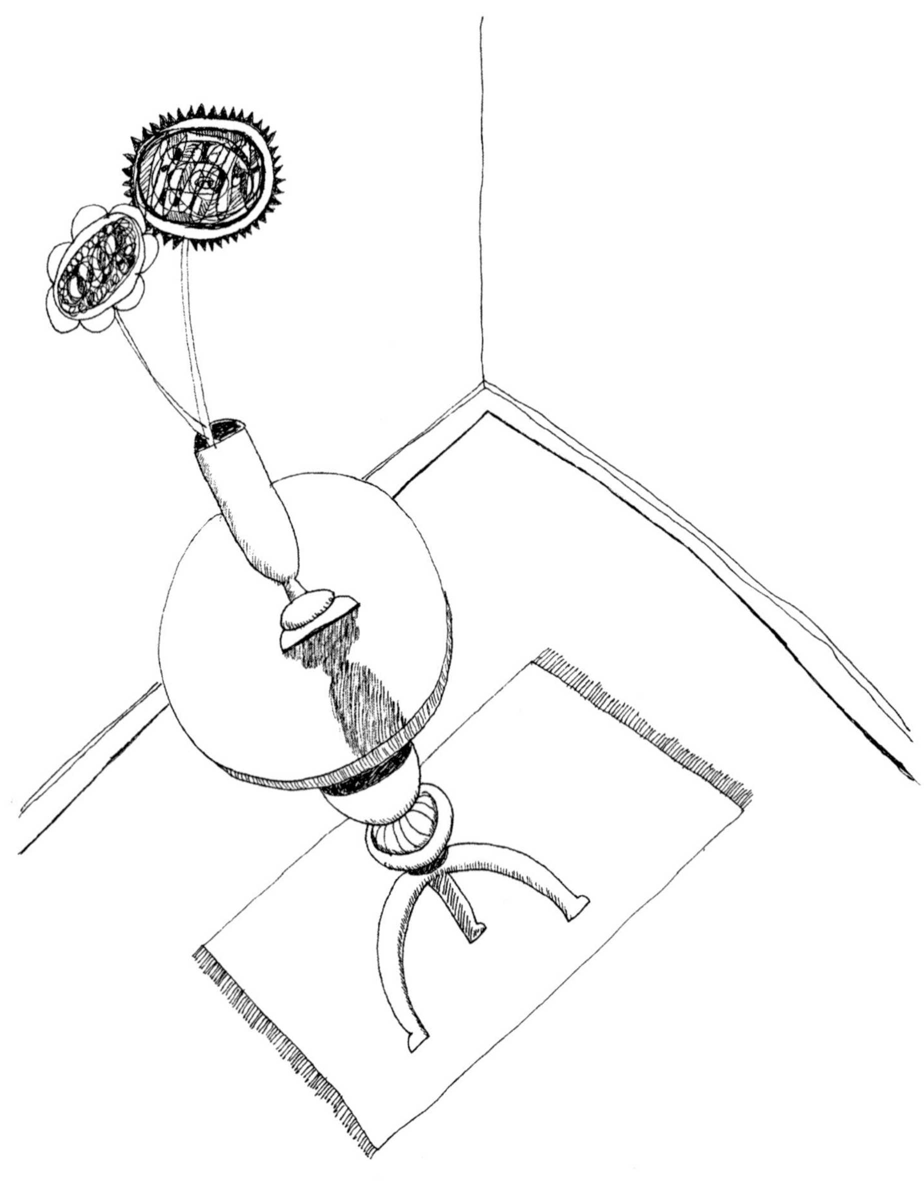

Writing a message to **N**obody, who couldn't care less. Still the words come pouring out, can't still them. Got to say what I got to say though nobody knows I'm saying it. Got to admit that's my fault—I am waiting for someone to come knocking on my door and say, Can I read what you've written?

The truth is, I *can't imagine* the process of getting these words out into the world—you can't get there from here. There is no path from the inside to the outside, no bridge across the gap. Got to build one, quick. All the prisoners will escape. All the words held in dungeons, the dungeons of the filled-up pages piling up on the floor going nowhere.

Time to go somewhere.

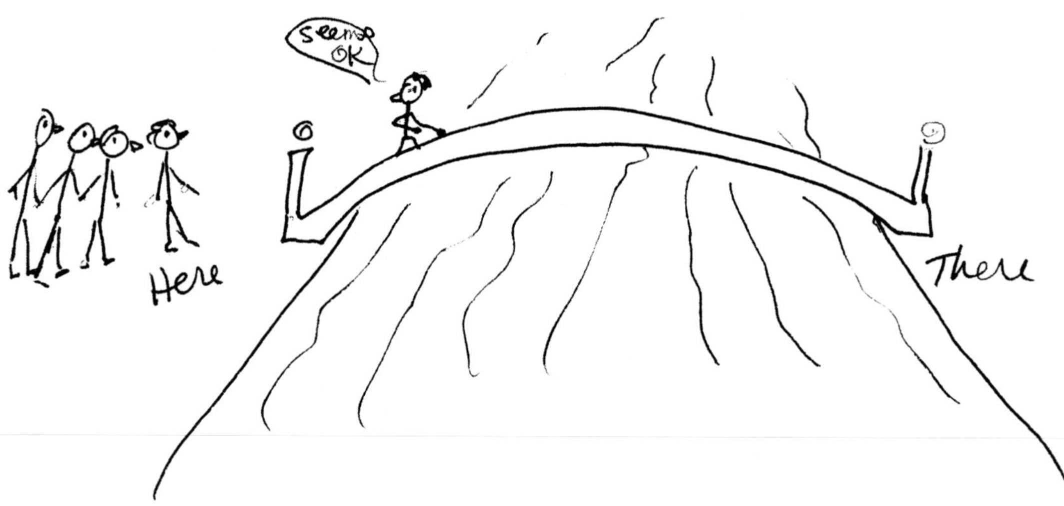

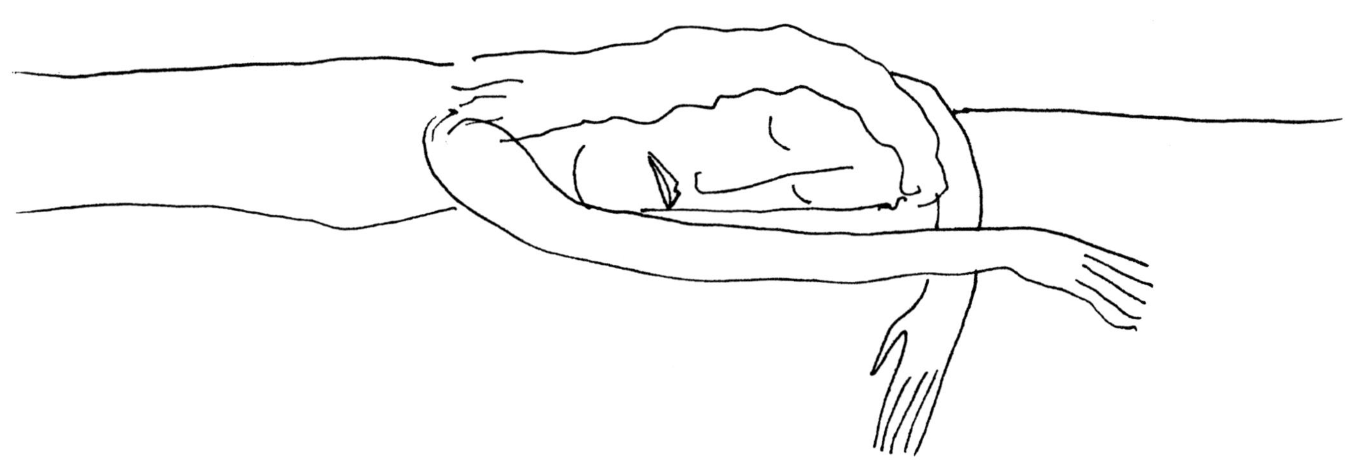

CPSIA information can be obtained at www.ICGtesting.com
Printed in the USA
BVOW061430251111

276794BV00005B/6/P